Corporate Criminality and Liability for Fraud

Through a rational reconstruction of orthodox legal principles, and reference to cutting-edge neuroscience, this book reveals some startling truths about the criminal law, its history and the fundamental doctrines that underpin the attribution of criminal fault. While this has important implications for the criminal law generally, the focus of this work is the development of a theory of corporate criminality that accords with modern theory of group agency, itself informed by advancements in contemporary philosophy and social science. The innovation it proposes is the theoretical and practical means by which criminal fault can be attributed directly to the corporate actor, where liability cannot or should not be reduced to its individual members.

Dr Alison Cronin holds a PhD specialising in corporate fraud and is a Senior Lecturer at the Department of Law, Bournemouth University, UK. Called to the Bar by the Honourable Society of the Inner Temple in 2004, her research interests are in the field of corporate and economic crime.

T0382829

Corporate Criminality and Liability for Fraud

Alison Cronin

Routledge
Taylor & Francis Group

LONDON AND NEW YORK

First published 2018
by Routledge

2 Park Square, Milton Park, Abingdon, Oxfordshire OX14 4RN
52 Vanderbilt Avenue, New York, NY 10017

Routledge is an imprint of the Taylor & Francis Group, an informa business

First issued in paperback 2020

British Library Cataloguing-in-Publication Data
A catalogue record for this book is available from the British Library

Library of Congress Cataloging-in-Publication Data
Names: Cronin, Alison, author.
Title: Corporate criminality and liability for fraud / Alison Cronin.
Description: Abingdon, Oxon [UK] ; New York : Routledge, 2018. |
Includes index.
Identifiers: LCCN 2017048538| ISBN 9781138744639 (hbk) |
ISBN 9781351716857
(web pdf) | ISBN 9781351716840 (epub) | ISBN 9781351716833
(kindle)
Subjects: LCSH: Corporations--Corrupt practices. | Corporation law--
Criminal provisions. | Criminal liability of juristic persons.
Classification: LCC K5216 .C76 2018 | DDC 345/.0263--dc23
LC record available at https://lccn.loc.gov/2017048538

ISBN: 978-1-138-74463-9 (hbk)
ISBN: 978-0-367-59201-1 (pbk)

Typeset in Galliard
by Swales & Willis Ltd, Exeter, UK

For Mr Cronin

Contents

Table of cases

Table of legislation

Statutory instruments

Australia

Preface

I suppose it was all rather predictable really, having been brought up by a mother who had worked for a bank before having me and a father who continued to work for a bank until his retirement. In those days it was all very different, banking was a personal business in which managers got to know their individual customers and were vested with discretion as regards lending and other decisions. The era of information technology, heralding first the invasion of the computer and then online banking, was yet to come. My father was already the assistant manager of a reasonably large high street branch before electronic calculators became available and affordable. The wheels of the banking world turned largely on manual systems of recording, reporting and auditing and, for the most part, communication was by snail mail. Cyber crime had not been "invented" but other forms of financial crime, and its prevention, seeped into my early consciousness as a result my father's work. If dinner was delayed, it was because my father was late home and this would be because the cashiers' tills could not be reconciled at the close of business. Every transaction, manually recorded, would need to be looked at to trace every last penny that had been handled during the day. Internal audits, in those days, meant that the use of every last postage stamp had to be noted and accounted for. This meticulous attention to detail never left my mother, who kept full records of just about everything until the day she passed away, from the minutiae of household expenditure to the books that she had read.

I have childhood memories of all the family sitting down for dinner every evening and, having enquired about our schooling, my father recounting the events of his day at work. I remember hearing about the dubious activities of some of the bank's customers, discovered that bank employees were not always above such behaviour themselves, and became relatively knowledgeable about various security procedures that, years on, I am still too cautious to disclose. With what was probably an unhealthy interest, I absorbed it all. I vividly recall my parents drilling my younger sister and me as to what we should do if we were snatched for ransom, a not infrequent form of extortion aimed at those, like bank managers, who had access to large sums of cash. It was of paramount importance that, in any such event, we were to relay particular code words via our abductors that would confirm that we had genuinely been taken. It was all rather exciting at the time. The only disappointment for a spirited young girl was that the opportunity never arose in which to employ the secret code. As my father's career progressed, he went "on the road" as a senior inspector for the bank. Away from branch management, and without personal access to any safe, the risk of abduction sharply declined. This job was interesting though, involving unannounced visits to branches across the region during which my father and his team checked for everything from internal and external security measures, managerial propriety, employee theft and customer service to staff appearance and standards of cleanliness in the public foyer. Internal accountability was high on the corporate agenda and the position of inspector was highly regarded.

It was only later, when my father was promoted back into management of a "big" branch, that I began to sense that things in the banking world were changing. Managers, not computers, continued to make lending decisions and they were still based on managerial discretion involving personal knowledge of the customer and his business. Whether performance targets were just being introduced at this time, whether they were assuming a greater prominence or whether they brought greater demands, I do not know. What I do remember is that the tone of the dinner conversation changed in a way that made me uneasy. It was clear that my father was, slowly but surely, becoming concerned that the exercise of his lending discretion was being subtly compromised. It was not that he felt restrained to lend less, but encouraged to lend more. This was not consistent with the erstwhile cautious approach in which the borrower's potential capacity to repay was the primary consideration. Responsible for a large number of members of staff, for whom a significant part of their remuneration depended upon the meeting of lending targets, the implicit pressure to lend more than he felt comfortable with bore heavily upon him. Profoundly troubled, he finally resolved his position through early retirement.

That my father's circumstances accommodated such a withdrawal from what, for him, was a matter of professional and personal conflict is not a luxury afforded to many. Indeed, he is the first to acknowledge that he was fortunate in this respect. With legitimate ambitions for commercial profit, or economic concerns for non-profit making organisations, it has become a target driven world which now leaves little room for such sensitivity. Having previous experience in retail, sales and in business, the distinction between entrepreneurialism on the one hand, sharp practice and deception on the other has become something of a personal fascination. It is not an easy line to draw for all sorts of reasons. Indeed, although much of the theoretical argument in this book is premised on the example of the mis-selling scandals that have pervaded the financial services industry, payment protection insurance (ppi) being the paradigm example, my personal experience in this respect has been entirely positive. Properly sold, it certainly saved our bacon, financially-speaking, when my husband became very ill and was unable to work for a considerable period.

When I came to practise the law, it is probably of little surprise that it was the criminal law that "caught me" and, no doubt to the consternation of my ever-supportive parents, it was criminal defence work that I was involved in. It is, however, a privilege to work in this capacity, not only for what can be achieved at a personal level for clients but also in the respect that the criminal justice system is rightly founded in the notion that the prosecution must prove its case. Defence work, quite rightly, tests that case and a reluctance or failure to do so would undermine our commitment to rule of law values and the basic principles of justice for which we should be proud. I enjoyed every aspect of defence work although it was the fraud cases that I found perhaps the most interesting. Now in academia, it is corporate fraud that has become my area of research. It is a problem that continues to pose challenges to those involved in the law and its enforcement and it is an area ripe for ongoing development and reform. I hope that this book provides some useful contribution in this area. It has been a joy to write and I am particularly grateful for the support of Christopher Harding and Stephen Copp throughout this endeavour and for the helpful comments provided by the anonymous reviewers who read the initial draft.

Alison Cronin
Bournemouth
September 2017

1 Criminal fraud and the problem of the corporate actor

1.1 Introduction: when is a fraud not a fraud?

While fraud is a global problem,[1] in 2016 it was estimated to be costing the UK economy alone a staggering £193 billion every year.[2] Cost can be defined as a misallocation of resources or resources that have been diverted from where they were intended.[3] Furthermore, although the methodology employed in the calculation of the Annual Fraud Indicator has become increasingly sophisticated,[4] encompassing more sectors by business and victim type, any such calculation is fraught with difficulties such that this figure is likely to be a gross underestimate of the real extent of fraud. There are inevitable gaps of unaccounted crime, not least because fraud is by its very nature a hidden crime and, even if detected by the victim, it is an offence that is under-reported or not recorded for a variety of reasons.[5] Furthermore, the Annual Fraud Indicator has traditionally focused on the costs sustained by the public and private sectors in relation to a number of specified frauds perpetrated against agencies, businesses and charities. One refinement in recent years has therefore been to estimate the loss caused to individuals through fraud and in 2016 this was placed at £9.7 billion, making up just 5% of the estimated total. In relation to frauds perpetrated against individuals, the current calculation is limited to just four

---

1 The Global Financial Crisis of 2008–9 cost c. $11.9 trillion, one-fifth of global output and a significant contributing factor was the USA's sub-prime mortgage market in which borrowers and lenders alike were dishonest as regards repayment capacity. As mortgagors defaulted, the seeds of the financial crisis were sown, see Geoffrey Smith and others, *Studying Fraud as White Collar Crime* (Basingstoke: Palgrave Macmillan 2011) 2.

2 Annual Fraud Indicator 2016, www.experian.co.uk/assets/identity-and-fraud/pkfexperian-fraud-indicator-report.pdf accessed 6 December 2016.

3 www.croweclarkwhitehill.co.uk/wp-content/uploads/sites/2/2017/02/crowe-the-financial-cost-of-fraud-2017.pdf accessed 30 June 2017, p 4, para 1.5.

4 www.gov.uk/government/uploads/system/uploads/attachment_data/file/118530/annual-fraud-indicator-2012.pdf accessed 7 December 2016.

5 The current methodology for the Annual Fraud Indicator is based on that previously developed by the National Fraud Agency, see 2016 www.experian.co.uk/assets/identity-and-fraud/pkfexperian-fraud-indicator-report.pdf accessed 6 December 2016 and 7 December 2016.

discrete categories: the estimated losses due to mass marketing frauds, identity fraud, private rental property fraud, and repayment meter scams. While there are recognised types of fraud that are still excluded from the scope of the enquiry, there are also economically harmful activities that have yet to be recognised as criminal and the employment of a broader conception of fraud would therefore render a significant increase in the estimated losses. For example, if the systemic mis-selling of financial products in recent years were to be reconceived as criminal acquisition rather than regulatory breach, a staggering £26 billion may be added to the figures from January 2011 to September 2016 to reflect mis-sold payment protection insurance (PPI) alone,[6] and this would be the tip of the iceberg. The Financial Ombudsman predicts that the conclusion to this particular scandal is still some years away[7] and notes that PPI complaints made up just 74% of the total lodged in the banking and finance sector during this period, the mis-selling of interest rate hedging schemes, packaged accounts, interest only mortgages, investments and other insurance products making up the remainder.[8] Although this particular raft of complaints may now have peaked, other practices of commercial mis-conduct are starting to attract similar attention. For example, it has been suggested that liability for mis-sold pension annuities may prove to be as extensive as the PPI scandal[9] and the banks may also be facing multi-billion-pound fines for selling toxic mortgages.[10] Indeed, in the aftermath of the global financial crisis, evidence is emerging of misconduct that has never before "occurred so systematically, in such a scale and across multiple jurisdictions."[11] Notwithstanding the widespread outrage, scrutiny and claims processes this has spawned, under the regulatory cloak of the Financial Conduct Authority (FCA) and its predecessor, the Financial Services Authority (FSA), this genre of

---

6 This is the amount paid out in refunds and compensation in that period, see https://www.fca.org.uk/consumers/payment-protection-insurance/monthly-ppi-refunds-and-compensation accessed 6 December 2016.

7 www.bbc.co.uk/news/business-30695720 accessed 6 January 2015.

8 www.financial-ombudsman.org.uk/news/speech/2013/CW-BILA-conference.pdf accessed 22 January 2015.

9 www.telegraph.co.uk/finance/personalfinance/pensions/11286965/Annuity-mis-selling-scandal-could-it-be-as-big-as-PPI.html accessed 3 October 2015.

10 www.dailymail.co.uk/news/article-4062858/Barclays-HSBC-Royal-Bank-Scotland-face-multi-billion-fines-toxic-mortgages.html accessed 28 December 2016.

11 Minouche Shafik, Bank of England Deputy Governor, Markets and Banking, "From 'ethical drift' to 'ethical lift': Reversing the tide of misconduct in global financial markets" speech given at the Federal Reserve Bank of New York Conference on 'Reforming Culture and Behaviour in the Financial Services Industry' October 20, 2016, www.bankofengland.co.uk/publications/Pages/speeches/default.aspx/Documents/speeches/2016/speech930.pdf accessed October 21,2016. See too the European Parliament, Directorate General for Internal Policies, Policy Dept A: Economic and Scientific Policy, Consumer Protection Aspects of Financial Services (2014), IP/A/IMCO/ST/2013-07 February 2014, www.europarl.europa.eu/RegData/etudes/etudes/join/2014/507463/IPOL-IMCO_ET(2014)507463_EN.pdf accessed 26 October 2016.

corporate wrongdoing has been framed as a regulatory breach, attracting civil remedies and sanctions, and has consequently escaped formal definition as fraud. Through such a conception the annual estimate of fraud excludes the sizeable losses borne by consumers and the analysis of this sector is therefore one-sided, confined to frauds committed by those who are not operating as regulated persons, namely customers who are committing offences against the financial providers. Accordingly, the quantitative estimate encompasses fraudulent insurance claims made against insurers and cheque, credit card and mortgage frauds perpetrated against regulated bodies.[12]

While the extensive losses sustained by consumers due to mis-sold products and commodities in the financial sector have been highly publicised, commercial wrongdoing of the trading standards or consumer protection ilk has attracted less attention in the press. Similarly, the Annual Fraud Indicator excludes consumer losses resulting from what is described as "unfair trading" and which therefore falls within the respective ambits of the Trading Standards Service and the Competition and Markets Authority. In this respect, it is acknowledged that the direct consumer detriment for the year from March 2015, estimated at £19.6 billion, is an underestimate.[13] While there may be a degree of overlap with the mass marketing category that is included, this amount is double the figure estimated in the Annual Fraud Indicator and does not touch the financial misconduct dealt with by the other, 200 or so, bodies working in the consumer protection system.[14] Were losses arising through sharp commercial practices of this nature to be integrated, through their categorisation as fraud, a dramatic increase to the current £193 billion annual cost, or misallocation of resources, would follow. With the possible exception of mass marketing scams, typically orchestrated by criminal organisations formed specifically for the illegitimate purpose, the current fraud analysis constructs the commercial entity qua victim and not perpetrator of crime. This one-dimensional account of the corporate form is, however, far removed from the observations made by Punch, some two decades ago, in his seminal work on corporate delinquency. In this respect, Punch articulated in terms of business organisations possessing an ineluctably ambiguous nature, providing ample illustration of the ways in which corporations commit serious violations of law during the course of conducting otherwise legitimate business. The corporate form not only provides the environment in which individuals can commit crime but can itself be a perpetrator of it.[15] Notwithstanding that potential for

---

12 Annual Fraud Indicator 2016 www.experian.co.uk/assets/identity-and-fraud/pkfexperian-fraud-indicator-report.pdf accessed 6 December 2016.
13 National Audit Office, Department for Business, Energy and Industrial Strategy, *Protecting Consumers from Scams, Unfair Trading and Unsafe Goods*, HC Session 2016–17, 16 December 2016.
14 Ibid 4.
15 Maurice E Punch, *Dirty Business: Exploring Corporate Misconduct* (London: Sage 1996).

causing serious criminal harms, most commercial activities are subject to the regulatory control of specialised agencies[16] with the result that commercial wrongdoing typically evades the ambit of mainstream criminal prosecution.

The selection of categories included in the Annual Fraud Indicator is thus logical in that it simply reflects the existing criminal/regulatory divide indicative of the different ways that wrongdoing is constructed in different social arenas. However, notwithstanding the historic and enduring perception of corporate wrongdoing as a matter of regulatory breach, if put to the test in the criminal courts many of the "unfair" trading and mis-selling practices that have hit the headlines may, in substance, be found to constitute criminal fraud. The generic offence is contained in the Fraud Act 2006 and can be made out either through the making of a false or misleading representation[17] where the defendant knows that the representation is, or might be, untrue or misleading,[18] by failing to disclose information that a person is legally obliged to disclose,[19] or by abusing a position occupied in relation to the financial interests of another.[20] If done dishonestly[21] and with an intention to make a gain for himself or another, or to cause a loss to or to expose another to a risk of loss,[22] a conviction can follow. While the mental characteristics of the offence, "dishonesty" and the "intention" to bring about one of the prescribed outcomes, seemingly import liability on the basis of individual human offenders who possess these metaphysical hallmarks of blameworthiness, the Fraud Act itself adverts to the commission of fraud by corporate bodies.[23] This possibility is, however, currently limited by the need to successfully apply the "identification principle" in the particular case. This means that a corporate conviction is possible only if an officer who is deemed to be a "directing mind and will" of the company has committed the fraud in question, with the requisite mental elements.[24] The mental elements of an offence, generically described by the Latin term "mens rea", are what particularly define the proscribed conduct as a truly criminal matter. Mens rea is what distinguishes a crime from a civil wrong or a so-called strict liability "public welfare" offence that can be made out irrespective of moral culpability. In the case of criminal charges, it is the identification doctrine that serves as the

---

16 The regulatory context has been described as "one in which a Government department or agency has (by law) been given the task of developing and enforcing standards of conduct in a specialised area of activity", Law Commission, *Criminal Liability in Regulatory Contexts* (Law Com No 195, 2010) para 1.9. At the time of this report, there were over 60 national regulators and 486 trading standards and local authorities with various powers to make criminal law, para 1.21.

17 Fraud Act 2006,s. 1(2)(a) ands. 2.

18 Fraud Act 2006,s. 2(2)(a) and (b).

19 Fraud Act 2006,s. 1(2)(b) ands. 3.

20 Fraud Act 2006,s. 1(2)(c) ands. 4.

21 Fraud Act 2006,s. 2(1)(a),s. 3(a),s. 4(1)(b).

22 Fraud Act 2006, s. 2(1)(b)(i) and (ii),s. 3(b)(i)and (ii),s. 4(1)(c)(i) and (ii).

23 Fraud Act 2006,s. 12.

24 *Tesco Ltd v Nattrass* [1972] AC 153 (HL).

mechanism to attribute the necessary mental state to the artificial corporate entity, the blameworthiness of the "directing mind" being equally attributable to the corporation which is perceived as that individual's alter ego. It is of note that in the context of business activity and regulatory contravention, regulations are typically drafted without a mens rea requirement such that the problem of attributing blameworthy mental states to the non-human legal entity is avoided. While this sidesteps the mens rea obstacle in the context of corporate misconduct, it is also true to say that regulatory breaches, requiring no proof of blameworthiness, do not attract the same moral opprobrium that attaches to truly criminal behaviour.[25] Whatever the gravity of the prohibited conduct, it is effectively reduced to a level akin to a breach of a public welfare offence, minimising the stigma and sense of culpability attached. In the context of fraud, individual wrongdoing is considered a truly criminal matter, whether a statutory offence or common law conspiracy to defraud, while corporate misconduct amounting to fraud, save for the exceptional circumstances in which the "identification principle" may apply, is typically confined to the regulatory sphere.

1.2 The location of corporate crime in the regulatory sphere

Corporate behaviour in commercial markets is largely shaped by regulations prescribed by the particular industry's regulatory authority. The regulatory agencies are also endowed with enforcement powers such that they are primarily responsible for identifying and addressing instances of regulatory breach. Accordingly, any discussion of the proposed expansion of the criminal liability of corporations must consider the traditional interplay between the criminal law and the regulatory regime. While this work does not propose a deconstruction of the whole regulatory edifice, a veritable industry in itself, it does seek to redraw the boundaries between the regulatory and the criminal in a way that reflects the contemporary understanding of the corporate form and corporate action. However, any exercise to rebalance the respective spheres cannot take place in a vacuum and an account of the law's evolution is necessary to understand the factors that have led to the current status quo. Without necessitating a detailed historiography, some reference to the birth and growth of the regulatory regime goes some way to explain why commercial wrongdoing came to be constructed within the regulatory framework in preference to the mainstream criminal law.

Although the criminal law has been used for some centuries to address the problem of individual traders who perpetrate frauds on the public at large, the recognition of the "corporate person" as a legal entity in its own right, with

25 Gerry Johnstone and Tony Ward, *Key Approaches to Criminology: Law and Crime* (London: Sage 2010).

distinct agency, is a more recent development.[26] The first so-called "corporate frauds" can be dated to the early 1700s[27] but it was not until the Victorian era that fraud as a widespread problem emerged, going hand in hand with the rise of industrial capitalism that was, of course, funded by joint stock projects.[28] These early criminal prosecutions for "corporate" frauds were, however, being brought against the individuals who were behind the corporation in the sense that they were playing a controlling or directing role.[29] At this time, one means to guard against financial crime was considered to be the mechanism of incorporation itself, with the requirement of company registration and the accompanying disclosure that this required.[30] Resonating with the English law's deeply entrenched doctrine of *caveat emptor*, this was an obvious response to new challenges, particularly those posed by the use of incorporation in dishonest schemes to lure would-be investors to part with their money in the expectation of large returns of profit. However, company registration and the concomitant disclosure regime was never expected to provide the ultimate solution to all corporate fraud and the limitations of the approach are both well documented and evidenced by the numerous subsequent piecemeal legal reforms that have followed.[31] The early developments in the law also reflected the ambiguous nature of the corporate form, which provides not only a novel environment for fraud but also a vehicle with which to perpetrate it. Similarly, that the early frauds were readily identifiable as the acts of the individuals behind the corporations is indicative of the simple pyramidal management structures typical of the first corporate forms. This practical reality was also resonant with the criminal law's theoretical adherence to individualism and the

26 Corporations have a legal existence and rights and duties distinct from those of the individual persons who form them; they enjoy perpetual succession, can sue and be sued, Co Litt 250a; 1 Bl Comm 468; *Salomon v Salomon* [1897] AC 22 (HL). The term 'legal person' can be applied to any entity that is legally distinct from its owners or members, e.g. nation states, local authorities.

27 See the accounts given by John Carswell, *The South Sea Bubble* (London: Cresset Press 1960); Virginia Cowles, *The Great Swindle* (London: Collins 1960); GP Gilligan, 'The Origins of UK Financial Services Regulation', (1997) 18(6) Co Law 167.

28 George Robb, *White Collar Crime in Modern England, Financial Fraud and Business Morality 1845–1929* (Cambridge: Cambridge University Press 1992); see too HA Shannon, 'The Coming of General Limited Liability', (1930–31) J Econ Hist 2 269; HA Shannon 'The Limited Companies of 1866–1883', (1933) J Econ Hist 4 295; RW Kostall, *Law and English Railway Capitalism 1825–75* (Oxford: Clarendon Press 1994): GR Searle, *Morality and the Market in Victorian Britain* (Oxford: Clarendon Press 1998).

29 See for example *R v Esdaile & others* (1858) 175 ER 696 known as the Royal British Bank trial.

30 Select Committee on Joint Stock Companies First Report, BPP, VII 1844 the *'Gladstone Committee Report'* and see George Robb, *White Collar Crime in Modern England, Financial Fraud and Business Morality 1845–1929* (Cambridge: Cambridge University Press, 1992).

31 Select Committee on the Financial Aspects of Corporate Governance (1992), the *'Cadbury Report'*, para 1.9, "Had a Code such as ours been in existence in the past, we believe that a number of the recent examples of unexpected company failures and cases of fraud would have received attention earlier."

conditions of individual liability.[32] Although the theory has endured, the characteristic simplicity of the early managerial frameworks is in stark contrast to the complex, diffuse and decentralised corporate structures that began to emerge in the 20th century. The initial primitive and the subsequent complex forms of organisational hierarchy have each brought distinct implications and challenges for the law. In the former, local traders and individuals behind the corporate form were men of a certain class and/or status and, historically, the local justices would have been reluctant to convict them as their own social peers.[33] Furthermore, the finding of personal criminal wrongdoing would have represented an unthinkable departure from the perception of criminality as a problem primarily confined to the lower social orders.[34] In such circumstances, the establishment of the regulatory regime, innovated through the enactment of the Factories Act 1833, provided a remedy by creating a central government agency with the power to make rules, enforce them and initiate prosecutions. The prohibitive provisions were characteristically drafted in the form of what is now described as a "strict liability" which, lacking a mens rea element, avoided the need to establish mental blameworthiness on the part of the factory owner. The use of such statutory regulation served to ensure basic standards of working conditions and they were relatively easy to enforce while involving no moral opprobrium.

Dispensing with the need to prove individual blame, the depersonalisation process would also have accorded with the developing law of corporations which, in striking contrast to the criminal law, prioritised the agency of the company over that of the individual owners and directors. Indeed, the general approach of the civil law has not varied in this respect and a court will only look beyond the corporate form to attribute individual civil liability in the rare situation that the stringent requirements for what is metaphorically described as "piercing the corporate veil" have been established.[35] Thus, the establishment and use of the regulatory regime neatly sidestepped the particular stigma associated with

32 RA Duff and Stuart Green (eds.), *Philosophical Foundations of Criminal Law* (Oxford: Oxford University Press 2011); Lindsay Farmer, *Criminal Law, Tradition, and Legal Order: Crime and the Genius of Scots Law 1747 to the Present* (Cambridge: Cambridge University Press 1997) 141.
33 WG Carson, 'Some Sociological Aspects of Strict Liability and the Enforcement of Factory Legislation' (1970) 33 MLR 396; WG Carson, 'White-Collar Crime and the Enforcement of Factory Legislation' (1970) 10 Brit J Criminology; WG Carson, 'The Conventionalisation of Early Factory Crime' (1979) 7 Int'l J Soc Law 37.
34 HW Arthurs, *'Without the law': Administrative Justice and Legal Pluralism in Nineteenth Century England* (Toronto: University of Toronto Press 1985); Alan Norrie, *Crime, Reason and History* (2nd ed, Cambridge: Cambridge University Press 2001); Nuno Garoupa and others, 'The Investigation and Prosecution of Regulatory Offences: Is There an Economic Case for Integration?' (2011) 70(1) CLJ 229–59, 233.
35 *Salomon v Salomon* [1897] AC 22 (HL). The civil law will only pierce the veil of incorporation if the company was essentially an alter ego vehicle for the defendant, *Caterpillar Financial Services (UK) Ltd v Saenz Corporation Ltd & Ors* [2012] EWHC 2888 (Comm).

the criminal law, overcame the prosecutorial and evidential hurdles consequent upon the need to prove individual mens rea at a senior level and was congruent with the fundamental principles of corporate law that were developing. This left the possibility of invoking the criminal law for the worst cases of legal violations that were considered to merit its full force. In the event of a violation considered truly criminal in character, the fault of the individual wrongdoer might then be correlated with the fault of the corporation. In its result, this mechanism broadly aligned to liability of a vicarious nature that was well established in the long-standing master and servant jurisprudence.[36] In such circumstances, the finding of corporate criminal liability would have had the practical advantage that the company would be the subject of any punitive fine incurred.

However, as the complexity of the corporate form grew, the correlation between it, as a distinct legal entity, and its owners and/or directors as individuals, became increasingly distant and more contrived. While the practical implications of a finding of corporate fault might have been attractive, the more remote the blameworthy act from the centre of ownership and/or control, the more difficult it would have been to attribute to the corporation the moral opprobrium that criminal conviction involves. Accordingly, the law developed coincidentally over time, on a case by case basis, responding to factual contexts that happened to both arise and be brought before the courts. In due course, a general principle of law was said to have been formulated such that the corporate entity would only be considered criminally liable if the wrongdoing was that of an individual who was senior enough to attract a correlation whereby the company could be considered his alter ego.[37] Throughout this period of the law's development, the continued and ongoing use of the regulatory regime, obviating the need to prove mens rea, provided a practical solution to the emerging problem of fault attribution in ever more structurally complex organisations. Indeed, the use of regulation to encourage compliance with specified standards in the commercial environment has flourished and, as a corollary, the accompanying enforcement process, as an alternative to mainstream criminal prosecution, has itself embedded in the legal framework.[38]

Typically, regulators enforce detailed and highly prescriptive regulations though a range of civil sanctions, backed up by the criminal law for only the

36 The respective nature of the liabilities differs in that the former is said to be attributed directly to the company while the latter is attributed vicariously on the basis of the relationship between the servant and the master.
37 This gradual development is considered in detail in Ch. 7.
38 The Royal Commission on Criminal Procedure, *Report on the Investigation and Prosecution of Criminal Offences in England and Wales: The Law and Procedure* (1980/81 Cmnd 8092-I and II, 1980/81)158, para 7.42. See also N Garoupa and others, 'The Investigation and Prosecution of Regulatory Offences: Is There an Economic Case for Integration?' (2011) 70 (1) CLJ 229, 233; HW Arthurs, *'Without the law': Administrative Justice and Legal Pluralism in Nineteenth Century England* (Toronto: University of Toronto Press 1985); Royal Commission on Practices and Proceedings of the Courts of Common Law, 5th Report (1833–34).

worst cases of breach.[39] Nonetheless, the role of the regulatory body is perceived more as advisory than prosecutorial and is clothed in an ethos that prefers to attain objectives via education and the encouragement of voluntary compliance[40] rather than the suppression of undesirable conduct by punishing wrongdoing.[41] With a traditional tendency to view prosecution as a last resort,[42] regulation has therefore been conceptualised outside the ambit of mainstream crime, and corporate wrongdoing, even of a serious character, has continued to attract a different moral compass.[43]

1.3 Regulation: the panacea for all corporate wrongdoing

Although the regulatory architecture was once seen as the panacea for all corporate wrongdoing, the extension of the reach of the criminal law to deal with financial misconduct is not the remote prospect it may once have been. The landscape is clearly changing, with statutory offences already enacted in the

39 Regulatory Enforcement and Sanctions Act 2008 enacted following Richard B Macrory (Better Regulation Executive), *Regulatory Justice: Making Sanctions Effective, Final Report* (Nov 2006).
40 Jeremy Rowan-Robinson and Paul Q Watchman, *Crime and Regulation: A Study of the Enforcement of Regulatory Codes* (London: T & T Clark 1990).
41 Genevra Richardson, 'Strict Liability for Regulatory Crime: The Empirical Evidence' (1987) Crim LR 295–306; Carolyn Abbot, *Enforcing Pollution Control Regulation* (Oxford: Hart 2009) cited by Nuno Garoupa and others, 'The Investigation and Prosecution of Regulatory Offences: Is There an Economic Case for Integration?' (2011) 70(1) CLJ 229–59. Even where successful, the average fine imposed is very low, see Law Commission, *Criminal Liability in Regulatory Contexts* (Law Com No 195, 2010) App. A, para A.15. This reluctance can be dated to our earliest attempts to deal with corporate fraud, see the early company legislation e. g. Joint Stock Companies Act 1844 and see too D Hay, 'Property, Authority and the Criminal Law' in D Hay and others (eds.), *Albion's Fatal Tree* (London: Allen Lane 1975); WR Cornish and G Clark, *Law and Society in England 1750–1950* (London: Sweet & Maxwell 1989); M Foucault, *Discipline and Punish: The Birth of A Prison* (Harmondsworth: Penguin 1977); KJM Smith, *Lawyers, Legislators and Theorists: Developments in English Criminal Jurisprudence 1800–1957* (Oxford: Oxford University Press 1998); Alan Norrie, *Crime, Reason and History* (2nd ed, Cambridge: Cambridge University Press 2001).
42 R Baldwin, 'The New Punitive Regulation' (2005) MLR 351; see too James Gobert, 'Corporate Criminality: New Crimes for the Times' (1994) Crim LR 722; Keith Hawkins, *Law As Last Resort* (Oxford: Oxford University Press 2002); Law Commission, *Criminal Liability in Regulatory Contexts* (Law Com No 195, 2010) App. A, para A.12–13.
43 Of note, when the Royal Commission provided the recommendations that formed the basis of the new Crown Prosecution Service in 1981, the ambit of the report was confined to mainstream crime, Royal Commission on Criminal Procedure (The Phillips Commission) 1977, reported in 1981, *The Investigation and Prosecution of Criminal Offences in England and Wales: The Law and Procedure* (Cmnd 8092-I and II, 1980/81). The Commission gave little attention to the non-police agencies, commenting that "prosecution is the weapon of final resort because they prefer to obtain their objectives by education and persuasion". See too Archibald Bodkin, 'The Prosecution of Offenders: English Practice' (1928) 1 Pol J 354–5; Howard Pendleton, *Criminal Justice in England: A Study in Law Administration* (New York: MacMillan 1931) vol 1; Joshua Rozenberg, *The Case for the Crown: The Inside Story of the DPP* (London: Thorsons 1987).

context of corporate offences for bribery[44] and tax evasion,[45] and there is a renewed political determination to deal with what has been described more generically as corporate liability for economic crime.[46] The question is no longer whether to criminalise serious corporate misconduct but how. With the growing recognition that corporations can both harbour criminals and develop a criminogenic autonomy,[47] the deficiencies of regulation in the financial sector, and the "light touch" approach that became synonymous with it, are already well documented with the need for a more robust regime now widely articulated.[48] Accordingly, this book does not set out to rehearse the arguments for the use of the criminal law in preference to the use of regulatory enforcement and, for this reason, a brief overview of the main justifications will suffice. A recent and more detailed discussion of this nature, which considers the rationale for criminalising corporate fraud in particular, can be found in the work of Copp and Cronin.[49]

44 Bribery Act 2010,s. 7, the corporate failure to prevent bribery offence.
45 Finance Act 2016, s. 162 and Sch.20; s. 166 inserts ss. 106B to 106H into the Taxes Management Act 1970 and introduces tougher sanctions, civil penalties and additional criminal offences for individuals who enable tax evasion. The Criminal Finances Act 2017, Pt. 3, s. 45 and s. 46, introduces offences of corporate failure to prevent UK and foreign tax evasion.
46 See, for example, Ministry of Justice, *Corporate Liability for Economic Crime*, Call for Evidence, 13 January 2017.
47 The Fair and Effective Markets Review: Implementation Report is available at www.bankofeng land.co.uk/markets/Documents/femr/implementationreport.pdf accessed October 26, 2016.
48 See e.g. the Parliamentary Commission on Banking Standards, *Changing Banking for Good*, 12 June 2013; HM Treasury, Bank of England and FCA, *Fair and Effective Markets Review*, Final Report, June 2015; New City Agenda and Cass Business School, *Cultural Change in the FCA, PRA and Bank of England, Practising What They Preach?*, 25 October 2016. For earlier discussions see e.g. James Gobert and Maurice Punch, *Rethinking Corporate Crime* (Oxford: Butterworths 2003); M Levi, *Regulating Fraud* (London: Tavistock 1987); Michael Levi, *The Economic Cost of Fraud Report for the Home Office* (London, NERA 2000); Michael Levi, 'The Roskill Fraud Commission Revisited: An Assessment' (2003) JFL 11(1), 38–44; Michael Levi, *The Phantom Capitalists* (Andover: Ashgate 2008); Michael Levi and others, *The Nature, Extent and Economic Impact of Fraud in the UK* (London: ACPO 2007); The Royal Commission on Criminal Justice *The Investigation, Prosecution and the Trial of Serious Fraud*: (London, HMSO 1993); JE Parkinson, *Corporate Power and Responsibility, Issues in the Theory of Company Law* (Oxford: Clarendon Press 2000); D Sugarman, 'Law Economy and the State in England 1750–1914: Some Major Issues' in D Sugarman (ed.) *Legality, Ideology and the State* (London: Academic Press 1983); Edward S Herman, *Corporate Control, Corporate Power* (Cambridge: Cambridge University Press 1981); Gary Slapper and Steve Tombs, *Corporate Crime* (Harlow: Longman 1999); GP Gilligan, 'The Origins of UK Financial Services Regulation', (1997) 18(6) Co Law 167–6; SP Shapiro, 'Collaring the Crime, Not the Criminal: Reconsidering the Concept of White Collar Crime' (1990) 55 Am Soc Rev 346–65; Gary Scanlan, 'Dishonesty in Corporate Offences, A Need for Reform?' (2002) 23(4) Co Law 114–19; Gary Scanlan, 'Offences Concerning Directors and Officers of a Company – Fraud and Corruption in the United Kingdom – the Future' (2008) 29(9) Co Law 264–71; JL Masters, 'Fraud and Money Laundering: The Evolving Criminalization of Corporate Non-compliance' (2008) JMLC 103.
49 Stephen Copp and Alison Cronin, 'The Failure of Criminal Law to Control the Use of Off Balance Sheet Finance During the Banking Crisis' (2015) 36(4) Co Law 99.

It is, however, worth observing that, although not attracting the same extent of international collaboration that the anti-corruption and tax evasion initiatives have required, many of the arguments for the criminalisation of corporations for bribery can also be made for fraud. In particular, the architects of the anti-bribery provisions at the European level were concerned with the efficacy of the civil law as a means of redress for the "victims" of bribery. At a national level, the limitations of the tortious approach have been clearly identified and these include the evidential difficulties that potential claimants face as well as the problem of the quantification of the loss suffered as a result of missing the opportunity to do business. While the quantification issue may be less difficult for victims of fraud who want to instigate a civil claim, considerable obstacles remain for those who do recognise that they have been defrauded, not least in relation to obtaining evidence sufficient to satisfy the burden of proof and the likelihood of a vast imbalance in both expertise and resources in favour of the corporate defendant.[50] In this respect, evidence has emerged in relation to claims brought by SMEs (small and medium-sized enterprises), who were particularly affected by financial mis-selling, that the banks exploited their superior position to discourage claimants from pursuing their cases, wearing them down through delays and cost accumulation. This was often exacerbated by the restructuring power of the banks allowing them to seize control over businesses, assets and balance sheets at the first indication of financial trouble.[51] Additionally, the availability of legal representation for claimants can be significantly reduced through the banks' pre-engagement of a plethora of legal firms with detailed restrictive terms preventing them from acting in any matter against the bank.[52] Further, businesses that otherwise managed to overcome the substantial financial and other hurdles may have been denied an action that could have been brought by a "private person" pursuant to s. 150 Financial Services and Markets Act 2000 for the contravention of an FSA rule by an authorised person, for example the duty to deal "fairly", since a company is not considered a "private person".[53]

In relation to widespread frauds of the mis-selling and mass-marketing genre, although victims may have a claim in both the tort of deceit and in

---

50 See for example berg Solicitors annual Banking Report (2016) at www.berg.co.uk accessed 30 April 2017. In that small and medium-sized enterprises (SMEs) are typically heavily reliant on bank loans to sustain and develop their businesses, they have been one of the biggest victims of mis-selling as regards the purchasing of derivative products the loans were conditional upon. Since the Financial Ombudsman Service provides access to compensation for awards up to just £150,000, with highly restrictive eligibility criteria that exclude most SME claims, and the High Court's Financial List only hears claims in excess of £50 million or those which involve issues of general importance to the financial markets, SMEs can only litigate in the usual way through the County and High Courts.

51 Abuse of this kind was the focus of the trial and conviction, in January 2017, of 6 former employees and associates for fraud in the HBOS Reading scandal, berg Solicitors annual Banking Report (2016) at www.berg.co.uk accessed 30 April 2017.

52 Michel Reznik, 'Injustice in Financial Services Disputes (Pt. 1)' (2017) 167 NLJ 7743, 18.

53 *Titan Steel Wheels Ltd v Royal Bank of Scotland Plc* [2010] EWHC 211 (Comm).

contract, the perpetrators tend to target numerous individuals for relatively small amounts of money such that the relative cost of bringing an action will be prohibitive for individual claimants. Consequently, consumer protection bodies often engage with wrongful trading complaints where there is widespread public harm but, since they serve an altogether different purpose, they do not obtain redress for individual complainants and often possess limited enforcement and/or prosecutorial powers. While the FSA and its successor, the FCA, have been instrumental in obtaining repayments and compensation for customers who were mis-sold financial products and derivatives, such as the PPI policies, it must be acknowledged that the regulatory provisions they enforce are designed primarily to address conduct that is not harmful in itself, but which may be conducive to harmful outcomes. In contrast, the criminal law is the normative response to harmful conduct where wrongdoers deserve the stigma associated with conviction because they have engaged in seriously reprehensible conduct.[54] In this respect, serious offences are defined as those involving dishonesty, intention, knowledge or recklessness[55] and the fraud-based offences have been specifically identified as meriting the invocation of the criminal law[56] since these involve a moral failing and not just a breach of a rule or a departure from a standard.[57] Applying these standards to the financial misconduct that has been witnessed in the last few decades, there is a real case for the intervention of the criminal law.

One of the oft-cited objections to a corporate crime regime is that criminal conviction and the accompanying potential for the courts to hand down tough sentences, such as high-level fines, is directly or indirectly detrimental to other acknowledged interests and innocent parties. These include, for example, the spectre of possible corporate insolvency, the diminution of employment opportunities, reduced regional prosperity, reduced investment in innovation and development, reduced tax revenue and the erosion of capital reserves and lending potential, in addition to the direct costs that would be borne by the shareholders and passed on to customers.[58] However, cogent counter-arguments have been made elsewhere for the operation of Darwinian principles in the market, for example in the context of cartel activity, where organisations are not viable but for the prohibited conduct (collusion).[59] Although corporate fraud frequently gives

---

54 Law Commission, *Criminal Liability in Regulatory Contexts* (Law Com No 195, 2010) 8, para 1.28.
55 Ibid 28, para 3.10.
56 Ibid 11, para 1.42.
57 Ibid 68, para 4.2.
58 See for example the Chancellor of the Exchequer's 2015 Mansion House speech, www.gov. uk/government/speeches/mansion-house-2015-speech-by-the-chancellor-of-the-exchequer accessed November 4, 2016.
59 Christopher Harding and Julian Joshua, *Regulating Cartels in Europe* (2nd ed, Oxford: Oxford University Press 2010) and citing in particular Massimo Motta, 'On Cartel Deterrence and Fines in the European Union' (2008) 29 European Competition Law Review.

rise to a more remote sense of harm than other crimes, and the extent of the harm is impossible to calculate accurately, it undoubtedly results in a misallocation of resources and an overall reduction in consumer welfare. Indeed, underlying the Fair and Effective Markets Review of 2015, recommendations were made to deliver "fair" markets and these were defined as "markets in which participants behave with integrity ... [and] that means participants should be confident that they will not be subject to fraud, deception, disinformation, misrepresentation, manipulation or coercion."[60] Beyond the quantifiable direct financial cost of fraud and the more elusive damage caused to consumer trust and to market operation generally, there is also the documented social cost of economic crime which includes small businesses being forced into bankruptcy, livelihoods ruined, opportunities lost and the inestimable impact on society and people's health and well-being.[61] As to the potentially far-reaching effect of punitive corporate fines, this is not the only sentencing option for corporate offenders. Indeed, a substantial body of work has previously been undertaken in this area that has provided some imaginative and useful alternatives to the financial penalty.[62] In any event, while such considerations may bear on the "public interest" stage of enquiry in the prosecutor's code (and the decision whether to prosecute) or on mitigation in the sentencing process, they have no bearing on the issue of criminal responsibility.

From an economic perspective, the relative costs of establishing, maintaining and complying with a regulatory regime can be compared with those that would be incurred in the use of the mainstream criminal law. Analysis reveals that the cost benefits of pursuing a simple general anti-fraud law appear to significantly outweigh those associated with highly-particularised regulations, the eye-watering costs of which further distort competition and damage overall market efficiency.[63] In the financial sector compliance costs are particularly high in that the FCA and the Prudential Regulation Authority (PRA) rulebooks,

---

60 HM Treasury, Bank of England, Financial Conduct Authority, *Fair and Effective Markets Review*, Final Report, 2015, 1.1.
61 New City Agenda and Cass Business School, *Cultural Change in the FCA, PRA and Bank of England, Practising What They Preach?*, 25 October 2016, p 13.
62 Anon, 'Corporate Crime: Regulating Corporate Behaviour Through Criminal Sanctions' (1979) 92 Harv L Rev, 1227; Brent Fisse, 'Reconstructing Corporate Criminal Law: Deterrence, Retribution, Fault and Sanctions' (1983) 56 S Cal L Rev 1141–246; James P Bonner and Beth N Forman, 'Bridging the Deterrence Gap: Imposing Criminal Penalties on Corporations and their Executives for Producing Hazardous Projects', (1993) 20 San Diego Justice Journal 1,1; Brent Fisse and John Braithwaite, *Corporations, Responsibility and Corporate Society* (Cambridge: Cambridge University Press 1993); Mary Kreiner Ramirez, 'The Science Fiction of Corporate Criminal Liability: Containing the Machine Through the Corporate Death Penalty' (2005) 47 Ariz L Rev 933–1002.
63 Copp S and Cronin A, 'The Failure of Criminal Law to Control the Use of Off Balance Sheet Finance During the Banking Crisis' (2015) 36(4) Co Law 99. See too Gary S Becker, 'Crime and Punishment: An Economic Approach' (1968) 76 J Pol Econ 169; Kenneth G Elzinga and William Breit, *The Anti-trust Penalties: A Study in Law and Economics* (New Haven: Yale University Press 1976); John Collins Coffee Jnr, 'Corporate Crime and Punishment: A Non-Chicago View of the Economics of Criminal Sanctions', (1980) 17 Am Crim L Rev 419–76;

guidance and supervisory statements, together comprise a staggering quantity of information in excess of 13,000 pages.[64] Similarly, the cost of compliance must be added to the operating costs of the regulators themselves and in relation to the FCA, PRA, Financial Ombudsman Service, Financial Services Compensation Scheme and Money Advice Service alone the total administrative costs are now almost £1.2 billion a year, a six fold increase since 2000.[65] It is also of note that where strong regulatory enforcement sanctions are imposed, as means to achieve optimum deterrence against the most serious breaches, a natural juridification of the regulation process occurs when more is at stake and defence rights and appeal procedures tend to dominate the process.[66]

The fact that large organisations provide positive outcomes does not negate the effects of harm that they can cause. It is not in doubt that the role of specialised agencies and the use of regulation is an invaluable means to encourage businesses to conform to industry standards and enforce prophylactic measures, however, there is also wide recognition that some violations, by their intrinsic nature or the particular harm that they cause, demand the full force of the criminal law.[67] Although there has been arguably little in the recent past to distinguish conduct which falls short of a minor disclosure requirement and that which is tantamount to criminal fraud, dishonesty affords fraud the immoral character of criminality. Furthermore, given that widespread misconduct of this nature has the potential to cause vast economic harm, nationally and globally, the question is not so much why companies should be criminalised, but where to draw the line between the regulatory and criminal spheres and how to construct a model of liability that accommodates the non-physiological nature of the corporation.

1.4 Corporate agency: corporations as autonomous actors

It is without doubt that the regulatory model provided the solution to both practical and theoretical difficulties associated with the criminalisation of collective "corporate" misconduct. However, the current architecture of, and

Richard A Posner, 'An Economic Theory of the Criminal Law' (1985) 85 Colum L Rev 1193–231; Kenneth G Dau-Schmidt, 'An Economic Analysis of the Criminal Law as a Preference-Shaping Policy' (1990) Duke Law Journal 1–38; Pat O' Malley, 'Risk, Power and Crime Prevention' (1992) 21 Economy and Society 252; Richard A Posner, *Economic Analysis of Law* (New York: Aspen 2007).

64 New City Agenda and Cass Business School, *Cultural Change in the FCA, PRA and Bank of England, Practising What They Preach?*, 25 October 2016 at http://newcityagenda.co.uk/wp-content/uploads/2016/10/NCA-Cultural-change-in-regulators-report_embargoed.pdf accessed May 21, 2017, p 38.

65 Ibid 58.

66 Christopher Harding and Julian Joshua, *Regulating Cartels in Europe* (2nd ed, Oxford: Oxford University Press 2010) 302.

67 Ibid; Richard B Macrory (Better Regulation Executive), *Regulatory Justice: Making Sanctions Effective, Final Report* (Nov 2006).

interrelationship between, the regulatory and criminal spheres is less the product of a unified overarching jurisprudence and more the progeny of an accumulation of responses to a number of various problems, influences and demands arising in the commercial forum at various different epochs. One of the predominant influences in this respect has been the criminal law's entrenched commitment to individualism, exclusively conceived in the form of the human person, and its failure to develop a theory of corporate agency to which responsibility can be assigned and that can accommodate principles of direct corporate liability. Accordingly, the term "corporate crime" inherently imports a notion of individuals committing offences in the corporate environment whereas, in contrast, violations described as "regulatory breaches" are more readily understood as the product of corporate agency. While it is accepted that companies can flout or fall foul of regulations and cause harm through their activities, it is generally perceived that only human agents can perpetrate real crime, whether acting alone or in concert. Flowing from this, references to "corporate fraud" commonly denote economic offences that are perpetrated by individual, typically "white collar",[68] workers or directors and, further, that the employer company is either the victim of, or the conduit for, the crime or provides the setting in which it is committed. In the criminal law the notion of the "corporate actor" imports a considerably narrower meaning than is afforded in other contexts and it certainly does not involve a broader appreciation of the corporation as an autonomous criminal actor in its own right. While it is readily accepted that, for example, nations can win wars, armies can commit atrocities, teams can lose matches and corporations win or lose contracts, the popular assumption that corporations cannot commit crime is stubbornly entrenched. Real crime, it seems, is only reducible to individuals.

Although reference to an organisational whole gives meaning to descriptions that would otherwise be lacking, for example "the team played well" illustrates much more than any account of each individual's performance,[69] and the language of blame is not necessarily limited by individualism,[70] the language of responsibility is laden with individualistic meaning. Notions such as rationality and autonomy and the use of words such as "person" and "actor" are metaphysically limiting.[71] This impediment is exacerbated in the context of the criminal

---

68 Edwin Sutherland, *White Collar Crime* (New York: Holt 1949).
69 Gellner E, 'Holism versus Individualism' in May Brodbeck (ed.), *Readings in the Philosophy of the Social Sciences* (New York: Macmillan 1968) 258, referred to by G R Sullivan, 'The Attribution of Culpability to Limited Companies' (1996) 55(3) CLJ 515, 538.
70 For example, when people blame organisations they are not blaming the "ox that gored, or pointing the finger at individuals behind the corporate mantle, they condemn the fact that the organisation either implemented a policy of non-compliance or failed to exercise its capacity to avoid the offence for which blame attaches", Brent Fisse and John Braithwaite, *Corporations: Crime and Accountability* (Cambridge: Cambridge University Press 1993) 25.
71 Celia Wells, 'Corporations: Culture, Risk and Criminal Liability' (1993) Crim LR Aug 551–66.

law whereby the analysis of any offence is by reduction to its physical and mental elements, articulated in terms of "actus reus" and "mens rea" respectively, which further marginalises corporate behaviour.[72] The notion of corporate criminal responsibility is intrinsically bound up with the need to establish mens rea, the guilty mind, which is considered the bedrock of culpability in the criminal law. The corporate entity may be able to sue and be sued, own property and have perpetual succession but it is considered wholly bereft of the physiology required for the criminal law's imposition of moral blame.

However, while some frauds that are perpetrated in the commercial context are readily identifiable as the acts of particular individuals, who have the requisite mens rea to attract criminal culpability that may or may not be attributable to the corporation, others are not reducible in the same way. For example, criminal harm may be the result of systemic and pervasive corporate practices that do not involve criminal intent on the part of any one or more of its individual members. Thus, if the mis-selling conduct referred to above were to be considered fraud, importing the recognition that it may be a dishonest practice,[73] it would not necessarily be possible or appropriate to prosecute the individual employees who were involved in the selling. In such circumstances, it is entirely conceivable that the honesty of the staff members would not be in doubt where, for instance, they simply sold a product or commodity that was a constituent of the range of products authorised and offered by the employer organisation and the sales conduct was a usual and encouraged part of the company activity, consistent with the corporate policy and part of a company-wide, and potentially industry-wide, practice.[74] Similarly, in the same circumstances there may be no individual criminal fault on the part of any one or more of the company's senior managers or directors to which corporate attribution under the identification principle could attach. Indeed, this was considered to be the case in the PPI mis-selling scandals in that, although the activity in question involved hundreds of firms over a number of years, only one senior executive was found to be at fault and fined,[75] while not one banking executive has been subject to any enforcement

---

72 Celia Wells, 'The Decline and Rise of English Murder: Corporate Crime and Individual Responsibility' (1988) Crim LR Dec 788. Harding also suggests that this has resulted in the anthropocentric mind-set which is at the heart of the individualist/holist impasse, Christopher Harding, *Criminal Enterprise: Individuals, Organisations and Criminal Responsibility* (Cullompton: Willan 2007).

73 Fraud Act 2006, ss. 2(1)(a), 3(a) and 4(1)(b). The dishonesty requirement will be discussed more fully in Ch. 4.

74 It should be noted that in his defence to the LIBOR manipulation prosecution Tom Hayes, the UBS and Citibank trader who was found guilty of eight counts of conspiracy to defraud in August 2016, was not successful in arguing that he was not dishonest for participating in what had been industry standard practice for 20 years.

75 This was the Chief Executive of the sofa retailer "Land of Leather", fined by the predecessor to the FCA, the Financial Services Authority.

action for either this or the mis-selling of interest rate swap agreements to SMEs.[76] This type of misconduct points more readily to the existence of a criminogenic corporate culture rather than the dishonesty of particular individuals. Accordingly, any "parasitic" attribution of corporate liability for fraud, based on the commission of an underlying fraud offence by an individual (or individuals), cannot work where the individuals involved in the "dishonest" conduct cannot as individuals be said to have been dishonest. This would rule out not only the application of the identification principle but also the "failure to prevent" model of corporate liability that has been mooted as the most likely statutory reform to be selected.[77]

The understanding that malpractice and criminal misconduct can be the product of a potentially deviant organisational "culture", rather than individual criminality, is now increasingly recognised, particularly in the financial sector.[78] This recognition accords with accepted theories of groups and collective action more readily acknowledged in other disciplines. It is accepted that individual members are influenced by the group context, to a lesser or greater extent, and behave differently than they would if acting outside of this setting. Furthermore, in addition to the possible influence of the organisational cultural norms on acts that can be reduced to the individual level, and the dynamic arising between the organisational whole and its members, corporate outcomes can be the result of numerous other contributing factors where there is a complex interplay between external demands and various internal forces, such as managers, standard procedures, and corporate policies and priorities.[79] This signals a departure from the historical focus on the individual in the analysis of socio-economic phenomena,[80] the basic elements of which comprise the assumption of rationality and what is called "methodological individualism"[81] in which social phenomena must first be explained by showing how they result from individual actions and then by

76 New City Agenda (a not-for-profit financial services think tank) and Cass Business School, *Cultural Change in the FCA, PRA & Bank of England, Practising What They Preach?*, 25 October 2016.
77 A more detailed discussion is set out below in Ch. 2.
78 See, for example, The Fair and Effective Markets Review: Implementation Report, www.bankofengland.co.uk/markets/Documents/femr/implementationreport.pdf accessed October 26, 2016.
79 James P Bonner and Beth N Forman, 'Bridging the Deterrence Gap: Imposing Criminal Penalties on Corporations and their Executives for Producing Hazardous Projects' (1993) 20 San Diego Justice Journal 1.
80 This practice became prominent with the Enlightenment and can be seen in the works of, for example, John Locke, John Stuart Mill and Jeremy Bentham, see Geoffrey M Hodgson, 'Meanings of Methodological Individualism' (2007) Journal of Economic Methodology, 14 (2) June, 211–26. See too the Austrian School of Economics, e.g. Robert Ahdieh, 'Beyond Individualism in Law and Economics' (2011) 91 BUL Rev 43, 43 citing Lars Udehn, 'The Changing Face of Methodological Individualism' (2002) 28 Ann Rev Soc 479, 484.
81 Robert Ahdieh, 'Beyond Individualism in Law and Economics' (2011) 91 BUL Rev 43.

reference to the intentional states that motivate the actors.[82] This reductionist approach to the behaviour of social institutions broadly equates to the need to examine subjective mens rea in the criminal law's treatment of the individual. However, while criminal law theory has become ever more entrenched in this individualist paradigm, economic theory has gone on to recognise group behaviour as a methodology.[83] In accordance with this development, sociologists have addressed the issue of interdependence where "people are not always independent actors, but are members of groups, and [that] such membership can sometimes affect their actions".[84] Agassi described this as "institutional individualism", in recognition that institutional structures exist and affect individual choices, while only individuals have aims and responsibilities. This account acknowledges that the influence of group and social structures can produce types of collective intention[85] albeit they are not evaluated as direct causes of phenomena.[86] The fact that members of highly structured organisations develop different norms and mores as members than those they hold outside the group environment is now well documented in sociology.[87]

The seed of institutional individualism may be located in the early realist, or natural entity, theory associated with von Gierke's work on legal and political philosophy in which he seemed to suggest the phenomena of a group psyche.[88]

82 M Weber, *Economy and Society* (Berkeley, University of California Press 2013) originally published posthumously in 1922. The phrase was originally coined by his student, Joseph Schumpeter in *Das Wesen und der Hauptinhalt Der Theoretischen Nationalokonomie* (Leipzig, Duncker and Humblot 1908) and in English the following year, Joseph Schumpeter, 'On the Concept of Social Value' (1909) QJ Econ 213, 231. See too Robert Ahdieh, 'Beyond Individualism in Law and Economics' (2011) 91 BUL Rev 43, 49.

83 Karl R Popper, *The Open Society and Its Enemies* (London: Routledge & Kegan Paul 1945) 2 vols; Joseph Agassi, 'Methodological Individualism' (1960) 11(3) British Journal of Sociology, Sept 244–70; Joseph Agassi, 'Institutional Individualism' (1975) 26(2) British Journal of Sociology, June 144–55.

84 Kenneth G Dau-Schmidt, 'Economics and Sociology: The Prospects for an Interdisciplinary Discourse on Law' (1997) Wis L Rev 389, 419; Robert Ahdieh, 'Beyond Individualism in Law and Economics' (2011) 91 BUL Rev 43.

85 See Karl R Popper, *The Poverty of Historicism* (London: Routledge & Kegan Paul 1957); JWN Watkins, 'Historical Explanation in the Social Sciences' (1957–58) British Journal for the Philosophy of Science 104; John R Searle, *The Construction of Social Reality* (London: Penguin 1996); Valerie P Hans, *Business on Trial* (New Haven: Yale University Press 2000).

86 Robert Ahdieh, 'Beyond Individualism in Law and Economics' (2011) 91 BUL Rev 43, 57.

87 Christopher Harding, *Criminal Enterprise: Individuals, Organisations and Criminal Responsibility* (Cullompton: Willan 2007) and referring in support to Peter A French, 'The Corporation as a Moral Person' (1979) 16 Am Phil Q 207 reprinted as ch 9 in Larry May and Stacey Hoffman (eds.), *Collective Responsibility, Group Based Harm and Corporate Rights* (Notre Dame, University of Notre Dame Press 1987).

88 Otto von Gierke, *Political Theories in the Middle Age* (trans FW Maitland, Cambridge: Cambridge University Press 1913) and FW Maitland's introduction vii–xiv. It is suggested that von Gierke's views were employed in fascist political theory to justify the dictatorial fascist state as an organism superior to the individuals of whom it is composed, see E Barker's Introduction in von

This view was widely endorsed at that time and found favour in the legal arena too as is evidenced in the works of some particularly eminent jurists.[89] For example, Maitland wrote, "if n men unite themselves in an organised body, jurisprudence, unless it wishes to pulverize the group, must see n + 1 persons".[90] Similarly, Dicey observed

> it is a fact which has received far too little notice from English lawyers, that, whenever men act in concert for a common purpose, they tend to create a body which, from no fiction of law, but from the very nature of things, differs from the individuals from whom it is constituted.[91]

The early realist theory held that group agents are emergent entities, with similar provenance to the metaphors used in the vitalist account of life, and treat group agency as the product of a mysterious force.[92] Although this view of the organisation was widely accepted at the turn of the 20th century, its demise may have been its association with the totalitarian image of society as fascism took over in Europe.[93] The advancement of realist philosophy in the criminal law was equally short-lived, its abrupt conclusion seemingly brought about in the narrow confine of concerns about trading with the enemy where

---

Gierke's *Natural Law and the Theory of Society 1550–1800 (*trans E Barker, Cambridge: Cambridge University Press 1934) lxxxiv–lxxxvii. It is also suggested that the recent re-emergence of the notion of the company as its own entity with a distinct personality is simply the application of the political philosophy of communitarianism to companies, Daniel J Morrissey, 'Toward a New/Old Theory of Corporate Social Responsibility' (1989) 40 Syracuse L Rev 1005, 1033–6, discussed in D French and others, *Mayson, French and Ryan on Company Law* (27th ed, Oxford: Oxford University Press 2010). See also G Teubner, 'Enterprise Corporatism: New Industrial Policy and the "Essence" of the Legal Person' (1988) 36 Am J Comp Law 130 in which Teubner says that the autopoietic, self-creating theory and its real personality derives from the fact that it has a socially binding self-description of an organised action system.

89 See, for example, FW Maitland, 'Moral Personality and Legal Personality' and 'Trust and Corporation' in HAL Fisher (ed.) *The Collected Papers of Frederick William Maitland* (Cambridge: Cambridge University Press 1911) vol 3, 210–319; Cecil Thomas Carr, *The General Principles of the Law of Corporations* (the Yorke prize essay for 1902, Cambridge: Cambridge University Press 1905).

90 FW Maitland, 'Moral Person and Legal Person' in HAL Fisher (ed.), *The Collected Papers of Frederick William Maitland* (Cambridge: Cambridge University Press 1911) 304, 316. See also the discussion in D French and others, *Mayson, French and Ryan on Company Law* (27th ed, Oxford: Oxford University Press 2010).

91 AV Dicey, 'The Combination Laws as Illustrating the Relation Between Law and Public Opinion in England During the 19th Century' (1904) Harv L Rev 511, 513; AV Dicey, *Law and Opinion in England* (2nd ed, London: Macmillan 1914) referred to by Christopher Harding, *Criminal Enterprise: Individuals, Organisations and Criminal Responsibility* (Cullompton: Willan 2007).

92 Christian List and Philip Pettit, *Group Agency* (Oxford: Oxford University Press 2011) 8. The vitalist account holds that life results from a vital force peculiar to living organisms, described in terms of a distinct fluid or spirit.

93 Ibid.

one of the contracting parties was an English corporation owned and directed by German nationals.[94] Influenced by libertarian politics, group agents came to be viewed as a fiction and nothing more than individual agents acting collaboratively.[95] This accorded with the view endorsed by proponents of the economic utilitarian movement such as Jeremy Bentham and legal theorist, John Austin.[96]

However, while resolute in its continued commitment to individualism, theorising in the criminal law was not completely dormant. For example, the jurist Winn made the following observation in the context of the law and corporate activity in the 1920s:

> Corporations have no thoughts of their own, for they have no brains to which thought images may pass; the brains of the corporators are their own brains and not the corporations. But the minds of the corporators, thinking in meeting assembled, exert a mutual influence which makes the definite purpose and firmness of attitude; when nine men of the like opinions unite to prove to attend the infallibility of their position, each will be strengthened, confirmed and rendered more obdurate by the support of others. Mutually stimulated they will go to excesses from which alone they would have shrunk. It is an inexplicable but plainly demonstrable phenomenon of the human mind that men do not think their own thoughts within groups; each mind contributes something to the group, and is influenced by the thought impulses which are in play around it.[97]

More recently, accompanied by the growth of inter-disciplinary research and insights from extra-legal disciplines, the criminal law's interest in collective theories has been revived, looking to identify groups with their own defining features, obligations and rights.[98] For example, Sullivan has added his theory of organisational "collective intention", observing that individual intention flows downwards from the collective,[99] and Celia Wells acknowledges the practical reality that people do not think as individuals but act as group participants influenced by institutional and cultural constraints.[100] Similarly, Lee conceives corporate criminal liability by comparison with a team of individuals who play a

---

94 *Daimler Co Ltd v Continental Tyre Co Ltd* [1916] 2 AC 307 (HL) and see David Foxton, 'Corporate Personality in the Great War' (2002) 118 LQT 428.
95 Christian List and Philip Pettit, *Group Agency* (Oxford: Oxford University Press 2011) 10.
96 Ibid 74.
97 Winn CRN, 'The Criminal Responsibility of Corporations' (1927–29) 3 CLJ 398, 406.
98 For example the critical legal studies movement, see Eli Lederman, 'Models for Imposing Corporate Criminal Liability: From Adaptation and Imitation toward Aggregation and The Search for Self-Identity' [2001] Buff Crim LR 642.
99 G R Sullivan, 'The Attribution of Culpability to Limited Companies' (1996) 55(3) CLJ 515.
100 Celia Wells, 'Corporations: Culture, Risk and Criminal Liability' (1993) Crim LR, Aug, 551–66.

part in the pursuance of shared goals.[101] On this account, moral agency rests on team participation in which team members share in both the achievements and failures of the team as a whole. Thus, when a participant commits a crime motivated by the corporate norms, both the individual wrongdoer and the corporation deserve punishment since this indicates condemnation of the organisation's norms and will influence the behaviour of the individuals who contribute to the creation of those norms. This subtle inter-dynamic between the individual and the organisation as a whole, described as "metaphysical holism",[102] is considered a variable dynamic such that a scale or spectrum of liability can be ascertained; fault ranging from that which is wholly attributable to the individual at one end to wholly organisational at the other.[103]

In accordance with this thinking, Ashworth acknowledges that while the law may be right to focus on the acts of individuals, often these can only be fully explained by reference to the social and structural context in which they take place, such as the structure and policies of a company.[104] Moreover, Ashworth also accepts that companies can gain a momentum and dynamic of their own which temporarily transcends the actions of individual officers. At this point the company itself is capable of both civil and criminal liability because it is the company which creates the structure and context for the individual's conduct.[105] Indeed, there is wide support in the legal academy for the holist view that organisations can become autonomous actors whose behaviour "transcends specific individual contributions"[106] and whose personality is

101 Ian B Lee, 'Corporate Criminal Responsibility as Team Member Responsibility' (2011) 31 (4) OJLS 755–81.

102 May Brodbeck, 'Methodological Individualisms: Definition and Reduction' (1958) 25 Philosophy of Science 1, 3–4 which is considered by Christopher Harding, *Criminal Enterprise: Individuals, Organisations and Criminal Responsibility* (Cullompton: Willan 2007).

103 Ibid. In agreement with Harding see also Peter A French, *Collective and Corporate Responsibility* (New York: Columbia University Press 1984) and also discussed in Celia Wells, *Corporations and Criminal Responsibility* (2nd ed, Oxford: Oxford University Press 2001).

104 Andrew Ashworth, *Principles of Criminal Law* (6th ed, Oxford: Oxford University Press 2009). Ashworth adds that individual autonomy is not lost in the process.

105 Ibid.

106 Peter A French, 'The Corporation as a Moral Person' (1979) 16 Am Phil Q 207, 211 and Peter A French, *Collective and Corporate Responsibility* (New York: Columbia University Press 1984); Celia Wells, *Corporations and Criminal Responsibility* (2nd ed, Oxford: Oxford University Press 2001) Ch. 4; James Gobert and Maurice Punch, *Rethinking Corporate Crime* (Oxford: Butterworths 2003); Christopher Harding, *Criminal Enterprise: Individuals, Organisations and Criminal Responsibility* (Cullompton: Willan 2007) 226, 227; Philip N Pettit, 'Responsibility Incorporated' (2007) 117 Ethics 171, 172; Law Commission, *Criminal Liability in Regulatory Contexts* (Law Com No 195, 2010) App. C, para C.26– C.28. This view is similar to acceptance of the state as an organisational actor in its own right in international law, see too R Scruton, 'Corporate Persons' (1989) Proceedings of the Aristotelian Society (supplementary series) 239; JA Quaid, 'The Assessment of Corporate Criminal Liability on the Basis of Corporate Identity: An Analysis' (1998) 423 McGill LJ 67, 78; Wells C and Elias J, 'Catching the Conscience of the King: Corporate Players on the

unique.[107] According to Harding, the underlying issue is one of ontology, rather than methodology, and whether it is possible to attribute responsibility to an organisation rather than to its individual members.[108] Although organisational rationality originates in human activity, it is the process of human interaction that can transform the character of the rationality such that a distinct corporate personality/culture can emerge with the potential to become the commanding determinant of organisational action.[109] As to the identification of a distinct corporate personality, Fisse and Braithwaite[110] suggest there are two crucial elements: functional autonomy and a distinct ethos.[111] Functional autonomy is most clearly expressed through the idea of

International Stage' in Philip Alston (ed.), *Non State Actors and Human Rights* (Oxford: Oxford University Press 2005) 155; Hegel, *The Philosophy of Right* (trans TM Knox, Oxford: Oxford University Press 2010) 279–83.

107 Jonathan Clough, 'Bridging the Theoretical Gap: The Search for a Realist Model of Corporate Criminal Liability' (2007) 18 Crim L F 267, 275–6. Clough states that the personality arises from various identifiable characteristics which include the corporate structure, goals, training provisions, compliance systems, reactions to past violations, incentives and remedial steps, "(t)hese are all matters which are under the control of those who manage the organisation". In French's language the 'conglomerate' replaces the 'aggregate' collective actor, suggesting that the attribution of agency applies to the former but not the latter since the conglomerate group actor is defined as being more than a sum of its parts, Peter A French, 'The Corporation as a Moral Person', (1979) 16 Am Phil Q 207 reprinted as Ch. 9 in Larry May and Stacey Hoffman (eds.), *Collective Responsibility, Group Based Harm and Corporate Rights* (Notre Dame, University of Notre Dame Press 1987) discussed by Christopher Harding, *Criminal Enterprise: Individuals, Organisations and Criminal Responsibility* (Cullompton: Willan 2007) Ch. 9; Pamela H Bucy, 'Corporate Ethos: A Standard for Imposing Corporate Criminal Liability' (1991) 75 Minn L Rev 1095, 1124; Brent Fisse and John Braithwaite, *Corporations, Crime and Accountability* (Cambridge: Cambridge University Press 1993).

108 Christopher Harding, *Criminal Enterprise: Individuals, Organisations and Criminal Responsibility* (Cullompton: Willan 2007).

109 Ibid. See also Larry May and Stacey Hoffman, *Collective Responsibility: Five Decades of Debate in Theoretical and Applied Ethics* (Lanham: Roman & Littlefield 1991).

110 Writing about the American experience, Fisse and Braithwaite start with the premise that corporate prosecutions undermine individual accountability and it is therefore in some way a shortcut by the prosecution, see Brent Fisse and John Braithwaite, *Corporations, Crime and Accountability* (Cambridge: Cambridge University Press 1993) and considered in Christopher Harding, *Criminal Enterprise: Individuals, Organisations and Criminal Responsibility* (Cullompton: Willan 2007). See too John Collins Coffee Jnr, 'No Soul to Damn, No Body to Kick, An Unscandalised Enquiry into the Problem of Corporate Responsibility' (1981) 79 Mich L Rev 386, 459; thereafter corporations are supposed to react by using internal disciplinary systems, see Richard A Posner, 'An Economic Theory of the Criminal Law' (1985) 85 Colum L Rev 1193, 1227–9. Fisse and Braithwaite perceive the problem as one of non-prosecution of individuals and the non-assurance of internal corporate accountability. Accordingly they propose a more responsive programme for achieving accountability. They do, however, refer to the situation in England and describe corporate criminal liability as having little practical significance compared with individuals.

111 Brent Fisse and John Braithwaite, *Corporations, Crime and Accountability* (Cambridge: Cambridge University Press 1993) and considered in Christopher Harding, *Criminal Enterprise: Individuals, Organisations and Criminal Responsibility* (Cullompton: Willan 2007).

the corporation's ability to dispense with human actors or its capacity to survive irrespective of human composition, described by Coleman as the "irrelevance of persons".[112] Drawing broadly on a functionalist theory of agency, List and Pettit, ascribe autonomy to group agents on an epistemological, rather than ontological, approach and go further in setting out the conditions that must be met for a group agent to be deemed responsible for a group action. These require the agent to be in a position to make normative judgments about the options it faces and have the control necessary to select between the options based on those judgements. The group agent can thus form and enact a "single mind", displaying beliefs and desires and acting upon them, and can communicate that mind to function within the space of mutually recognised obligations.[113]

In his account, Harding suggests organising the criteria of agency into two main types, one relating to structure and the capacity for autonomous action, the other relating to role.[114] The structure and capacity for autonomous action would link with the individual human members in a purposeful activity such that it would distinguish the corporation from the crowd or other random collectivity. The structural conditions would comprise a decision making process, organisational apparatus and an identity over time, characterised by the irrelevance of persons, and producing a functional autonomy of action in addition to a representative role in the pursuit of a common purpose.[115] The representational aspect of organisational agency is particularly significant in that it facilitates an appreciation of both the "driving force and ethos" of the organisation and the way in which it presents itself as a legitimate actor. The purposive element of identity gives meaning to the behaviour of the organisation, distinguishing it from the individual members, and it may produce a culture or ethos with patterns of behaviour and certain expectations within the structural whole. The

---

112 James S Coleman, *The Asymmetric Society: Organisational Actors, Corporate Power and the Irrelevance of Persons* (New York: Syracuse University Press 1982).

113 Christian List and Philip Pettit, *Group Agency* (Oxford: Oxford University Press 2011) 176. For a contrary view see Eli Lederman, 'Criminal Law, Perpetrator and Corporation: Rethinking a Complex Triangle', (1985) 76 J Crim L and Criminology 285340; Eli Lederman, 'Models for Imposing Corporate Criminal Liability: From Adaptation and Imitation toward Aggregation and the Search for Self-Identity' [2001] Buff Crim LR 642, 690. Lederman argues that since the modification of the group agent is contingent on the efforts of those in the higher managerial ranks who have the power to influence the corporate hierarchy, criminal liability should be exclusively individual. This view is dispelled by List and Pettit who argue that although founders of any corporate entity bear some responsibility for how the group functions as a result of its design, it leaves in place the responsibility of the group which is doing what the designers made it possible to do. The designers' responsibility in relation to the group's later actions is like the parents' responsibility in relation to their grown-up children.

114 Christopher Harding, *Criminal Enterprise: Individuals, Organisations and Criminal Responsibility* (Cullompton: Willan 2007).

115 Ibid.

organisation can then be viewed as a moral or legal agent in the sense that it is appropriate and meaningful to consider it responsible, rather than individuals.[116]

The notion of a corporate ethos that can determine the conduct of individuals who perform an organisational role different from their role as individuals is widely accepted.[117] Thus, the ethos, or distinctive culture, is what gives meaning to the attribution of corporate responsibility[118] and this is reflected in the Australian Criminal Code which adopts the concept of corporate culture as a means to reflect corporate blameworthiness.[119] Although the physical elements of the offence are attributed to the corporation on the basis of vicarious liability,[120] s. 12.3(1) provides that, "if intention, knowledge or recklessness is a fault element ... [it] must be attributed to a body corporate that expressly, tacitly or impliedly authorised or permitted the commission of the offence". The means by which this can be established includes, at s. 12.3(2) (c) and (d) instances in which it is proved that a "corporate culture existed within the body corporate that directed, encouraged, tolerated or led to non-compliance with a relevant provision" or there was a failure to "create and maintain a corporate culture that required compliance with the relevant provision."[121] Corporate culture is defined as "an attitude, policy, rule, course of conduct or practice existing within the body corporate generally or in the part of the body corporate in which the relevant activities takes (sic) place".[122] In his seminal work, Punch elaborates the concept in these terms:

116 Ibid. This view is supported by Virginia Held, 'Can a Random Collection of Individuals be Morally Responsible?' (1970) J Phil 68 reprinted as Ch. 6 in Larry May and Stacey Hoffman (eds), *Collective Responsibility, Group Based Harm and Corporate Rights* (Notre Dame: University of Notre Dame Press 1987) and Gellner E, 'Holism v Individualism' in May Brodbeck (ed.), *Readings in The Philosophy of the Social Sciences* (New York: Macmillan 1968) 258.

117 James S Coleman, *The Asymmetric Society: Organisational Actors, Corporate Power and the Irrelevance of Persons* (New York: Syracuse University Press 1982); Larry May and Stacey Hoffman (eds.), *Collective Responsibility, Group Based Harm and Corporate Rights* (Notre Dame: University of Notre Dame Press 1987) 8182; Maurice Punch, *Dirty Business: Exploring Corporate Misconduct* (London: Sage 1996) Ch. 5.

118 Brent Fisse and John Braithwaite, *Corporations, Crime and Accountability* (Cambridge: Cambridge University Press 1993) and Pamela H Bucy, 'Corporate Ethos: A Standard for Imposing Corporate Criminal Liability' (1991) 75 Minn L Rev 1095, 1124, both considered in Christopher Harding, *Criminal Enterprise: Individuals, Organisations and Criminal Responsibility* (Cullompton: Willan 2007).

119 Australian Criminal Code 1995, Pt. 2.5. See too Australian Standing C'ttee of Attorneys-General, Criminal Law Officers C'ttee, Model Criminal Code, Discussion Draft, Ch. 2 General Principles of Criminal Responsibility 501.3.1, 501.3.2, discussed in Christopher Harding, *Criminal Enterprise: Individuals, Organisations and Criminal Responsibility* (Cullompton: Willan 2007).

120 Australian Criminal Code 1995, Pt. 2.5, s. 12.2.

121 Australian Criminal Code 1995, Pt. 2.5, s. 12.3(2)(c).

122 Australian Criminal Code 1995, Pt. 2.5, s. 12.3(6).

specific companies, and parts of companies, have often a separate style of doing things manifested in subtle, semi-conscious ways of thinking and acting. The corporate ethos is the functional equivalent of attitude that in human actors are used as bases for moral judgment.[123]

Taken in the round, it is suggested that the process of organisations and individuals engaging in group activity may generate autonomous activity which need not be identified anthropocentrically or in terms of the sum of its parts[124] and, on this view, the moral responsibility of corporations derives from social process rather than elusive attributes of personhood.[125] Recognition of the dynamic nature of the organisation, and that corporate group agency exists, is now instilled in mainstream thinking in the criminal law.

1.5 Capturing corporate intention

Given the dynamic interdependent relationship between the organisation and its individual members, the question remains as to how the line should be drawn between organisational and individual responsibility generally or in particular contexts. Assuming it is possible to identify all the relevant individual participants in a group action, it may still be important to hold the group agent responsible. For example, the individuals may be blameless or ignorant of the harm they bring about together; the individual participation may make little difference to it; or they may be acting under such pressure that they cannot be held fully responsible for their contribution to a bad outcome.[126] Furthermore, organisations can obscure internal accountability and it is often difficult for enforcement agencies to prosecute individuals even where criminality is evident.[127] The failure to recognise corporate responsibility makes it possible for high level individuals to benefit from the deficit of corporate responsibility, through a structural distancing from the harmful activity,[128] and

---

123 Maurice Punch, *Dirty Business: Exploring Corporate Misconduct* (London: Sage 1996) following Ouchi WG, 'Organisational Culture' (1985) Annual Review of Sociology 457, both considered in Christopher Harding, *Criminal Enterprise: Individuals, Organisations and Criminal Responsibility* (Cullompton: Willan 2007).

124 Larry May and Stacey Hoffman, *Collective Responsibility: Five Decades of Debate in Theoretical and Applied Ethics*, (Lanham: Roman & Littlefield 1991).

125 Brent Fisse and John Braithwaite, *Corporations: Crime and Accountability* (Cambridge: Cambridge University Press 1993) 24.

126 Werhane PA and RE Freeman, 'Corporate Responsibility' in Hugh La Follette (ed.), *The Oxford Handbook of Practical Ethics* (Oxford: Oxford University Press 2003) discussed in Christian List and Philip Pettit, *Group Agency* (Oxford: Oxford University Press 2011) 165.

127 Brent Fisse, *Howard's Criminal Law* (5th ed, London: Sweet & Maxwell 1990) 591 and referring to Jack Katz, 'Concerted Ignorance: The Social Construction of Cover Up' (1979) 8 Urban Life 295.

128 Christian List and Philip Pettit, *Group Agency* (Oxford: Oxford University Press 2011) 167.

also for corporations to tender employees as scapegoats for prosecution.[129] Aside
from the potential to offend basic principles of justice by denying the agency
of the organisation,[130] there are strong developmental rationales for finding
corporations responsible. The imposition of corporate liability is likely to
incentivise shareholders to establish checks on the board and management[131]
and more broadly it is hoped that it will stimulate appropriate internal
disciplinary action and the development of effective internal controls.[132] It
must not be forgotten that collective blameworthiness is a well-recognised
phenomenon, examples of which can be found in the reports of inquiries
such as those following the Herald of Free Enterprise and Aberfan
disasters.[133]

Notwithstanding the broad-ranging justifications for the attribution of
corporate fault and the breadth of support for a model of realist, or
holist, liability[134], the focus of this work is the specific problem of corporate
fraud where the dishonest practice cannot be reduced to dishonesty at
an individual level. In this respect the basis of liability remains to
be determined,[135] as does the choice of legal mechanism that might
be employed. Since the notion of "intention" is at the heart of most
philosophical justifications of individual liability and moral blameworthiness,
the overriding concern is how the artificial entity may be said to behave
with any such human characteristic or sentiment.[136] Intention as a mark
of corporate culpability has therefore remained in doubt[137] with the
consequence that proposals for reform commonly avoid trying to "squeeze
corporate square pegs into the round holes of criminal law doctrines devised
with individuals in mind".[138] However, although the language of responsibility might be hard to apply in the context of corporate liability, there is

129 Brent Fisse, *Howard's Criminal Law* (5th ed, London: Sweet & Maxwell 1990) 593.
130 Ibid.
131 Christian List and Philip Pettit, *Group Agency* (Oxford: Oxford University Press 2011) 166.
132 Brent Fisse, *Howard's Criminal Law* (5th ed, London: Sweet & Maxwell 1990) 591, 597.
133 Brent Fisse, *Howard's Criminal Law* (5th ed, London: Sweet & Maxwell 1990) 591.
134 Celia Wells, *Corporations and Criminal Responsibility* (2nd ed, Oxford: Oxford University
     Press 2001) citing Anon, 'Corporate Crime: Regulating Corporate Behaviour Through
     Criminal Sanctions' (1979) 92 Harv L Rev, 1227.
135 Celia Wells, *Corporations and Criminal Responsibility* (2nd ed, Oxford: Oxford University
     Press 2001) citing Anon, 'Corporate Crime: Regulating Corporate Behaviour Through
     Criminal Sanctions' (1979) 92 Harv L Rev, 1227.
136 See for example GR Sullivan, 'The Attribution of Culpability to Limited Companies'
     (1996) 55(3) CLJ, Nov 515, 532, 537 and his reference to Peter Arenella, 'Convicting
     the Morally Blameless: Reassessing the Relationship between Legal and Moral Account-
     ability' (1992) 39 UCLA Rev 1511; S Wolf, 'The Legal and Moral Responsibility of
     Organisations' in J Rowland Pennock and John W Chapman (eds.) *Criminal Justice* (New
     York: Lieber-Atherton 1985) 276–9.
137 See the discussion in Ian B Lee, 'Corporate Criminal Responsibility as Team Member
     Responsibility' (2011) 31(4) OJLS 755, 761.
138 James Gobert, 'Corporate Criminality: New Crimes for the Times', (1994) Crim LR 722.

clear academic support for expansive definition of the notion such that it can be said that corporations can and do act intentionally.[139]

According to French, the "Corporation's Internal Decision Structure"[140] provides the framework for the expression of corporate intention which transcends the intention of individuals or groups of individuals when corporate decisions are taken in accordance with the organisation's "established policies".[141] The concept of a decision-making structure is widely accepted as the cornerstone of a theory of organisational intention as is the requirement that the decision-making capacity will succeed any change in corporate personnel. A further refinement suggests that there must also be enforcement of standards of conduct of individuals in the group.[142] This approach is supported by organisational theory in that corporations tend to have intricate structures which place responsibility for specific aspects on different

---

139 Peter A French, 'The Corporation as a Moral Person' (1979) 16 Am Phil Q 207, 211; Peter A French, *Collective and Corporate Responsibility* (New York: Columbia University Press 1984); Philip Pettit, 'Responsibility Incorporated' (2007) 117 Ethics 171, 172.

140 Peter A French, *Collective and Corporate Responsibility* (New York: Columbia University Press 1984) 41. French identifies three elements that comprise the 'Corporate Internal Decision Structure': an organisational flow chart, procedural rules and corporate policies. Erskine suggests that the conglomeration must also have a conception of itself as a unit, T Erskine, 'Assigning Responsibilities to Institutional Moral Agents: The Case of States and "Quasi-states"' in T Erskine (ed.) *Can Institutions Have Responsibilities? Collective Moral Agency and International Relations* (Basingstoke: Palgrave Macmillan 2003). Dan-Cohen provides an account similar to French but claims that the reality of the structure need not depend on any human association; a humanless corporation can exist as an intelligent, computer-directed decision-making system, Mier Dan-Cohen, *Rights, Persons and Organisations: A Legal Theory for a Bureaucratic Society* (Berkeley: University of California Press 1986) discussed in GR Sullivan's 'The Attribution of Culpability to Limited Companies' (1996) 55(3) CLJ, Nov 515, 534. Whether system-guided responses can be taken to be states of mind cognate with human states is a contested philosophical question, see Daniel C Dennett 'Intentional Systems' in Daniel C Dennett (ed.) *Brainstorms: Philosophical Essays on Mind and Psychology*, (Cambridge, Mass: MIT Press 1978); John R Searle, *Intentionality: An Essay in the Philosophy of Mind* (Cambridge: Cambridge University Press 1983); Daniel C Dennett, *The Intentional Stance* (Cambridge, Mass: MIT Press 1987).

141 Peter A French, 'The Corporation as a Moral Person' (1979) 16 Am Phil Q 207, 213; Peter A French, *Collective and Corporate Responsibility* (New York: Columbia University Press 1984) 44. It must be said that Sullivan is highly critical of this approach, he says it is not obvious why one should look for culpability within the company structure rather than among the individuals responsible for maintaining that structure, GR Sullivan, 'The Attribution of Culpability to Limited Companies' (1996) 55(3) CLJ, Nov 515–46, 536.

142 See for example, Peter A French, 'The Corporation as a Moral Person' (1979) 16 Am Phil Q 207, 211; Peter A French, *Collective and Corporate Responsibility* (New York: Columbia University Press 1984). French's account is criticised by GR Sullivan who argues that company procedures do not arise spontaneously and are not the equivalent of a virgin birth, Sullivan GR, 'The Attribution of Culpability to Limited Companies' (1996) 55(3) CLJ 515–46, 536. He says that the organisational structure is ultimately the product of human agency, however sophisticated and automated the company's procedures might be.

departments.[143] If corporations lack intention in the sense that they do not have the capacity to entertain a cerebral mental state, it is suggested that they certainly do exhibit their own special kind of intention in the form of corporate policy,[144] which represents the culmination of decisions made. Of significance, corporations also have the capacity to change their policy and their procedures.[145] Moreover, Pettit submits that group agents not only act intentionally but can also form "evaluative beliefs".[146] Since the organisation can make value judgments and can then act in consequence, it can be held responsible for its acts in the same way that any individual actor can.[147] Further, Bonner and Forman recognise that criminal harm can result not just from the influence of particular individuals but also from the complex inter-play between managers, standard operating procedures, corporate priorities, market demands and various other forces at work within corporations.[148] In such circumstances, the essence of corporate crime is the behaviour of corporations, not individuals, and the level of intervention must therefore be organisational rather than individual if it is to be effective.[149]

Corporations may lack feelings and emotions but it is widely agreed that this absence does not negate the quality of autonomy.[150] On the contrary, it is argued that the lack of emotions and feelings promotes rather than hinders considered rational choice and in this respect the corporation is arguably the paradigm responsible actor.[151] Large corporations have available, and can make use of, far more information than is possible for one individual to compute.[152] Furthermore, with perpetual succession, the corporate form is

---

143 Celia Wells, *Corporations and Criminal Responsibility* (2nd ed, Oxford: Oxford University Press 2001).

144 Peter A French, *Collective and Corporate Responsibility* (New York: Columbia University Press 1984); Brent Fisse and John Braithwaite, *Corporations, Crime and Accountability* (Cambridge: Cambridge University Press 1993) 26.

145 Warner M, *Organisational Choice and Constraint* (Westmead: Saxon House 1977).

146 Philip Pettit, 'Responsibility Incorporated' (2007) 117 Ethics 171, 186–7. See too Christian List and Philip Pettit, *Group Agency* (Oxford: Oxford University Press 2011).

147 Ibid. Lee challenges Pettit's account suggesting that it is not fair "to assume that anyone or anything that makes value judgments is a member of our moral community, such that moral rights and duties subsist between us and them, the violation of which would be the kind of 'bad value judgment' that rightly attracts blame", Ian B Lee, 'Corporate Criminal Responsibility as Team Member Responsibility' (2011) 31(4) OJLS 755–81 at 764.

148 J Bonner and B Forman, 'Bridging the Deterrence Gap: Imposing Criminal Penalties on Corporations and their Executives for Producing Hazardous Projects' (1993) 20 San Diego Justice Journal 1,1 cited in Celia Wells, *Corporations and Criminal Responsibility* (2nd ed, Oxford: Oxford University Press 2001).

149 Steven Box, *Power, Crime and Mystification* (London: Tavistock 1983] 70.

150 Michael McDonald, 'The Personless Paradigm' (1987) 37 UTLJ 212; Brent Fisse and John Braithwaite, *Corporations, Crime and Accountability* (Cambridge: Cambridge University Press 1993) 30–1.

151 Ibid.

152 Michael McDonald, 'The Personless Paradigm' (1987) 37 UTLJ 212.

"immortal" and this renders it better able to bear responsibility for its deeds than humans, whose sins die with them.[153]

Now described as the "holist" model,[154] the recognition of organisational autonomy accords with what was described, and widely accepted, over a century ago as the "realist" theory of corporations.[155] As an account of corporate criminal liability it is also consistent with the basic and enduring principles of corporate theory and company law which stress the independence of the corporate entity as distinct from the individuals associated with it.[156] It is also of note that while criminal lawyers have tended to confine their thinking to the context of companies engaging in commercial activity,[157] organisational theory has much broader application. If the decision-making personality is the hallmark of moral agency, many other "organisations" can possess moral agency, whether they are incorporated or not. This applies equally to non-commercial collectivities and, for example, to the government and the state; certainly international lawyers in the context of the International Criminal Court have no problem with the concept of state responsibility for a range of illegal acts.[158] In contrast, the criminal law remains entrenched in the individualist paradigm, viewing the company as a collection of individuals and corporate wrongdoing as a derivative of individual liability, and for as long as it does so it will lack the conceptual tools necessary to address corporate liability.[159] This conclusion is borne out by the fact that Parliament has enacted statutory offences in the areas of corporate manslaughter, corruption and tax evasion, each of which involve a bespoke model of corporate fault attribution that judiciously avoid confronting the "intention", or mens rea, stumbling block.

153 Ibid; Eli Lederman, 'Models for Imposing Corporate Criminal Liability: From Adaptation and Imitation toward Aggregation and The Search for Self-Identity' [2001] Buff Crim LR 642.
154 Eli Lederman, 'Models for Imposing Corporate Criminal Liability: From Adaptation and Imitation toward Aggregation and The Search for Self-Identity' [2001] Buff Crim LR 642.
155 Neil Cavanagh, 'Corporate Criminal Liability: An Assessment of the Models of Fault' (2011) 75 JCL 414 refers to the realist-based models.
156 Eli Lederman, 'Models for Imposing Corporate Criminal Liability: From Adaptation and Imitation toward Aggregation and The Search for Self-Identity' [2001] Buff Crim LR 642.
157 Brent Fisse and John Braithwaite, *Corporations: Crime and Accountability* (Cambridge: Cambridge University Press 1993); Celia Wells, *Corporations and Criminal Responsibility* (2nd ed, Oxford: Oxford University Press 2001); James Gobert and Maurice Punch, *Rethinking Corporate Crime* (Oxford: Butterworths 2003).
158 Christopher Harding, *Criminal Enterprise: Individuals, Organisations and Criminal Responsibility* (Cullompton: Willan 2007).
159 Celia Wells, 'Corporations: Culture, Risk and Criminal Liability' (1993) Crim LR Aug 551–6; Brent Fisse and John Braithwaite, 'The Allocation of Responsibility for Corporate Crime: Individualism, Collectivism and Accountability' (1988) 11 Sydney L Rev 468. Similarly, Harding points out that in a society that is increasingly characterised by the presence and impact of organisations and organisational structures, the dominant role of the classic individualist model may now be doubted, Christopher Harding, *Criminal Enterprise: Individuals, Organisations and Criminal Responsibility* (Cullompton: Willan 2007).

It is the aim of this book to resolve the intractable problem of corporate agency and responsibility in the criminal law. In so doing, it steers an innovative departure from the various constructions of corporate liability currently in use as well as the alternative proposals that have been mooted to date. Each of the existing and proposed models implicitly concede defeat to the criminal law's mainstay doctrine of mens rea and the commitment to individualist and subjectivist methodology that this seems to demand. It is without doubt the need to prove mens rea that has been the real obstacle to the common law's development of an overarching theory and general construct of corporate criminality and it is this doctrine that will now be considered.

1.6 Mens rea and metaphysics: the stumbling block of the criminal law

The foundation of criminal liability has long been expressed in the Latin maxim *"actus non facit reum nisi mens sit rea"*[160] which is crudely interpreted as "whatever the deed a man may have done, it cannot make him criminally punishable unless his doing of it was actuated by a legally blameworthy attitude of mind".[161] Conforming to utilitarian and Enlightenment thinking, it is therefore the blameworthy mental state, the "mens rea" element, as set out in each offence definition, that acts as the modern hallmark of moral culpability. Furthermore, the criminal law's individualist ideal demands that the defendant's state of mind is a matter of subjective assessment, in preference to an assessment by reference to an objective standard of behaviour.[162] One particular consequence of this metaphysical approach to individual culpability is that the corporate body, absent of any mental state upon which liability can be established, has come to be viewed as a fiction. In contrast to the realist thinking that pervades other disciplines, the fiction theory views the corporation exclusively as a legal entity with no transcendent reality:[163]

> The artificial legal person called the corporation has no physical existence. It exists only in contemplation of law. It has neither body, parts, nor passions. It cannot wear weapons or serve in the wars. It can be neither loyal, nor disloyal. It cannot compass treasons. It can be neither friend nor enemy. Apart from its corporators it can have neither thoughts, wishes, nor intentions, for it has no mind other than the minds of the corporators.[164]

---

160 See Lord Kenyon C.J. in *Fowler v Padget* (1798) 7 TR 509; Lord Goddard C.J. in *Harding v Price* [1948] 1 KB 695.
161 JW Cecil Turner, *Russell on Crime* (12th ed, London: Stevens & Sons 1964) vol 1.
162 For example *R v G & Another* [2004] 1 AC 1034 (HL) provides a recent example of the objective test of recklessness being replaced in favour of a subjective test.
163 Hart HLA, 'Definition and Theory in Jurisprudence' (1954) 70 LQR 37.
164 See Buckley LJ's dissenting judgment in *Daimler Co Ltd v Continental Tyre and Rubber Co (GB) Ltd* (1915) 1 KB 893 (CA) 916.

This "individualistic anchor" is widely recognised as the real "stumbling block to corporate liability",[165] with the attendant perception that the purely legal entity has "no soul to damn; no body to kick".[166] Thus, in the criminal law, the fictionist view has prevailed over the alternative realist theory of organisations, with the consequence that corporations have not been considered autonomous, responsibility-bearing actors in their own right. Similarly, as regards offences considered "truly criminal" and which, therefore, contain specified mens rea elements, it would seem that the courts have laboured to find a mechanism by which the necessary blameworthy mental state might be attributed to the artificial person. In response to this "metaphysical obstacle", the common law developed a doctrine by which a corporation can be found criminally culpable, but only if the individual who is deemed to be its "directing mind and will" is himself guilty of the offence in question.[167] As the orthodox interpretation of this legal evolution, it will suffice at this stage to explain that the individual's mens rea can be considered the mens rea, or moral guilt, of the corporate form on the basis that the company is, in essence, his alter ego. While the shortcomings of this interpretation will be discussed later, the deficiencies of the principle itself were perhaps most clearly articulated in relation to its application in highly publicised "corporate manslaughter" cases. For a considerable period in the 1980s and 1990s, it was the specific offence of corporate manslaughter that became the narrow focal point of discussion about corporate criminality generally. This was ostensibly driven by public and media outcry in the face of a number of transport tragedies and the significant criticism that the law attracted at the time in its failure to convict the companies whose operating procedures amounted to serious breaches of safety standards resulting in numerous fatalities, to both employees and members of the public. In March 1987, 187 people were killed in the Herald of Free Enterprise disaster, there were 167 fatalities on Piper Alpha in July 1988 and, just five months later, 35 rail passengers lost their lives at Clapham. Over the years, the names Kings Cross, Marchioness, Southall, Paddington, Hatfield and Potters Bar added to the public chorus demanding that profit-driven corporate perpetrators be brought to account for the manslaughter offence in preference to some nominal health and safety breach. The first case to recognise that manslaughter was an offence that could be committed by a company was in relation to the Herald of Free Enterprise ferry disaster, a case which now provides a well-known illustration of the difficulties associated with the common law identification doctrine. Notwithstanding the fact that the organisation was found to be infected from top to bottom with an "attitude of sloppiness" as regards safety,

---

165 Law Commission, *Criminal Liability in Regulatory Contexts* (Law Com No 195, 2010) Celia Wells, App. C, para C.47.

166 John Collins Coffee Jnr, 'No Soul to Damn, No Body to Kick: An Unscandalised Inquiry into the Problem of Corporate Punishment' (1981) 79 Mich L Rev 386.

167 Attributed to Viscount Haldane L.C. in *Lennard's Carrying Co Ltd v Asiatic Petroleum Ltd* [1915] AC 705 (HL).

the prosecution was unable to prove that any of the five senior managers should have known of the risks of sailing with the ship's bow open and it was therefore unsuccessful in it its attempt to prosecute P & O for corporate manslaughter.[168]

One of the implications of the identification, or alter ego, principle is therefore that large companies with complex and decentralised organisational structures are likely to evade prosecution while smaller companies, with directors more likely to be involved in the day to day business activities, will offer "low-hanging fruit" for prosecution.[169] Thus, the current common law test of corporate responsibility "works best in cases where it is needed least [small businesses] and works worst in cases where it is needed most [big businesses]".[170] It is widely recognised that, as a method of liability attribution, "it fails to reflect the reality of the modern day large multinational corporation ... [and] it produces what many regard as an unsatisfactory narrow scope for criminal liability".[171] Furthermore, the need to identify the criminality of an individual of sufficient seniority, as a precursor to corporate prosecution, incurs evidential problems which tend to increase as the size of the company increases.[172] Indeed, the shortcomings of this model of liability are so well documented that there has been legislative intervention in the various contexts of corporate manslaughter, corruption, bribery and offshore tax evasion, each having attracted the enactment of bespoke statutory offences to deal specifically with the corporate offender. In each case, the statutory provisions base criminal liability on innovative models that avoid reference to any mens rea element, the classic hallmark of crime, and thus neatly sidestep the metaphysical issue. In each case, moral disapproval or blameworthiness, which defines the fault as of a criminal culpability rather than civil wrong, is imported through an alternative means.

However, as regards the fraud offence, the finding of corporate criminality still turns on the successful application of the common law identification principle. Notwithstanding the government's commitment at the time to address major commercial frauds,[173] the Fraud Act 2006 did not contain any innovation in this respect.[174] Although s. 12 explicitly recognises that the fraud

168   *P & O European Ferries (Dover) Ltd* (1990) 93 Cr App R 72.
169   *R v Kite & OLL Ltd*, The Times, 8 Dec 1994; *R v Jackson Transport (Ossett) Ltd, R v Roy Bowles Transport Ltd*, 10 Dec 1999. See also T Woolf, 'The Criminal Code Act 1995 (Cth) - Towards a Realist Vision of Corporate Criminal Liability' (1997) Crim L J 257.
170   James Gobert and Maurice Punch, *Rethinking Corporate Crime* (Oxford: Butterworths 2003) 63.
171   David Ormerod, *Smith & Hogan's Criminal Law* (12th ed, Oxford: Oxford University Press 2008) 249, a view shared by Gobert, see James Gobert, 'Corporate Criminality: Four Models of Fault' (1994) 14(3) LS 393, 395.
172   Mark Hsaio, 'Abandonment of the Doctrine of Attribution in favour of Gross Negligence Test in the Corporate Manslaughter and Corporate Homicide Act 2007' (2009) 30(4) Co Law 110, 111.
173   The government sought to respond to the public perception that 'those responsible for major crimes of the commercial sphere have managed to avoid justice', Law Commission, *Report on Fraud* (Law Com No 276, July 2002) Introduction and p 3, para 3.
174   The Fraud Act 2006 came into force on the 17 January 2007.

offence can be perpetrated by a corporate actor, confirming the definition of "person" provided in the Interpretation Act 1978,[175] the corporate conviction for fraud still turns on the commission of an underlying fraud offence by an officer considered to be a "directing mind". Consequently, there remains a discernible disparity between the contemporary political rhetoric and the practical reality. As it happens, the Law Commission had already dismissed the applicability of the new generic fraud offence to corporate misconduct,[176] deferring instead to the existing framework comprising the regulatory regime and individualised offences,[177] referred to as "specialist branches of fraud, which require separate consideration".[178] Given that one of the aims of the Fraud Act was to simplify the law, by replacing the highly-particularised deception offences contained in the Theft Acts of 1968 and 1978,[179] and that it "would be aimed at encompassing fraud in all its forms",[180] this has been disappointing. Similarly, the continued tendency to draft the regulatory offences as matters of strict liability[181] perpetuates the conception of corporate wrongdoing as mere technical infringement rather than criminal wrong.[182]

While it must be acknowledged that there are a variety of potential disincentives to criminal proceedings for corporate fraud, this book is specifically concerned with the doctrinal obstacle that has been identified. Political, judicial and prosecutorial reluctance may be explained on any number of perspectives, the lack of resources for example, the relative complexity of fraud trials or the lobbying power of large corporations. Each of these aspects merit investigation, however, an evaluation of their influence is not the aim here; this work is concerned primarily with a narrow examination of the substantive law with a view to potential law reform. This becomes increasingly urgent, not least because the "failure to prevent" offence, employed in the fight against corporate bribery and tax evasion, is increasingly seen as the model of choice. The inadequacy of

---

175 Fraud Act 2006,s. 12 deals with the liability of company officers for fraud offences committed by the company. Schedule 1 of the Interpretation Act 1978 also stipulates that where an act refers to a 'person' this is taken to include a body of persons corporate or unincorporate.

176 Law Commission, *Report on Fraud* (Law Com No 276, 2002) 11, para 2.26.

177 For example, Theft Act 1968,s. 17 false accounting ands. 19 false statements by company directors; Financial Services and Markets Act 2000,s. 397(1) and (2) misleading statements and practices;s. 206 Insolvency Act 1986 fraud etc. in anticipation of winding up.

178 Law Commission, *Report on Fraud* (Law Com No 276, 2002) 12, para 2.27. The explanation given was that the decision to keep "specialist branches of fraud" separate followed consultation between regulator and regulated in the context of misleading market practices to help draw the line between sharp practice and criminal practice.

179 The Fraud Act offence replaces for example the Theft Act 1968,s. 15 obtaining property by deception;s. 15A obtaining a money transfer by deception;s. 16 obtaining a pecuniary advantage,s. 20 procuring the execution of a valuable security; Theft Act 1978,s. 1 obtaining services,s. 2 inducing a creditor to wait for or forego payment by deception.

180 Law Commission, *Report on Fraud* (Law Com No 276, July 2002) 3, para 4.

181 Discussed in *Lim Chin Aik v The Queen* [1963] AC 160 (PC), Singapore.

182 Gerry Johnstone and Tony Ward, *Key Approaches to Criminology: Law and Crime* (London: Sage 2010).

this approach to address widespread and systemic fraud, of a nature already touched upon, will be elaborated further below as part of a detailed evaluation of the whole range of current legal responses and proposals. It will illustrate how the proposed corporate offences of the "failure to prevent" and "negligence" genres will miss the mark where there is no dishonesty, and therefore no offence, on the part of an individual employee. The discourse will demonstrate the need to add to the existing identification principle, negligence-based and "failure to prevent" range of responses, explaining in particular why they are incapable of dealing with the peculiar nature of corporate fraud and providing broader arguments for their rejection.

1.7 The aim of this book

This book enters new territory in the search for a model by which criminal liability can be attributed directly to a corporation for the substantive fraud offence. As the law currently stands, an organisation characterised by pervasive and systemic fraudulent conduct is frequently beyond the reach of the criminal courts. The identification doctrine has no application since the dishonesty that needs to be proved cannot be reduced to individual offenders at a senior level. Similarly, proposals to extend corporate liability for failure to prevent lower level employees committing fraud are also parasitic in nature and organisations will continue to evade liability if the individuals involved are not dishonest and therefore not guilty of fraud. Filling that lacuna, this book builds on the now accepted theory that organisations can gain an autonomy and dynamic of their own, apart from the agency of its individual members, and it reveals how mens rea, the classic indicia of true criminality, can be attributed directly to an organisation.

The theoretical basis by which dishonesty and intention can be attributed directly to an organisation will be achieved through traditional black letter law analysis. This will reconstruct the orthodox canons of fault, expressed as the voluntariness, actus reus and mens rea doctrines, together with the evidential presumptions they invoke. In so doing, this book builds on earlier works that depict the criminal law's gradual shift from fault based on "manifest liability" to the "mens rea" model premised in subjective individualism which focuses on the defendant's state of mind.[183] In contrast to the subjectivist account, the model of manifest liability was based on the observation of the overt act and then the appearance of the act by reference to the defendant's character. It is in relation to

---

183 See for example, Nicola Lacey's works, 'In Search of the Responsible Subject: History, Philosophy and Criminal Law Theory' (2001) 1 64 MLR 350–71; 'Responsibility and Modernity in Criminal Law' (2001) 9 Journal of Political Philosophy 249–77; 'Space, Time and Function: Intersecting Principles of Responsibility across the Terrain of Criminal Justice' (2007) 1 Criminal Law and Philosophy 233–50; GP Fletcher, *Rethinking Criminal Law* (Boston: Little, Brown and Co 1978).

the account of the "mens rea" model that this work breaks new ground, exposing how the fundamental concepts of subjective fault have themselves undergone striking transformation over the last century. Of note, it reveals that the current approach to the attribution of criminal responsibility represents the cumulative effect of coincidental and unrelated judicial interventions over a period of time and in so doing it paves the way for a rational reconstruction of the law. This approach, the historical reconstruction of the law, is advantageous in that it accommodates the discovery that reforms can resurrect aspects of long forgotten initiatives from the past, obviating the need to depart from the existing framework of the English common law system and traditional legal methodology. The implication of reordering and restating the orthodox planks of liability is that the means to attribute liability directly to a corporation is not only accommodated but that it is done in such a way that it preserves the overall integrity and coherence of the criminal law, without disturbing or dismantling its existing structure.[184] The use of the fault concepts, as originally conceived, and accompanying presumptive approaches lead to a refined version of the "manifest" approach which refocuses critical attention on the appearance of the act in question. The traditional black letter law methodology, and the conclusion it produces, is further supported by recent neuroscientific advances which demonstrate a surprising compatibility with the criminal law's predominant subjectivist ideology. The result not only contributes an overarching theory of corporate criminality but has exciting implications for our understanding of subjective individualism and principles of criminal law generally.

Given the growing recognition of the realist nature of organisations, this work is premised on the assumption that a collective group can act as an autonomous and responsibility-bearing agent in its own right. With this in mind, Chapter 2 provides an evaluation of the various current legal responses to corporate criminality generally and the main proposals for reform. Illustrating fraud's peculiar nature in comparison to other criminal offences, the suitability and deficiencies of each of the models will be examined in order to clarify the lacuna this book seeks to fill.

As the primary aim is a rational reconstruction of the law, with a view to effecting a practical reform, traditional "black letter law" analysis has an important role in this work, both in identifying and giving order to underlying legal principles. However, in viewing the law as an internal and self-sustaining set of principles[185] this analysis does not advert to any external factors which have shaped it and the empirical shortcomings of this approach have therefore been counterbalanced with the addition of inter-disciplinary and socio-legal

---

184 Pauline C Westerman, 'Open or Autonomous? The debate on legal methodology as a reflection of the debate on law', in Mark van Hoecke (ed.), *The Methodologies of Legal Research* (Oxford: Hart 2011) 88.

185 See e.g. M McConvill and Wing Hong Chui (eds.) *Research Methods for Law* (Edinburgh: Edinburgh University Press 2007).

methods.[186] Similarly, since language provides both the framework for the law and interprets it, and language is naturally fluid, contextual and susceptible to subjective interpretation,[187] knowledge of the real significance of legal conceptions in earlier periods is crucial to understanding the law in retrospect.[188] The genealogies of the criminal law's concepts of fault that are presented are therefore discussed by reference to the changing use of and meaning of legal terminology that has shaped their current conception.

Taken together, Chapters 3 and 4 focus on the profound changes that the fundamental canons of the substantive law have undergone and the consequent erosion of the traditional evidential presumptions that accompanied them. They reveal that successive but unconnected judgments clothed in ambiguous language served not only to reshape the classic indicia of blame, the voluntariness and mens rea doctrines, but also led to the erroneous understanding that the presumption of voluntariness reversed the burden of proof while the presumption of intention challenged the whole subjectivist edifice of the criminal law. In cumulative effect, but one that had been neither fashioned nor pre-determined, the refined "manifest" approach to fault attribution inherent in the orthodox canons was submerged in favour of an enlarged and distorted mens rea doctrine. Although the conceptual and evidential shift has had implications for the criminal law generally, it has had a particularly profound effect in frustrating the development of any theory of corporate responsibility.

Notwithstanding the common law's transformation of the nature and scope of the fault concepts, the criminal law's actus reus/mens rea construct, which separates the physical from the mental elements of an offence, is largely associated with Enlightenment thinking and its emphasis on subjective individualism. In that the strict division of the mental and the physical realms also accorded with the then prevailing Cartesian dualist philosophy, Chapter 5 considers the criminal law's framework by reference to the contemporary philosophy of "mind and action" which is supported by recent discoveries in mainstream neuroscience. While the aim is not to contribute to the existing literature on the philosophy of

---

186 The criminal law is widely recognised to be the product of a piecemeal response to the challenge of social control in changing eras, see e.g. Alan Norrie, *Crime, Reason and History* (2nd ed, Cambridge: Cambridge University Press 2001); L Farmer, 'The Obsession With Definition: The Nature of Crime and Critical Legal Theory' (1996) S & LS 5:57; L Farmer, 'Bringing Cinderella to the Ball: Teaching Criminal Law in Context' (1995) MLR 58(5) 756; Duff, RA and Stuart P Green (eds.), *Philosophical Foundations of Criminal Law* (Oxford: Oxford University Press 2011); D Husak, *Overcriminalization, The Limits of the Criminal Law* (Oxford: Oxford University Press 2008).
187 Reza Banaker and Max Travers (eds.), *Theory and Method in Socio-legal Research* (Oxford: Hart 2005) 133; see too Peter Goodrich, *Legal Discourse Studies in Linguistics, Rhetoric and Legal Analysis* (London: Macmillan 1986); Brian Bix, *Law, Language, and Legal Determinacy* (Oxford University Press 1996); Alfred Phillips, *Lawyers' Language: The Distinctiveness of Legal Language* (London: Taylor and Francis 2002).
188 JWC Turner, 'The Mental Element in Crimes at Common Law', in L Radzinowicz and JWC Turner (eds.), *The Modern Approach to Criminal Law* (London: Macmillan 1948) 195.

criminal law, the findings provide surprising support for both the realist nature of groups and the reinstatement of the revised "manifest" approach to fault attribution using the traditional evidential presumptions. While having broad implications for the modern interpretation of the subjectivist account of criminal law, this thinking impacts specifically on what has been the primary obstacle to a theory of corporate liability, dissolving the metaphysical limitation of the mens rea doctrine as it was previously understood.

Having reconstructed the criminal law's orthodox "manifest" approach to fault attribution and confirmed its compatibility with contemporary mind/action philosophy and advances in neuroscience, Chapter 6 focuses specifically on the identification principle of corporate liability as a creature of the common law.

Now identified as the landmark authority for the emergence of the fiction theory of organisations, with its articulation of the "directing mind" principle, *Lennard's Carrying Co Ltd* [1915][189] is considered in its philosophical and legal context and reveals that, at the time, this judgment was not taken to contribute anything remarkable to the law, or to develop any new principle of liability, in either the civil or criminal law. The black letter law analysis that follows demonstrates that authoritative status now afforded to the judgment was due to its retrospective elevation in *Tesco v Nattrass* [1972][190] in the midst of a growing judicial reluctance to convict in the absence of mens rea,[191] as the inflated doctrine was then understood or, to be more accurate, misunderstood. Consequently, the basis upon which the identification principle rests can now be narrowly defined such that, in appropriate circumstances, the shortcomings of this approach and its perceived bar to the direct attribution of corporate liability melt away.

In conclusion, the architecture of the criminal law is not only fashioned by its response to historical contingency but is also the creature of the empirical shortcomings associated with the internalised black letter law methodology of the common law. Aside from its isolationist nature, clinging to individualism as other disciplines have developed group theories of action, its language dependent approach has not afforded recognition that the meaning and significance of language can change over time. In this way, orthodox principles of criminal law have been the subject of gradual reconceptualisation with particularly far-reaching implications in the context of the law's approach to corporate liability. The rational reconstruction of the law reveals a framework that can accommodate corporate liability and the attribution of fault directly to the corporation where wrongdoing cannot be reduced to participation at an individual level. Accordingly, Chapter 7 builds on this substantive theory to advance practical and procedural refinements that are necessary for the direct attribution with which capacity and criminal intent can be directly attributed to a corporation without offending the subjectivist ideology.

---

189 *Lennard's Carrying Co Ltd v Asiatic Petroleum Ltd* [1915] AC 705 (HL).
190 *Tesco Ltd v Nattrass* [1972] AC 153 (HL).
191 Something already evidenced in *Sweet v Parsley* [1970] AC 132 (HL).

Bibliography

Books

Abbot C, *Enforcing Pollution Control Regulation* (Oxford: Hart 2009)

Alston P (ed.), *Non State Actors and Human Rights* (Oxford: Oxford University Press 2005)

Arthurs HW, *'Without the law': Administrative Justice and Legal Pluralism in Nineteenth Century England* (Toronto: University of Toronto Press 1985)

Ashworth A, *Principles of Criminal Law* (6th ed, Oxford: Oxford University Press 2009)

Banaker R and Travers M (eds.), *Theory and Method in Socio-legal Research* (Oxford: Hart 2005)

Bix B, *Law, Language, and Legal Determinacy* (Oxford: Oxford University Press 1996)

Box S, *Power, Crime and Mystification* (London: Tavistock 1983)

Brodbeck M (ed.), *Readings in the Philosophy of the Social Sciences* (New York: Macmillan 1968)

Carr CT, *The General Principles of the Law of Corporations* (the Yorke prize essay for 1902, Cambridge: Cambridge University Press 1905)

Carswell J, *The South Sea Bubble* (London: Cresset Press 1960)

Coleman JS, *The Asymmetric Society: Organisational Actors, Corporate Power and the Irrelevance of Persons* (New York: Syracuse University Press 1982)

Cornish WR and Clark G, *Law and Society in England 1750–1950* (London: Sweet & Maxwell 1989)

Cowles V, *The Great Swindle* (London: Collins 1960)

Dan-Cohen M, *Rights, Persons and Organisations: A Legal Theory for a Bureaucratic Society* (Berkeley: University of California Press 1986)

Dennett DC (ed.), *Brainstorms: Philosophical Essays on Mind and Psychology*, (Cambridge, Mass: MIT Press 1978)

Dennett DC, *The Intentional Stance* (Cambridge, Mass: MIT Press 1987)

Dicey AV, *Law and Opinion in England* (2nd ed, London: Macmillan 1914)

Duff RA and Green S (eds.), *Philosophical Foundations of Criminal Law* (Oxford: Oxford University Press 2011)

Elzinga KG and Breit W, *The Anti-trust Penalties: A Study in Law and Economics* (New Haven: Yale University Press 1976)

Erskine T (ed.) *Can Institutions Have Responsibilities? Collective Moral Agency and International Relations* (Basingstoke: Palgrave Macmillan 2003)

Farmer L, *Criminal Law, Tradition, and Legal Order: Crime and the Genius of Scots Law 1747 to the Present* (Cambridge: Cambridge University Press 1997)

Fisher HAL (ed.) *The Collected Papers of Frederick William Maitland* (Cambridge: Cambridge University Press 1911) vol 3

Fisse B, *Howard's Criminal Law* (5th ed, London: Sweet & Maxwell 1990)

Fisse B and Braithwaite J, *Corporations, Responsibility and Corporate Society* (Cambridge: Cambridge University Press 1993)

Fisse B and Braithwaite J, *Corporations: Crime and Accountability* (Cambridge: Cambridge University Press 1993)

Fletcher GP, *Rethinking Criminal Law* (Boston: Little, Brown and Co 1978)

Foucault M, *Discipline and Punish: The Birth of A Prison* (Harmondsworth: Penguin 1977)

French D and others, *Mayson, French and Ryan on Company Law* (27th ed, Oxford: Oxford University Press 2010)

French PA, *Collective and Corporate Responsibility* (New York: Columbia University Press 1984)

Gobert J and Punch M, *Rethinking Corporate Crime* (Oxford: Butterworths 2003)

Goodrich P, *Legal Discourse Studies in Linguistics, Rhetoric and Legal Analysis* (London: Macmillan 1986)

Hans VP, *Business on Trial* (New Haven: Yale University Press 2000)

Harding C, *Criminal Enterprise: Individuals, Organisations and Criminal Responsibility* (Cullompton: Willan 2007)

Harding C and Joshua J, *Regulating Cartels in Europe* (2nd ed, Oxford: Oxford University Press 2010)

Hawkins K, *Law As Last Resort* (Oxford: Oxford University Press 2002)

Hay D and others (eds.), *Albion's Fatal Tree* (London: Allen Lane 1975)

Hegel, *The Philosophy of Right* (trans TM Knox, Oxford: Oxford University Press 2010)

Herman ES, *Corporate Control, Corporate Power* (Cambridge: Cambridge University Press 1981)

Husak D, *Overcriminalization, The Limits of the Criminal Law* (Oxford: Oxford University Press 2008)

Johnstone G and Ward T, *Key Approaches to Criminology: Law and Crime* (London: Sage 2010)

Kostall RW, *Law and English Railway Capitalism 1825–75* (Oxford: Clarendon Press 1994)

La Follette H (ed.), *The Oxford Handbook of Practical Ethics* (Oxford: Oxford University Press 2003)

Levi M, *Regulating Fraud* (London: Tavistock 1987)

Levi M, *The Phantom Capitalists* (Andover: Ashgate 2008)

List C and Pettit P, *Group Agency* (Oxford: Oxford University Press 2011)

May L and Hoffman S (eds.), *Collective Responsibility, Group Based Harm and Corporate Rights* (Notre Dame: University of Notre Dame Press 1987)

May L and Hoffman S, *Collective Responsibility: Five Decades of Debate in Theoretical and Applied Ethics* (Lanham: Roman & Littlefield 1991)

M McConvill and Wing Hong Chui (eds.) *Research Methods for Law* (Edinburgh: Edinburgh University Press 2007)

Norrie A, *Crime, Reason and History* (2nd ed, Cambridge: Cambridge University Press 2001)

Ormerod D, *Smith & Hogan's Criminal Law* (12th ed, Oxford: Oxford University Press 2008)

Parkinson JE, *Corporate Power and Responsibility, Issues in the Theory of Company Law* (Oxford: Clarendon Press 2000)

Pendleton H, *Criminal Justice in England: A Study in Law Administration* (New York: MacMillan 1931) vol 1

Pennock JR and Chapman JW (eds.), *Criminal Justice* (New York: Lieber-Atherton 1985)

Phillips A, *Lawyers' Language: The Distinctiveness of Legal Language* (London: Taylor and Francis 2002)

Popper KR, *The Open Society and Its Enemies* (London: Routledge & Kegan Paul 1945) 2 vols

Popper KR, *The Poverty of Historicism* (London: Routledge & Kegan Paul 1957)

Posner RA, *Economic Analysis of Law* (New York: Aspen 2007)

Punch ME, *Dirty Business: Exploring Corporate Misconduct* (London: Sage 1996)

Radzinowicz L and Turner JWC (eds.), *The Modern Approach to Criminal Law* (London: Macmillan 1948)

Robb G, *White Collar Crime in Modern England, Financial Fraud and Business Morality 1845–1929* (Cambridge: Cambridge University Press 1992)

Rowan-Robinson J and Watchman PQ, *Crime and Regulation: A Study of the Enforcement of Regulatory Codes* (London: T & T Clark 1990)

Rozenberg J, *The Case for the Crown: The Inside Story of the DPP* (London: Thorsons 1987)

Searle GR, *Morality and the Market in Victorian Britain* (Oxford: Clarendon Press 1998)

Searle JR, *Intentionality: An Essay in the Philosophy of Mind* (Cambridge: Cambridge University Press 1983)

Searle JR, *The Construction of Social Reality* (London: Penguin 1996)

Slapper G and Tombs S, *Corporate Crime* (Harlow: Longman 1999)

Smith G and others, *Studying Fraud as White Collar Crime* (Basingstoke: Palgrave Macmillan 2011)

Smith KJM, *Lawyers, Legislators and Theorists: Developments in English Criminal Jurisprudence 1800–1957* (Oxford: Oxford University Press 1998)

Sugarman D (ed.), *Legality, Ideology and the State* (London: Academic Press 1983)

Sutherland E, *White Collar Crime* (New York: Holt 1949)

Turner JWC, *Russell on Crime* (12th ed, London: Stevens & Sons 1964) vol 1

Van Hoecke M (ed.), *The Methodologies of Legal Research* (Oxford: Hart 2011)

Von Gierke O, *Political Theories in the Middle Age* (trans FW Maitland, Cambridge: Cambridge University Press 1913)

Von Gierke O, *Natural Law and the Theory of Society 1550–1800* (trans E Barker, Cambridge: Cambridge University Press 1934)

Warner M, *Organisational Choice and Constraint* (Westmead: Saxon House 1977)

Weber M, *Economy and Society* (Berkeley: University of California Press 2013)

Wells C, *Corporations and Criminal Responsibility* (2nd ed, Oxford: Oxford University Press 2001)

Journal articles

Anon, 'Corporate Crime: Regulating Corporate Behaviour Through Criminal Sanctions' (1979) 92 Harv L Rev, 1227

Ahdieh R, 'Beyond Individualism in Law and Economics' (2011) 91 BUL Rev 43

Agassi J, 'Methodological Individualism' (1960) 11(3) British Journal of Sociology, Sept 244–270

Agassi J, 'Institutional Individualism' (1975) 26(2) British Journal of Sociology, June 144–155

Arenella P, 'Convicting the Morally Blameless: Reassessing the Relationship between Legal and Moral Accountability' (1992) 39 UCLA Rev 1511

Baldwin R, 'The New Punitive Regulation' (2005) MLR 351

Becker GS, 'Crime and Punishment: An Economic Approach' (1968) 76 J Pol Econ 169

Bodkin A, 'The Prosecution of Offenders: English Practice' (1928) 1 Pol J 354

Bonner JP and Forman BN, 'Bridging the Deterrence Gap: Imposing Criminal Penalties on Corporations and their Executives for Producing Hazardous Projects', (1993) 20 San Diego Justice Journal 1, 1

Brodbeck M, 'Methodological Individualisms: Definition and Reduction' (1958) 25 Philosophy of Science 1

Bucy PH, 'Corporate Ethos: A Standard for Imposing Corporate Criminal Liability' (1991) 75 Minn L Rev 1095

Carson WG, 'Some Sociological Aspects of Strict Liability and the Enforcement of Factory Legislation' (1970) 33 MLR 396

Carson WG, 'White-Collar Crime and the Enforcement of Factory Legislation' (1970) 10 Brit J Criminology

Carson WG, 'The Conventionalisation of Early Factory Crime' (1979) 7 Int'l J Soc Law 37

Cavanagh N, 'Corporate Criminal Liability: An Assessment of the Models of Fault' (2011) 75 JCL 414

Clough J, 'Bridging the Theoretical Gap: The Search for a Realist Model of Corporate Criminal Liability' (2007) 18 Crim L F 267

Coffee JC Jnr, 'Corporate Crime and Punishment: A Non-Chicago View of the Economics of Criminal Sanctions', (1980) 17 Am Crim L Rev 419–476

Coffee JC Jnr, 'No Soul to Damn, No Body to Kick, An Unscandalised Enquiry into the Problem of Corporate Responsibility' (1981) 79 Mich L Rev 386

Copp S and Cronin A, 'The Failure of Criminal Law to Control the Use of Off Balance Sheet Finance During the Banking Crisis' (2015) 36(4) Co Law 99

Dau-Schmidt KG, 'An Economic Analysis of the Criminal Law as a Preference-Shaping Policy' (1990) Duke Law Journal 1

Dau-Schmidt KG, 'Economics and Sociology: The Prospects for an Interdisciplinary Discourse on Law' (1997) Wis L Rev 389

Dicey AV, 'The Combination Laws as Illustrating the Relation Between Law and Public Opinion in England During the 19th Century' (1904) Harv L Rev 511

Farmer L, 'Bringing Cinderella to the Ball: Teaching Criminal Law in Context' (1995) MLR 58(5) 756

Farmer L, 'The Obsession With Definition: The Nature of Crime and Critical Legal Theory' (1996) S & LS 5:57

Fisse B, 'Reconstructing Corporate Criminal Law: Deterrence, Retribution, Fault and Sanctions' (1983) 56 S Cal L Rev 1141–1246

Fisse B and Braithwaite J, 'The Allocation of Responsibility for Corporate Crime: Individualism, Collectivism and Accountability' (1988) 11 Sydney L Rev 468

Foxton D, 'Corporate Personality in the Great War' (2002) 118 LQT 428

French PA, 'The Corporation as a Moral Person' (1979) 16 Am Phil Q 207

Garoupa N and others, 'The Investigation and Prosecution of Regulatory Offences: Is There an Economic Case for Integration?' (2011) 70(1) CLJ 229–259

Gilligan GP, 'The Origins of UK Financial Services Regulation' (1997) 18(6) Co Law 167

Gobert J, 'Corporate Criminality: Four Models of Fault' (1994) 14(3) LS 393

Gobert J, 'Corporate Criminality: New Crimes for the Times' (1994) Crim LR 722

Hart HLA, 'Definition and Theory in Jurisprudence' (1954) 70 LQR 37

Held V, 'Can a Random Collection of Individuals be Morally Responsible?' (1970) J Phil 68

Hodgson GM, 'Meanings of Methodological Individualism' (2007) Journal of Economic Methodology, 14(2) June, 211–226

Hsaio M, 'Abandonment of the Doctrine of Attribution in Favour of Gross Negligence Test in the Corporate Manslaughter and Corporate Homicide Act 2007' (2009) 30(4) Co Law 110

Katz J, 'Concerted Ignorance: The Social Construction of Cover Up' (1979) 8 Urban Life 295

Lacey N, 'In Search of the Responsible Subject: History, Philosophy and Criminal Law Theory' (2001) 1 64 MLR 350–371

Lacey N, 'Responsibility and Modernity in Criminal Law' (2001) 9 Journal of Political Philosophy 249–277

Lacey N, 'Space, Time and Function: Intersecting Principles of Responsibility Across the Terrain of Criminal Justice' (2007) 1 Criminal Law and Philosophy 233–250

Lederman E, 'Criminal Law, Perpetrator and Corporation: Rethinking a Complex Triangle', (1985) 76 J Crim L and Criminology

Lederman E, 'Models for Imposing Corporate Criminal Liability: From Adaptation and Imitation toward Aggregation and The Search for Self-Identity' [2001] Buff Crim LR 642

Lee IB, 'Corporate Criminal Responsibility as Team Member Responsibility' (2011) 31(4) OJLS 755–781

Levi M, 'The Roskill Fraud Commission Revisited: An Assessment' (2003) JFL 11(1), 38–44

Masters JL, 'Fraud and Money Laundering: The Evolving Criminalization of Corporate Non-compliance' (2008) JMLC 103

McDonald M, 'The Personless Paradigm' (1987) 37 UTLJ 212

Morrissey DJ, 'Toward a New/Old Theory of Corporate Social Responsibility' (1989) 40 Syracuse L Rev 1005

Motta M, 'On Cartel Deterrence and Fines in the European Union' (2008) 29 European Competition Law Review

O' Malley P, 'Risk, Power and Crime Prevention' (1992) 21 Economy and Society 252

Ouchi WG, 'Organisational Culture' (1985) Annual Review of Sociology 457

Pettit PN, 'Responsibility Incorporated' (2007) 117 Ethics 171

Posner RA, 'An Economic Theory of the Criminal Law' (1985) 85 Colum L Rev 1193–1231

Quaid JA, 'The Assessment of Corporate Criminal Liability on the Basis of Corporate Identity: An Analysis' (1998) 423 McGill LJ 67

Ramirez MK, 'The Science Fiction of Corporate Criminal Liability: Containing the Machine Through the Corporate Death Penalty' (2005) 47 Ariz L Rev 933–1002

Reznik M, 'Injustice in Financial Services Disputes (Pt 1)' (2017) 167 NLJ 7743

Richardson G, 'Strict Liability for Regulatory Crime: The Empirical Evidence' (1987) Crim LR 295–306

Scanlan G, 'Dishonesty in Corporate Offences, A Need for Reform?' (2002) 23(4) Co Law 114–119

Scanlan G, 'Offences Concerning Directors and Officers of a Company – Fraud and Corruption in the United Kingdom – the Future' (2008) 29(9) Co Law 264

Schumpeter J, 'On the Concept of Social Value' (1909) QJ Econ 213

Scruton R, 'Corporate Persons' (1989) Proceedings of the Aristotelian Society (supplementary series) 239

Shannon HA, 'The Coming of General Limited Liability', (1930–31) J Econ Hist 2 269

Shannon HA, 'The Limited Companies of 1866–1883', (1933) J Econ Hist 4 295

Shapiro SP, 'Collaring the Crime, Not the Criminal: Reconsidering the Concept of White Collar Crime' (1990) 55 Am Soc Rev 346

Sullivan GR, 'The Attribution of Culpability to Limited Companies' (1996) 55(3) CLJ 515

Teubner G, 'Enterprise Corporatism: New Industrial Policy and the "Essence" of the Legal Person' (1988) 36 Am J Comp Law 130

Udehn L, 'The Changing Face of Methodological Individualism' (2002) 28 Ann Rev Soc 479

Watkins JWN, 'Historical Explanation in the Social Sciences' (1957–58) British Journal for the Philosophy of Science 104

Wells C, 'The Decline and Rise of English Murder: Corporate Crime and Individual Responsibility' (1988) Crim LR Dec 788

Wells C, 'Corporations: Culture, Risk and Criminal Liability' (1993) Crim LR Aug 551–566

Winn CRN, 'The Criminal Responsibility of Corporations' (1927–29) 3 CLJ 398

Woolf T, 'The Criminal Code Act 1995 (Cth) – Towards a Realist Vision of Corporate Criminal Liability' (1997) Crim L J 257

Official materials

Law Commission, *Criminal Liability in Regulatory Contexts* (Law Com No 195, 2010)

Law Commission, *Report on Fraud* (Law Com No 276, July 2002)

Levi M, *The Economic Cost of Fraud Report for the Home Office* (London, NERA 2000)

Macrory RB, (Better Regulation Executive), *Regulatory Justice: Making Sanctions Effective, Final Report* (Nov 2006)

Ministry of Justice, *Corporate Liability for Economic Crime*, Call for Evidence, 13 January 2017

National Audit Office, Department for Business, Energy and Industrial Strategy, *Protecting Consumers from Scams, Unfair Trading and Unsafe Goods*, HC Session 2016–17, 16 December 2016

Parliamentary Commission on Banking Standards, *Changing Banking for Good*, 12 June 2013

Royal Commission on Criminal Justice *The Investigation, Prosecution and the Trial of Serious Fraud*: (London, HMSO 1993)

Royal Commission on Criminal Procedure, *Report on the Investigation and Prosecution of Criminal Offences in England and Wales: The Law and Procedure* (1980/81 Cmnd 8092-I and II, 1980/81)

Royal Commission on Practices and Proceedings of the Courts of Common Law, 5th Report (1833–34)

Select Committee on the Financial Aspects of Corporate Governance (1992), the '*Cadbury Report*'

Select Committee on Joint Stock Companies First Report, BPP, VII 1844 the '*Gladstone Committee Report*'

Reports

HM Treasury, Bank of England and FCA, *Fair and Effective Markets Review*, Final Report, June 2015

Levi M and others, *The Nature, Extent and Economic Impact of Fraud in the UK* (London: ACPO 2007)

New City Agenda and Cass Business School, *Cultural Change in the FCA, PRA and Bank of England, Practising What They Preach?*, 25 October 2016

Websites

www.bankofengland.co.uk/markets/Documents/femr/implementationreport.pdf accessed Oct 26, 2016

www.bankofengland.co.uk/publications/Pages/speeches/default.aspx/Documents/speeches/2016/speech930.pdf accessed Oct 21, 2016

www.bbc.co.uk/news/business-30695720 accessed Jan 6, 2015

www.berg.co.uk accessed Apr 30, 2017

www.croweclarkwhitehill.co.uk/wp-content/uploads/sites/2/2017/02/crowe-the-financial-cost-of-fraud-2017.pdf accessed June 30, 2017

www.europarl.europa.eu/RegData/etudes/etudes/join/2014/507463/IPOL-IMCO_ET(2014)507463_EN.pdf accessed Oct, 2016

www.experian.co.uk/assets/identity-and-fraud/pkfexperian-fraud-indicator-report.pdf accessed Dec 6, 2016

www.fca.org.uk/consumers/payment-protection-insurance/monthly-ppi-refunds-and-compensation accessed Dec 6, 2016

www.financial-ombudsman.org.uk/news/speech/2013/CW-BILA-conference.pdf accessed Jan 22, 2015

www.giffordlectures.org/Browse.asp?PubID=TPTPTR&Volume=O&Issue=O&ArticleID=6 accessed May 15, 2014

www.gov.uk/government/speeches/mansion-house-2015-speech-by-the-chancellor-of-the-exchequer accessed Nov 4, 2016

www.gov.uk/government/uploads/system/uploads/attachment_data/file/118530/annual-fraud-indicator-2012.pdf accessed Dec 7, 2016

www.telegraph.co.uk/finance/personalfinance/pensions/11286965/Annuity-mis-selling-scandal-could-it-be-as-big-as-PPI.html accessed Oct 3, 2015

www.dailymail.co.uk/news/article-4062858/Barclays-HSBC-Royal-Bank-Scotland-face-multi-billion-fines-toxic-mortgages.html accessed Dec 28, 2016

2 Corporate fraud
The case for a new approach

2.1 Review of the current legal responses and proposals

The common law's so-called "identification principle" limits a finding of corporate criminal liability to instances of wrongdoing in which the individual who is deemed to be the "directing mind and will" of the corporation is himself guilty of the offence in question.[1] While this model of attribution works adequately where the company has a relatively simple, pyramidal managerial framework, it is widely acknowledged that large corporations with typically complex organisational structures and decentralised responsibility are likely to evade prosecution.[2] The same can be said where corporate policy and decision-making is the product of other corporate policies and procedures rather than the result of individual decisions.[3] Moreover, as a basis of fault, the identification principle serves less to deter criminal conduct and more to motivate senior managers to distance themselves from, or "turn a blind eye" to, questionable or dubious practices. It also acts as a disincentive for the internal reporting of suspected illegality[4] and the introduction of individual accountability measures. Furthermore, the need to identify the criminality of an individual of sufficiently senior rank, as a precursor to corporate prosecution, incurs evidential problems which inevitably increase as the size of the company increases.[5] This problem is compounded by organisations obscuring accountability when under investigation and resorting

---

1 This terminology is attributed to Viscount Haldane L.C., *Lennard's Carrying Co Ltd v Asiatic Petroleum Ltd* [1915] AC 705 (HL).
2 For its application in the prosecution of the small company in *R v Kite & OLL Ltd.*, The Times, 8 Dec 1994; see too HMRC 'Tackling Offshore Tax Evasion: A New Corporate Criminal Offence of Failure to Prevent the Facilitation of Evasion' (Consultation document, 16 July 2015); D. Ormerod, *Smith & Hogan's Criminal Law* (Oxford: Oxford University Press, 2008) 249; J. Gobert, 'Corporate Criminality: Four Models of Fault' (1994) 14(3) LS 393, 395.
3 C.M.V. Clarkson, 'Kicking Corporate Bodies and Damning Their Souls' [1996] MLR 557, 561.
4 HMRC "Tackling Offshore Tax Evasion: A New Corporate Criminal Offence of Failure to Prevent the Facilitation of Evasion" (Consultation document, 16 July 2015).
5 M. Hsaio, 'Abandonment of the Doctrine of Attribution in favour of Gross Negligence Test in the Corporate Manslaughter and Corporate Homicide Act 2007' (2009) 30(4) Co Law 110, 111.

to other evasive strategies such as transferring personnel out of the legal jurisdiction[6] or deliberately covering up evidence.[7] The limitations of the common law identification principle are now so well recognised that bespoke statutory reforms have been enacted in the areas of corporate manslaughter,[8] bribery[9] and tax evasion[10] and further reform is being considered in other areas of economic crime.

The Corporate Manslaughter and Corporate Homicide Act 2007 was the first of the statutes to introduce a distinct basis to address corporate liability where the common law identification principle was seen to be particularly inadequate. It is applicable where death arises as a consequence of the way in which an organisation's activities are managed or organised by its senior management is a substantial element of what amounts to a gross breach of the duty of care owed to the deceased by the organisation.[11] The liability incurred under this model is truly "corporate" in the sense that it is not predicated on the commission of a manslaughter offence by any individual officer or employee. Furthermore, framed in the language of gross negligence, as is its common law equivalent for manslaughter perpetrated by individuals,[12] the problematic issue of mens rea does not arise, the negligence concept being based on the failure to meet reasonable standards of conduct.

It is worth observing that the Corporate Manslaughter and Corporate Homicide Act 2007 came into force in 2008[13] after more than a decade of public outcry over a number of high-profile transport disasters[14] that had highlighted the deficiencies of the common law principle. During this period, a solution was mooted in the form an extension to the common law identification doctrine, referred to as the aggregation principle, and this was raised specifically in the case following the sinking of the Herald of Free Enterprise.[15] In the absence of individual culpability at the directing mind level, it was suggested that the organisation should be attributed with the individual knowledge of its employees, on a vicarious basis, such that the

---

6 Brent Fisse, *Howard's Criminal Law* (5th ed, London: Sweet & Maxwell 1990) 591; Brent Fisse and John Braithwaite, *Corporations, Crime and Accountability* (Cambridge: Cambridge University Press 1993) 38.

7 Jack Katz, 'Concerted Ignorance: The Social Construction of Cover-up' (1979) 8 Urban Life 295.

8 Corporate Manslaughter and Corporate Homicide Act 2007.

9 Bribery Act 2010, s. 7.

10 Criminal Finances Act 2017, Pt. 3, ss. 45 and 46.

11 Corporate Manslaughter and Corporate Homicide Act 2007, s. 1(1) and (3).

12 Gross negligence manslaughter.

13 Coming into force on April 6, 2008.

14 E.g. in March 1987, 187 people were killed in the Herald of Free Enterprise disaster, 167 died on Piper Alpha in July 1988 and five months later 35 rail passengers died at Clapham. Other fatalities occurred at Kings Cross, Southall, Paddington, Hatfield and Potters Bar, and on the Marchioness river boat.

15 *P & O European Ferries (Dover) Ltd* (1990) 93 Cr App R 72.

knowledge could then be aggregated at the corporate level so as to produce a collective knowledge to which corporate blameworthiness could attach. However, while this approach avoided the need to locate fault in one individual at the senior, "directing mind" level, the notion of aggregated liability faced fierce academic criticism. Aside from the evidential issues that would arise where there are a number of witnesses with individual knowledge components,[16] the primary concern was that aggregation would operate to turn otherwise innocent acts or omissions into criminal acts[17] and that the sum of the knowledge could exceed that of the individual parts.[18] Not only was the composite knowledge suggested artificial in nature, it singularly failed to reflect the notion of corporate fault.[19] The question of the level of seniority required of the individuals with knowledge relevant to the wrongdoing[20] would remain and, importantly, it was observed that collective knowledge is not synonymous with collective intention, which is the mental attitude towards that body of knowledge, such that intention is non-aggregable.[21] In the event, the prosecution of *P & O Ferries* failed,[22] and in a judicial review arising out of the same facts it was also held that a case against one defendant could not be fortified by evidence against another.[23] At the same time, the Law Commission was also refusing to acknowledge the possibility of aggregation as a basis of corporate liability.[24]

In Australia, the recognition of the realist nature of organisations had shaped the criminal law somewhat earlier, the "corporate culture model" originating in the Australian Criminal Code 1995. As an innovation emerging from a common law jurisdiction it is worthy of consideration but also the acknowledgement that,

---

16 GR Sullivan, 'The Attribution of Culpability to Limited Companies' (1996) 55(3) CLJ 515.

17 See e.g. Eli Lederman, 'Models for Imposing Corporate Criminal Liability: From Adaptation and Imitation toward Aggregation and The Search for Self-Identity' (2001) Buff Crim LR 642.

18 James Gobert, 'Corporate Criminality: New Crimes for the Times' (1994) Crim LR 722.

19 Caron Beaton-Wells & Brent Fisse, *Australian Cartel Regulation* (Cambridge: Cambridge University Press 2011) 241 and citing TA Hagemann and J Grinstein, 'The Mythology of Aggregate Corporate Knowledge: A Deconstruction' (1997) 65 Geo Wash L Rev 210; Brent Fisse, 'Reconstructing Corporate Criminal Law: Deterrence, Retribution, Fault and Sanctions', S Cal L Rev, 56 (1983) 1141, 1189–90.

20 James Gobert, 'Corporate Criminality: New Crimes for the Times' (1994) Crim LR 722.

21 Eli Lederman, 'Models for Imposing Corporate Criminal Liability: From Adaptation and Imitation toward Aggregation and The Search for Self-Identity' (2001) Buff Crim LR 642.

22 At the time of the P&O case, negligence manslaughter was known as 'reckless manslaughter'. It comprised two elements: first, a person was reckless if he did an act which in fact created an obvious and serious risk of causing physical injury and second, he had either failed to give any thought to the possibility of the existence of such a risk or had recognised some risk and had nonetheless gone on to do that act. In P&O the judge halted proceedings and directed acquittals of the seven defendants, finding that none had been reckless.

23 *R v HM Coroner for East Kent, ex p Spooner* (1989) 88 Cr App R 10.

24 Law Commission, *A Criminal Code for England and Wales* (Law Com No 177, 1989) vol 1, para 30(2).

as an approach to corporate crime, it is not one that has been influential or adopted in English law. Under the Code, the actus reus element of the offence is imposed under the principle of vicarious liability, and is not restricted to the conduct of an individual who represents a directing mind.[25] The Code also provides the means by which to attribute mens rea to the corporation where there is evidence of a blameworthy corporate culture. However, the Code is not of general application, being applicable in limited circumstances and only in relation to some federal offences including those perpetrated against Common-wealth entities. The concept of the corporate culture appears to require proof of conditions and attitudes that exist within the organisation and it is this aspect that may be particularly challenging. It would appear that the evidence of socio-logical experts would be relevant in this respect. Further, given that the corporate environment typically accommodates many diverse cultures, the concept of fault based on some homogenous culture is problematic.[26] Indeed, general dissatisfac-tion with the construction of corporate fault as contained in the Code appears borne out by the provisions of the Competition and Consumer Act 2010 (Cth.) which expressly exclude its application.[27] It is also of note that since the code only provides the mechanism to attribute intention, recklessness and knowledge to a corporation, the usefulness of any further examination of the model in the context of fraud, a classic dishonesty offence, is questionable.[28]

Alternative bases for corporate liability have also been proposed, one of which was the concept of reactive corporate fault, advanced by Fisse, which would recognise instances where corporate blameworthiness could be imposed not by reference to the occurrence of the harmful act but, subsequently, by reference to the inadequacy of the organisation's response. More precisely, liability would be incurred where there had been an unreasonable failure on the part of the organisation to devise and implement adequate preventative or corrective measures in response to the commission of the actus reus of an offence by one or more of its members.[29] This model would depart from traditional principles of criminal law in that the mens rea, or blameworthy attitude, would not coincide temporally with the harmful act itself and, in suggesting that the corporation would attract liability for the substantive offence that was the cause of the harm, it would do so on the basis that the mens rea did not match the actus reus. This led to claims that, on such an approach, the corporate offence would not be equivalent to the substantive offence in terms of turpitude and could therefore be challenged as an affront to the principle of

---

25 Australian Criminal Code 1995, s. 12.2.
26 Caron Beaton-Wells and Brent Fisse, *Australian Cartel Regulation* (Cambridge: Cambridge University Press 2011) 231.
27 Competition and Consumer Act 2010 (Cth.) s. 6AA(2).
28 Australian Criminal Code 1995.
29 Brent Fisse, 'Reconstructing Corporate Criminal Law: Deterrence, Retribution, Fault and Sanctions' (1983) 56 S Cal L Rev 1141, 1195.

fair labelling.[30] However, the recognition of corporate fault based on a failure to respond to harm resulting from its activities has some appeal and it may be that such an approach would be better conceived as a distinctive form of corporate culpability. Of note, it is from the reactive fault perspective that French went on to propose the "extended principle of accountability"[31] and the "principle of responsive adjustment".[32] The extended accountability would impose liability for the unintended effects that the company "was willing to have occur as a result ... of his actions"[33] while responsive adjustment liability would look to the measures taken to prevent the recurrence of an untoward event caused by it.[34] On either version, reactive or responsive, the agency of the organisation itself is recognised and corporate liability would not be imposed on a parasitic basis that would require that an underlying criminal offence had been committed by an individual member. Furthermore, both versions are innovative in focusing on the construction of fault by reference to the sufficiency of the corporate response to the harmful conduct in question. In this respect the problem of proving corporate mens rea, as it is conceived in the traditional terms of intention, recklessness or knowledge, is avoided.

Otherwise, suggestions for a construct of corporate culpability have tended to be framed as forms of negligence. Since negligence is premised in the assessment of conduct by reference to objective standards of reasonableness, it is an approach that also circumvents the problem of mens rea where corporate entities are concerned. In addition, the negligence-based approach is particularly attractive in that it responds to the fact that corporate crime is often envisaged as the result of an omission rather than a positive act. Indeed, Fisse and Braithwaite have suggested that the predominant form of corporate fault is more likely to be negligence than intention if an anthropomorphised notion of corporate intention is not at the heart of responsibility.[35] In this respect, Lederman has advocated a model which appears to be one of negligence in substance. He suggests that the concept of group mens rea should be perceived unconventionally, with objective and constructive elements, such that liability is premised on the gap between the social expectation of the corporate behaviour and its actual conduct.[36] Similarly, Gobert has observed that mens rea is only one means to address the issue of

---

30 See GR Sullivan, 'The Attribution of Culpability to Limited Companies' (1996) 55(3) CLJ 515.

31 Peter A French, *Collective and Corporate Responsibility* (New York: Columbia University Press 1984) 134.

32 Ibid 156.

33 Ibid 134.

34 Ibid 156.

35 Brent Fisse and John Braithwaite, *Corporations: Crime and Accountability* (Cambridge University Press 1993) 29.

36 Eli Lederman, 'Models for Imposing Corporate Criminal Liability: From Adaptation and Imitation toward Aggregation and The Search for Self-Identity' [2001] Buff Crim LR 642. Sullivan also proposed that an organisation's conduct should be assessed by compliance or non-compliance with prescribed standards, albeit rejecting the realist notion of corporations

blameworthiness, an alternative may be to ask whether the company could have taken steps to identify and avoid the occurrence of harm, whether it was reasonable to do so, and whether it did so in fact or otherwise acted with due diligence.[37] He proposes that liability might be predicated on an implied duty, namely a duty incumbent upon the company to prevent crime, arising on the basis that the state allows companies to carry on business for profit under its protective umbrella of law in exchange for them being able to operate within the legal structure. Consequently, the company has a duty not to conduct its business in a way that exposes innocent individuals to the dangers of harms proscribed by the state's criminal laws.[38] With this in mind, Gobert and Punch have adverted to negligence liability based on an obligation to put systems in place that would avert crime, the failure to do so being a reflection of the way that the company has chosen to do its business.[39] The substance of this account of negligence has now come to fruition in the specific contexts of bribery and tax evasion, albeit expressed in terms of a strict corporate liability for "failure to prevent" the commission of the offence with the availability of a due diligence defence.

This development occurred with the coming into force of the Bribery Act 2010[40] which, after the earlier enactment of the Corporate Manslaughter etc. Act,[41] added a second statutory model of corporate criminal responsibility. This act is distinctive in that liability is not based on wrongdoing at the senior management level but on the organisation's "failure to prevent" its employees or associates, at any level of the corporate hierarchy, bribing another to the advantage of the company. Although the corporate fault is premised on vicarious liability for its employees' acts, the apparent variance with fundamental values of justice[42] associated with this form of strict liability fault attribution is tempered by the adequate procedures/due diligence defence that accompanies it.[43] The novelty of the Act therefore lies in the creation of a serious corporate offence combined with a defence that requires the demonstration of regulatory-type compliance.[44] The statutory corporate liability for the "failure to prevent" bribery sits in tandem with the common law "identification doctrine" under which

---

and advocating vicarious liability with a due diligence defence, G R Sullivan, 'The Attribution of Culpability to Limited Companies' (1996) 55(3) CLJ 515.

37 James Gobert, 'Corporate Criminality: New Crimes for the Times', (1994) Crim LR 722, referring to LH Leigh 'The Criminal Liability of Corporations and Other Groups' (1977) 9 Ottawa L Rev 247, 287.

38 Ibid.

39 James Gobert and Maurice Punch, *Rethinking Corporate Crime* (London: Butterworths 2003).

40 Coming into force on July 1, 2011

41 Corporate Manslaughter and Corporate Homicide Act 2007.

42 See e.g. Brent Fisse, 'The Social Policy of Corporate Criminal Responsibility' (1978) 6 Adelaide LR 361–412, 366; L H Leigh, 'The Criminal Liability of Corporations and Other Groups: A Comparative View' (1982) Michigan LR 1508–29, 1514.

43 Bribery Act 2010, s. 7(2).

44 S. Gentle, 'The Bribery Act 2010' [2011] CLR 101.

corporate culpability for the substantive offence can still be established where sufficiently senior officers have been involved in bribing, being bribed or bribing foreign public officials.[45] Thus, the statutory "failure to prevent" model adds to the type of corporate criminal liability that can be incurred and it increases the scope of the liability that is parasitic in nature by the inclusion of the ineffective control of "rogue" employees at lower organisational levels.[46] In this respect, the model still relies upon individuals acting criminally within the company and there is no real departure from the individualist paradigm.[47] However, the "failure to prevent" basis of fault not only avoids the problematic attribution of mens rea to the corporation, through a version of essentially strict liability, it also overcomes the practical evidential difficulties that are exacerbated in the corporate context by placing the evidential onus on the corporate defendant to show due diligence. The availability of Deferred Prosecution Agreements, and accompanying opportunity for a reduction in penalty, serves as a strong incentive for corporations to self-report when their anti-bribery regime has been ineffective and to cooperate fully in the following investigation. Taken together, the early admission of the offence and the reversal of the evidential onus in relation to the defence means that the individual witnesses required to give evidence will generally do so on behalf of their employer company and not against it. Such an approach alleviates potential conflicts of personal interest and concerns about loyalty that inevitably arise where the evidential onus rests entirely on the prosecution and employees are key prosecution witnesses.

Deferred Prosecution Agreements became part of the Serious Fraud Office's enforcement armoury in February 2014 and can only be used, with judicial approval, once corporate criminal proceedings have been commenced. However, the effect is to defer the prosecution on specified terms which typically include the payment of a financial penalty, compensation and the implementation of an internal compliance programme. If the terms are met within the specified period, the proceedings are discontinued.[48] The rationale for the development of the "failure to prevent" model of corporate liability is that it encourages organisations to take reasonable steps, and put in place adequate procedures, to promote corporate good governance and, with the potential availability of Deferred Prosecution Agreements, to self-report

---

45 Bribery Act 2010, ss. 1, 2, 6.
46 The conviction of an individual is not a prerequisite to corporate liability.
47 Cavanagh argues that since corporate fault is "qualitatively different from human fault" the failure to prevent approach, formulated in this way, is not a suitable means to impose criminal liability on a corporation, Neil Cavanagh, 'Corporate Criminal Liability: An Assessment of the Models of Fault' (2011) 75 JCL 414.
48 Crime and Courts Act 2013, Sch. 17 and Criminal Procedure Rules 2015, Pt. 11. In October 2014 sentencing guidelines on financial penalties for companies convicted of economic crimes came into force and these inform the level of any penalty imposed under a DPA, www.sentencingcouncil.org.uk/wp-content/uploads/Fraud_bribery_and_money_laundering_of fences_-_Definitive_guideline.pdf accessed 22 May 2017.

when the commission of an offence has been discovered. In economic terms, there is a benefit in transferring the responsibility of policing to the corporation itself rather than the state incurring the costs and practical difficulties involved in monitoring the activities of the corporation's individual members.[49] Indeed, this model has been considered successful enough in the context of bribery that, when the relevant provisions of the Criminal Finances Act 2017 come into force, it will provide the basis for corporate liability for the facilitation of tax evasion[50] and it appears to be the favoured approach as regards reform proposals in relation to other corporate economic crimes, including fraud.[51]

2.2 The peculiar problem of fraud: the need for a new approach

It is clear that there is widespread acknowledgement of what Harding refers to as a spectrum of responsibility within an organisational context, ranging from conduct at one extreme that is wholly attributable to individuals to conduct at the other extreme that is wholly corporate, with varying degrees of mutual influence and interdependence in between. Once over the "tipping point", it would appear that organisations commit different offences from individuals,[52] the outcome being distinctive in terms of role, offending conduct and identity of the actor.[53] The distinctiveness of the corporate wrongdoing provides the justification for employing alternative mechanisms of fault attribution that avoid the actus reus/mens rea construct of crime that has proved so problematic in the context of corporate wrongdoing.

The suggestion of a negligence-based approach is particularly attractive in that it is assessed by reference to standards of behaviour that are considered reasonable in the circumstances and therefore avoids the metaphysical issue associated with the traditional construct of crime defined by notions of intention or recklessness. Negligence also responds to the fact that corporate crime is often envisaged as the result of an omission rather than a positive act and the failure to do some act, or to do it inadequately, is readily caught within its conception of fault. However, while the objective approach that is characteristic of negligence

---

49 Discussed in Brent Fisse, *Howard's Criminal Law* (5th ed, London: Sweet & Maxwell 1990) 617–20 and referring to Canada, Law Reform Commission, Working Paper 16, Criminal Responsibility for Group Action, p. 31.

50 Criminal Finances Act 2017, Pt. 3, ss. 45 and 46. See also HMRC "Tackling Offshore Tax Evasion: A New Corporate Criminal Offence of Failure to Prevent the Facilitation of Evasion", (Consultation document, 16 July 2015) paras 2.17 and 2.18, p 10.

51 See www.gov.uk/government/news/new-plans-to-tackle-corporate-fraud accessed June 26, 2016; Ministry of Justice, 'Call for Evidence on Corporate Liability for Economic Crime' 13 Jan to 24 Mar 2017.

52 Harding suggests this is necessary to delimit individual responsibility, Christopher Harding, *Criminal Enterprise: Individuals, Organisations and Criminal Responsibility* (Cullompton: Willan 2007).

53 With the possibility of different sanctions to convey judgements of responsibility, ibid.

has been unobjectionable for the imposition of civil liability, it has not carved much of a place in the criminal law[54] because it offends the criminal law's central canon of subjective individualism.[55] Negligence is not generally considered serious enough to attract the stigma reserved for truly criminal wrongdoing characterised by moral blameworthiness. References to objective standards in the criminal law are relatively few and far between and are usually confined to the assessment of sub-elements of an offence or defence, rather than being employed as the determinant characteristic of fault.[56] Further, in contrast to the civil law, the criminal law has traditionally focused its attention on those who exercise their rational choice as expressed in the doing of some positive act, and who do so intending or being reckless as to the harmful consequence that may follow. Accordingly, in relation to liability for a failure to act, the criminal law has not resorted to negligence principles, which are suited to attributing liability for omissions, but has taken an alternative approach to develop a basis upon which culpability can be established. Aside from the specific drafting of omission liability contained in various statutory offences,[57] the common law has identified limited circumstances in which a duty to act arises and where a failure to do so, in a way that can be reasonably expected, can give rise to criminal culpability. Thus, a common law duty to act can arise by virtue of a contractual obligation,[58] by virtue of the public office of the individual[59] or, for example, where an individual has created a danger.[60] However, a culpable omission will facilitate a conviction for the substantive offence on the basis of the mens rea required for that offence, and not on the basis of negligence. For instance, if a person innocently causes a fire and subsequently appreciates the risk of damage it may cause, he can be convicted of arson for the failure to do something reasonable to minimise the risk he has created.[61] In such a case, the fault element is subjective recklessness, as is required to make out the offence.[62] In the criminal law a duty to act can also arise where the defendant owes the victim a "duty of care", this concept deriving from the law of negligence in the civil law. Typical examples are where there is a special relationship, such as between parent and child[63] or doctor and patient.

---

54 There are some exceptions, e.g. some driving offences, and elements of other offences and defences include reference to an objective standard.
55 See e.g. *R v G& Another* [2003] UKHL 50 in which the objective approach to recklessness in criminal damage was rejected in favour of subjective assessment.
56 E.g. in the context of constructive manslaughter, the prosecution must prove that the defendant committed an unlawful act, with the requisite subjective mens rea of that crime, and then that the act was "dangerous". It is dangerousness that is considered objectively.
57 E.g. a motorist's liability for a failure to provide a police officer with a breath specimen when properly required, Road Traffic Act 1988, s. 6.
58 *R v Pittwood* (1902) 19 TLR 37.
59 *R v Dytham* [1979] QB 722.
60 *R v Miller* [1983] 2 AC 161.
61 Ibid.
62 Criminal Damage Act 1971, s. 1.
63 *R v Gibbons and Proctor* (1918) 13 Cr App R 134.

Again, in such circumstances the criminal conviction will be for the substantive offence, for example murder[64] or gross negligence manslaughter, if the failure to act amounts to a breach of the duty of care.[65] The common law's construction of fault on the basis of gross negligence is exceptional and is confined to manslaughter. As a controversial basis upon which to justify the imposition of criminal liability, the conviction for manslaughter on this basis is strictly confined to circumstances in which the negligence is considered "gross" such that it goes "beyond a mere matter of compensation ... [showing] such disregard for the life and safety of others as to amount to a crime against the State and conduct deserving punishment".[66]

A brief survey of the application of negligence in the criminal law thus reveals that it is not considered a primary indicium of fault. Although it has been uncontroversial as a proposed basis of corporate fault, it is not generally sufficient to establish individual criminal culpability. Whilst suited to situations where harm caused is the result of a failure to act, or a failure to act in accordance with standards that are considered reasonable, it is employed merely as a yardstick by which to measure the reasonableness of a defendant's behaviour where a duty to act exists. Otherwise, in the context of manslaughter, where fatality is the result of a breach of a duty of care owed, the breach must be so bad as to be considered gross.

Accordingly, in its proposed application as a general hallmark of criminality for corporations, negligence would convey far less opprobrium than the traditional canons of fault, expressed in the concepts of intention, subjective recklessness, knowledge and dishonesty. In the context of serious wrongdoing it would fail to satisfy the criminal law's expressive function which is considered the best way to control corporate power.[67] Since liability framed as the breach of a prescribed standard of conduct is more akin to regulatory non-compliance, corporate liability so framed would lack the reputational detriment, and deterrent bite, that accompanies a conviction for "real" crime. While there is an argument to the effect that the rights of group persons are not on a par with those enjoyed by natural persons,[68] such that a lower threshold of criminal wrongdoing might be justified, the recognition of an organisation as a responsible agent demands equivalence in the perception of the gravity of the misconduct. Furthermore, there is evidence that where liability is imposed on this basis, organisations invest in compliance to create a strong impression of diligent compliance efforts, which is rarely challenged but which masks underlying deviance.[69] The effect, described as the paradox of

---

64 Ibid.
65 *R v Stone and Dobinson* [1977] QB 354.
66 *R v Bateman* [1925] All ER 25, per Lord Hewart C.J..
67 William S Laufer, *Corporate Bodies and Guilty Minds* (Chicago: University of Chicago Press 2006) 154.
68 Christian List and Philip Pettit, *Group Agency* (Oxford: Oxford University Press 2011) 180.
69 Ibid Ch. 4.

moral hazard, is to ensure that employees' wrongdoing will be conceived as an individual rather than a corporate act, the "compliance firewall" serving to shift the risk of liability and loss. As the pressure to produce results inevitably continues, the unpalatable result is that corporate deviance is often tolerated or tacitly encouraged and levels of diligence actually decrease.[70]

Furthermore, in the specific context of fraud, there is also the problem that principles of negligence liability are based on the breach of a duty of care and this strict limitation means that no liability can attach in relation to losses suffered by persons to whom no duty of care is owed. A finding of such a relationship between the perpetrator and the victim of fraud would be extremely unlikely and would leave much corporate fraud beyond the reach of the law. Even if a duty of care could be established, while corporate negligence may adequately express the nature of the wrongdoing for some behaviours in some contexts, the commission of fraud by negligence is unlikely to be one of them.[71] Integral to the notion of fraud is behaviour intended to make a gain or to cause a loss, or expose another to a risk of loss,[72] and that it is done dishonestly.[73] The offence definition must capture the true nature of the criminality and an offence of negligently committing fraud simply does not reflect the character of the wrongdoing. It must also be noted that fraud is peculiar in that it defies definition, it is not an activity in itself but the way in which an otherwise lawful activity is performed.[74] There is a fine line between fraud and the general rough-and-tumble of the markets[75] and the concept of dishonesty is what delineates the two. Thus, for example, the fact that a statement may be both true and at the same time misleading undermines any approach to fraud by false representation[76] that does not encompass the element of dishonesty.[77]

The "failure to prevent" model of corporate liability is more promising in terms of consistency with criminal law doctrine. Although this has been categorised as a form of negligence liability, by virtue of the statutory defence of taking reasonable precautions,[78] it can also be analysed as the imposition of

---

70 Ibid.
71 The same argument has been made in relation to the cartel offence which is not concerned with negligently causing a prohibited result, but with intentional agreements not to compete with competitors, Caron Beaton-Wells and Brent Fisse, *Australian Cartel Regulation* (Cambridge: Cambridge University Press 2011) 233.
72 Fraud Act 2006, ss. 2(1)(b)(i) and (ii), 3(b)(i) and (ii), 4(1)(c)(i) and (ii).
73 Ibid ss. 2(1)(a), 3(a), 4(1)(b).
74 Paul McGrath, *Commercial Fraud and Civil Practice* (Oxford: Oxford University Press 2009) 3.
75 S Buell, 'Good Faith and Law Evasion' (2011) 58 UCLA LR 611.
76 Contrary to Fraud Act 2006, ss. 1(2)(a) and 2.
77 Stephen Copp and Alison Cronin, 'The Failure of Criminal Law to Control the use of Off Balance Sheet Finance During the Banking Crisis' (2015) 36(4) Co Law 99.
78 Caron Beaton-Wells and Brent Fisse, *Australian Cartel Regulation* (Cambridge: Cambridge University Press 2011) 219.

a duty to prevent the offence which, if not prevented, would incur liability. Although there may still be concerns of corporate evasion through use of the "compliance firewall" and "scapegoating", this construction does accord with the criminal law's general approach to omissions liability and would render the approach to corporate fraud consistent with that taken in the contexts of bribery and tax evasion. Not only is economy to be found in the use of a familiar framework, employed in conjunction with the Deferred Prosecution Agreement, the development of the law in this way would achieve much that the architects of the proposed "responsive" models of liability sought to achieve. Self-reporting and cooperation with enforcement agencies is incentivised and emphasis is placed on corporations to develop effective, rather than cosmetic,[79] preventative due diligence policies and procedures. Expressed as a "corporate failure to prevent fraud", the offence definition would accord with the nature of the wrongdoing and the imposition of fault would not involve a "mix and match" approach to the traditional actus reus/mens rea construction that was involved in the reactive fault concept proposed. As a supplement to the common law identification doctrine, which facilitates a corporate conviction for fraud based on the culpability of a senior officer, the corporate "failure to prevent" offence would provide the means by which an organisation could be made liable in relation frauds perpetrated by lower level "rogue" employees, without resort to the use of vicarious liability. The addition of such an approach to corporate fraud is to be recommended. This would result in a range of offences available to suit various circumstances. The Fraud Act 2006 would continue to deal with instances of individuals who perpetrate fraud in the corporate context but are nonetheless criminally liable as individuals. The common law identification principle would still address instances where the individual fraudster is a "directing mind" such that his guilt can be attributed to the corporation. A statutory offence of "corporate failure to prevent fraud" would be added to inculpate organisations who had failed to put in place procedures adequate to prevent the commission of fraud by lower level officers, employees and associates.

However, while the addition of a "failure to prevent" offence is widely hailed as the panacea to all corporate fraud, and it does accord with the realist theory of organisations, it is still parasitic in its approach to corporate liability. Corporate liability on this model can only be imposed where a "rogue" employee or associate has committed an underlying fraud offence.[80] Given that fraud is unique, it is not the activity itself but the accompanying dishonesty that is determinative of guilt, not all frauds will be reducible to individuals

---

79 William S Laufer, Corporate Bodies and Guilty Minds (Chicago: University of Chicago Press 2006) Ch. 4.

80 This may not be dependent upon the individual's prosecution or conviction, there may be public interest or other considerations militating against such action.

engaged in the activity. While there will be cases of fraud perpetrated by the "directing mind" of the company and cases involving "rogue" employees who are acting dishonesty, there will undoubtedly be other instances in which individual culpability will not result, because the individual himself is not dishonest. Circumstances such as this are not insignificant in terms of potential quantity and extent of loss, given the evidence of the numerous mis-selling scandals that are still coming to light. In the absence of dishonesty at the individual level, the fraudulent activities are more appropriately recognised as those of the corporation itself, expressed through policies determined via its decision making structure or the consequence of numerous divergent factors which have led to a criminogenic corporate culture. Indeed, to restrict the attribution of corporate liability to a parasitic basis may serve only to inculpate carefully selected scapegoats while the risk-averse organisation remains unscathed and undeterred.

It is clear that, to address the problem of *corporate* corporate fraud, an altogether different basis of liability is needed to supplement the identification doctrine and the mooted failure to prevent approach. It must accord with the realist nature of corporate action and be capable of establishing corporate fault of a quality that does not rely on an underlying offence having been committed by an individual.[81] It must also accommodate a notion of dishonesty since that is the determinative characteristic of fraud.

What remains consistent across the literature is the acceptance that the traditional actus reus/mens rea construct of crime is not a suitable mechanism with which to establish corporate liability. Accordingly, all of the realist approaches adopted and proposed thus far have supplied an alternative basis of fault, such as of the negligence or "failure to prevent" ilk, notwithstanding wide academic agreement that corporations can and do act intentionally or recklessly.[82] While the limitations of the language of metaphysical responsibility and anthropomorphism have been recognised, there has been no challenge to the validity of the actus reus/mens rea construct itself, as it is now understood. Having accepted this paradigm, with little further enquiry, the literature in this area therefore lacks analysis of the fundamental blocks used to determine criminality per se. In particular, the suggestion that corporate conduct might be assessed by reference to dishonesty is absent, appearing perhaps to be uncomfortably close to the requirement of a subjective state of mind. This book fills that lacuna, accepting the 'realist' nature of corporations, and providing a corrective re-interpretation of the actus reus/mens rea doctrine. In so doing it reveals how corporations can, where appropriate, be convicted of the substantive offence of fraud.

81 Neil Cavanagh, 'Corporate Criminal Liability: An Assessment of the Models of Fault' (2011) 75 JCL 414.
82 Celia Wells, 'The Decline and Rise of English Murder: Corporate Crime and Individual Responsibility' (1998) Crim LR, Dec 788.

Bibliography

Books

Beaton-Wells C and Fisse B, *Australian Cartel Regulation* (Cambridge: Cambridge University Press 2011)

Fisse B, *Howard's Criminal Law* (5th ed, London: Sweet & Maxwell 1990)

Fisse B and Braithwaite B, *Corporations, Crime and Accountability* (Cambridge: Cambridge University Press 1993)

French PA, *Collective and Corporate Responsibility* (New York: Columbia University Press 1984)

Gobert J and Punch M, *Rethinking Corporate Crime* (London: Butterworths 2003)

Harding C, *Criminal Enterprise: Individuals, Organisations and Criminal Responsibility* (Cullompton: Willan 2007)

Laufer WS, *Corporate Bodies and Guilty Minds* (Chicago: University of Chicago Press 2006)

List C and Pettit P, *Group Agency* (Oxford: Oxford University Press 2011)

McGrath P, *Commercial Fraud and Civil Practice* (Oxford: Oxford University Press 2009)

Ormerod D, *Smith & Hogan's Criminal Law* (Oxford: Oxford University Press 2008)

Journal articles

S Buell, '*Good Faith and Law Evasion*' (2011) 58 UCLA LR 611

Cavanagh N, '*Corporate Criminal Liability: An Assessment of the Models of Fault*' (2011) 75 JCL 414

Clarkson CMV, '*Kicking Corporate Bodies and Damning Their Souls*' [1996] MLR 557

Copp S and Cronin A, '*The Failure of Criminal Law to Control the use of Off Balance Sheet Finance During the Banking Crisis*' (2015) 36(4) Co Law 99

Fisse B, '*The Social Policy of Corporate Criminal Responsibility*' (1978) 6 Adelaide LR 361

Fisse B, '*Reconstructing Corporate Criminal Law: Deterrence, Retribution, Fault and Sanctions*' (1983) 56 S Cal L Rev 1141

Gentle S, '*The Bribery Act 2010*' [2011] CLR 101

Gobert J, '*Corporate Criminality: Four Models of Fault*' (1994) 14(3) LS 393

Gobert J, '*Corporate Criminality: New Crimes for the Times*' (1994) Crim LR 722

Hagemann TA and Grinstein J, '*The Mythology of Aggregate Corporate Knowledge: A Deconstruction*' (1997) 65 Geo Wash L Rev 210

Hsaio M, '*Abandonment of the Doctrine of Attribution in favour of Gross Negligence Test in the Corporate Manslaughter and Corporate Homicide Act 2007*' (2009) 30(4) Co Law 110

Katz J, '*Concerted Ignorance: The Social Construction of Cover-up*' (1979) 8 Urban Life 295

Lederman E, '*Models for Imposing Corporate Criminal Liability: From Adaptation and Imitation toward Aggregation and The Search for Self-Identity*' (2001) Buff Crim LR 642

Leigh LH, '*The Criminal Liability of Corporations and Other Groups*' (1977) 9 Ottawa L Rev 247

Leigh LH, '*The Criminal Liability of Corporations and Other Groups: A Comparative View*' (1982) Michigan LR 1508

Sullivan GR, '*The Attribution of Culpability to Limited Companies*' (1996) 55(3) CLJ 515

Wells C, '*The Decline and Rise of English Murder: Corporate Crime and Individual Responsibility*' (1998) Crim LR, Dec 788

Official materials

HMRC, '*Tackling Offshore Tax Evasion: A New Corporate Criminal Offence of Failure to Prevent the Facilitation of Evasion*' (Consultation document, 16 July 2015)

Law Commission, *A Criminal Code for England and Wales* (Law Com No 177, 1989)

Ministry of Justice, '*Call for Evidence on Corporate Liability for Economic Crime*' 13 Jan to 24 Mar 2017

Websites

www.gov.uk/government/news/new-plans-to-tackle-corporate-fraud accessed June 26, 2016

www.sentencingcouncil.org.uk/wp-content/uploads/Fraud_bribery_and_money_laundering_offences_-_Definitive_guideline.pdf accessed May 22, 2017

3 Orthodoxy and the twin canons of criminal fault

3.1 Mental states and the tale of shifting sands

The classic basis of criminality is said to be contained in the Latin maxim "*actus non facit reum nisi mens sit rea*",[1] which has been crudely paraphrased as 'whatever the deed a man may have done, it cannot make him criminally punishable unless his doing of it was actuated by a legally blameworthy attitude of mind'.[2] While the maxim appears simply to bifurcate the physical and mental elements of the offence, referring to actus reus and mens rea, the common law recognised two distinct mental states until well into the 20th century. According to the orthodox approach, the first of these states was "voluntariness" and this was the primary determinant of criminal fault applicable to every offence, common law or statutory.[3] Voluntariness indicates the actor's mental attitude to his conduct and not to the consequences of it[4] and, although a mental state that is to be assessed subjectively, a claim of involuntariness is a denial of the actus

---

1 Expressed by Coke, 3 Inst 6, it derives from St Augustine's, "*ream linguam non facit nisi mens rea*" which was later used as the test of guilt for perjury, Leges Henrici Primi 5, s. 28, see JW Cecil Turner, *Kenny's Outlines of Criminal Law* (17th ed, Cambridge: Cambridge University Press 1958) 13.

2 JW Cecil Turner, *Russell on Crime* (12th ed, London: Stevens & Sons 1964) vol 1, 22, "the word *reum* is an adjective which does not qualify the noun *actus* but does qualify the implied noun *hominem*: it is therefore a subjective epithet and signifies legally guilty, punishable as a criminal ... on the other hand the word *rea* does qualify the noun *mens* but not in the same subjective sense (hence the grammatical clumsiness of the whole maxim ...)".

3 See e.g. John Austin, 'The Province of Jurisprudence Determined' (1832) in John Austin and Robert Campbell (eds.), *Lectures on Jurisprudence* (orig. pub 1874, Kissinger Legacy 2010). Austin's early 19th century analysis of criminal responsibility had involved two mental states, the first concerning bodily action, the second the effects of such actions. Fragments of this thinking appeared in the Criminal Law Commission Fourth Report of 1839 identifying that one element was the actor's mental state in relation to his act, the second his mental state in relation to its consequences, Criminal Law Commission Fourth Report of Her Majesty's Commissioners on Criminal Law 1839 (168) XIX.

4 JW Cecil Turner, *Kenny's Outlines of Criminal Law* (17th ed, Cambridge University Press 1958) 27.

reus.[5] The second mental state was "mens rea". In contrast to the modern understanding, it was narrowly defined, requiring that the defendant must have foreseen a particular consequence of his act if he was to attract culpability,[6] and it applied only to common law offences.

The development of the twin fault concepts in the common law criminal jurisdiction, introducing first the concept of voluntariness and thereafter "mens rea", in its restrictive sense, was a gradual process.[7] In its earliest period, when the law served only to regulate the payment of compensation for harm caused, there was no need to establish any blameworthy mental state whatsoever.[8] However, when the idea of punishment developed, criminal liability came to depend on moral guilt, namely that the individual knew that he was doing wrong.[9] Initially decided by objective standards, the defendant's mind, actual or presumed, became relevant[10] and it was recognised that moral guilt could not be attributed to a person who had acted involuntarily. Thereafter, an advance was made when the accused was allowed to plead that his act was harmless in itself and that he had not foreseen that it would cause the harm that it did. Finally, it was recognised that although the act was harmful, a defendant could plead that he had not foreseen that it would cause harm.[11] The fundamental distinction between the two mental states, voluntariness and mens rea, formed the subject of Turner's seminal work which was published in the 1936 Cambridge Law Journal and his article will provide the touchstone for this discussion.[12]

Of note, Turner's analysis was confined to an examination of common law offences since the actus reus/mens rea construct of crime, articulated in the Latin maxim, had no application to the statutory offences which could be drafted in any way Parliament chose.[13] This distinct categorisation of common law and statutory offences meant that they were considered as separate areas of law, with their own principles, and in the same publication Jackson's "sister" article specifically addressed the interpretation of criminal statutes.[14] The need to distinguish the sources of law was so fundamental that even in the 1960s

---

5 Ibid 26, 27.

6 JWC Turner, 'The Mental Element in Crimes at Common Law' (1936–38) 6 CLJ 31, 32.

7 Nicola Lacey, 'In Search of the Responsible Subject: History, Philosophy and Criminal Law Theory' (2001) 64 MLR 350–71; Nicola Lacey, 'Responsibility and Modernity in Criminal Law' (2001) 9 Journal of Political Philosophy 249–77; Nicola Lacey, 'Space, Time and Function: Intersecting Principles of Responsibility across the Terrain of Criminal Justice' (2007) 1 Criminal Law and Philosophy 233–50.

8 JWC Turner, 'The Mental Element in Crimes at Common Law' (1936–38) 6 CLJ 31, 34.

9 JW Cecil Turner, *Kenny's Outlines of Criminal Law* (17th ed, Cambridge University Press 1958) 13.

10 JWC Turner, 'The Mental Element in Crimes at Common Law' (19–38) 6 CLJ 31, 35.

11 JWC Turner, 'The Mental Element in Crimes at Common Law' (1936–38) 6 CLJ 31, 35–6.

12 JWC Turner, 'The Mental Element in Crimes at Common Law' (1936–38) 6 CLJ 31.

13 RM Jackson, 'Absolute Prohibition in Statutory Offences' (19–38) 6 CLJ 83.

14 Turner acknowledges the work of RM Jackson in the same edition dealing with the mental element as regards statutory offences.

Turner refused to attempt to formulate general principles of mental elements that might apply equally to both:

> that task is ... futile, for it leads to a situation in which a clear picture of the common law principles becomes obscured amongst the tangles of statutory crime. It should not be forgotten that criminal law is the instrument of criminal policy, and that statutes creating new crimes are the attempts of the legislature to give effect to the criminal policy of the moment. The legislature is therefore primarily concerned to find the best method of dealing with the particular mischief which it is at that moment seeking to repress, and its decisions ... are not as a rule reached by any careful regard for general principles of an abstract kind. The result is that, as things are, the statutory crimes as a whole mass, cannot be brought under a simple scheme of general principles of criminal liability.[15]

The only mental state required in common law and statutory offences alike was that of voluntariness,[16] albeit this requirement was implied in both instances, as Stephen J, in *R v Tolson* (1889) had recognised.[17]

As regards criminal liability in the common law offences, Turner identified three elemental rules:

1   It must be proved that the conduct of the accused caused the actus reus.
2   It must be proved that the conduct was voluntary and,
3   It must be proved that the accused must have foreseen that certain consequences were likely to follow on his acts or omissions.[18]

Whereas rule 1 dealt solely with causation, rules 2 and 3 required evidence as to the defendant's state of mind and, although it had often been overlooked, Turner emphasised that that the difference between the two mental states was an essential one. Whereas Turner's rule 2 required voluntariness of conduct, rule 3 referred to mens rea which, unlike today's ubiquitous use of

---

15 JW Cecil Turner, *Russell on Crime* (12th ed, Stevens & Sons 1964) vol 1, 64–5.
16 Parliament could exclude the need to prove even this primary mental element and did so, albeit controversially, see *R v Larsonneur* (1934) 24 Cr App R 74 (CCA); *Winzar v CC Kent* (1983) The Times, 28 March, DC in which the defendant was convicted of being found drunk on a highway, contrary to Licensing Act 1872, s. 12, having been taken there by the police. Although Parliament had exceptionally dispensed with even this requirement in these cases, it is not clear whether *Larsonneur* had reached the judicial and academic consciousness at the time of the Cambridge Law Journal's publication since it did not feature in the 1935 edition of Courtney Stanhope Kenny, *A Selection of Cases Illustrative of English Criminal Law* (8th ed, Cambridge: Cambridge University Press 1935) or Robert Ernest Ross and Maxwell Turner, *Archbold's Criminal Pleading, Evidence and Practice* (30th ed, London: Sweet & Maxwell 1938).
17 *R v Tolson* (1889) 23 QBD 168, 187 (Stephen J).
18 JWC Turner, 'The Mental Element in Crimes at Common Law' (1936–38) 6 CLJ 31, 32–3.

the term, was narrowly confined to foresight and, further, the nature and extent of the foresight was fixed by law and specifically defined, different for each common law crime. Accordingly, a lawyer needed to know the particular consequences that were appropriate to each offence.[19] The individual significance of the respective mental states is that "(t)he state of a man's mind is relevant to finding out, first, if the act he did is to be imputed to him, and secondly, if he realised the probable consequences."[20] Voluntariness, denoting imputation, went to capacity, and served as the hallmark of the responsibility-bearing actor whether the offence was one of common law or statutory origin.

3.2 Voluntariness explored

Recognition that the conduct of the accused must be voluntary occurred at a comparatively early stage in the law, with evidence that the doctrine dates back as far as 1471.[21] Although conviction turns on proof that the defendant is acting voluntarily, the law presumes that a person does so.[22] Accordingly, if a defendant denies a charge on the basis that he was not acting voluntarily, it is for him to raise evidence in order to rebut the presumption. The presumption of voluntariness therefore operates to overcome the prosecution problem of proving a subjective mental state, albeit a claim of "involuntariness" amounts to a denial of the actus reus, the authorship of the act. Well-rehearsed examples in the criminal law include acting while being unconscious, asleep, afflicted by St Vitus' dance, disabled from driving while under attack by a swarm of bees[23] and other instances of reflex action where the actor physically experiences a "total destruction of voluntary control".[24]

An act cannot be said to be voluntary or willed if a person cannot physically control it[25] and, in today's terminology and categorisation, the claim would be described as a defence of either automatism or insanity (insane automatism),

---

19 JWC Turner, 'The Mental Element in Crimes at Common Law' (1936–38) 6 CLJ 31, 33.
20 RM Jackson, 'Absolute Prohibition in Statutory Offences' (1936–38) 6 CLJ 83, 91.
21 In support of the wider doctrine, Turner pointed to Hale who described a 1471 case in which a servant who had shot his master in mistake for a trespasser was acquitted, JWC Turner, 'The Mental Element in Crimes at Common Law', in L Radzinowicz and JWC Turner (eds.) *The Modern Approach to Criminal Law* (2nd ed, London: Macmillan 1948) 212, citing Kelynge 41 fn2 and Foster, CC & CL 264–5, fn 3.
22 JWC Turner, 'The Mental Element in Crimes at Common Law' (1936–38) 6 CLJ 31; Ashworth and Horder describe this in terms of the "normal presumption of free will", Andrew Ashworth and Jeremy Horder, *Principles of Criminal Law* (7th ed, Oxford: Oxford University Press 2013) 24.
23 *Hill v Baxter* [1958] 1 QB 277, 286.
24 *A-G's Reference* (No 2 of 1992) [1993] 99 Cr App R 429; see too the discussion in David Ormerod, *Smith and Hogan's Criminal Law* (13th ed, Oxford: Oxford University Press 2011) 58.
25 HLA Hart, *Punishment and Responsibility* (Oxford: Clarendon Press 1968) 181.

depending on the cause of the loss of control.[26] In addition to involuntariness, in the physical sense, the doctrine encompassed the notion of "non-voluntariness", which was essentially a denial of mental volition. The distinction between literal involuntariness and metaphorical non-voluntariness was itself a refinement of the early concept[27] and examples of non-voluntary behaviour included acts performed under mistake, duress or by necessity.

Support for the broad scope of the orthodox doctrine is elicited from early institutional texts and authorities which typically equate examples of non-voluntariness with involuntariness. For example, the 1935 edition of Kenny's provides detailed discussion of *R v Tolson* (1889),[28] a case in which Martha Tolson appealed her conviction for bigamy, a statutory offence,[29] on the basis that she had reasonably believed that her former husband was dead. Although the statutory provision contained no mental state, Cave J. stated that a reasonable belief in the existence of circumstances which, if true, would make the act for which a prisoner was indicted an innocent act had always been held to be a good defence. He observed that an "honest and reasonable mistake stands in fact on the same footing as absence of reasoning faculty, as in infancy or perversion of the faculty, as in lunacy".[30] That this reasoning related to capacity, and thus to voluntariness, was supported by Stephen J.[31]:

> In all cases whatever, competent age, sanity, and some degree of freedom from some kinds of coercion are assumed to be essential to criminality, but I do not believe they are ever introduced into any statute by which any particular crime is defined ... With regard to knowledge of fact, the law, perhaps, is not quite so clear, but it may, I think, be maintained that in every case knowledge of fact is to some extent an element of criminality as much as competent age and sanity.[32]

---

26 See Law Commission, *Criminal Liability: Insanity and Automatism*, discussion paper, 23 July 2013, para 1.41.

27 KJM Smith and William Wilson, 'Impaired Voluntariness and Criminal Responsibility: Reworking Hart's Theory of Excuses – the English Judicial Response' (1993) 13 OJLS 69.

28 *R v Tolson* (1889) 23 QBD 168, cited in Courtney Stanhope Kenny, *A Selection of Cases Illustrative of English Criminal Law* (supplement by E Garth Moore, 8th ed, Cambridge: Cambridge University Press 1935).

29 The offence is set out at Offences Against the Person Act 1861 (24 & 25 Vict c 100), s. 57.

30 *R v Tolson* (1889) 23 QBD 168, 181 (Cave J.).

31 Stephen J. also discussed *R v Prince* (1872–75) LR 2 CCR 154 in his judgment in *R v Tolson* (1889) 23 QBD 168, 190. Concurring with Brett J. in that case, he observed there was a general principle that a mistake of fact on reasonable grounds would make a prisoner guilty of no offence and that this excuse is implied into every criminal offence. Recognising that the majority had not dissented from the principle, Stephen J. explained it had simply been the case that it had not been held to apply fully to each part of the statutory section in question and that the legislature had intended, as it was free to do, that some of the prohibited acts were done at the actor's peril. Accordingly, the statute was interpreted such that mistake as to the girl's age would not exculpate, however, a mistaken belief of the father's consent, or not knowing that she was in anyone's possession, would.

32 *R v Tolson* (1889) 23 QBD 168, 187 (Stephen J.).

Of note, he continued:

> To take an extreme illustration, can anyone doubt that a man who, though he might be perfectly sane, committed what would otherwise be a crime in the state of somnambulism, would be entitled to be acquitted? And why is this? Simply because he would not know what he's doing ...[33]

Similarly, the 1938 edition of *Archbold's*,[34] observed that the capacity to commit crime presupposes an act of understanding and an exercise of will[35] and compared physical involuntariness (where "A by force takes the hand of B in which is the weapon, and therewith kills C, A is guilty of murder, but B is excused") with acts performed under compulsion or coercion.[36]

The recognition that acting under a mistake could negate voluntariness accords with the criminal law's focus on individual autonomy expressed in freedom of agency and capacity to choose.[37] Indeed, to "proceed to conviction without proof of voluntary conduct would be to fail, in the most fundamental way, to show respect for individuals as rational, choosing beings".[38] Since the notion of rational choice implies a process of selecting between options, calculating or weighing up potential courses of conduct, there is an assumption that the actor has some perception of the circumstances in which he operates; choice cannot be exercised in a void. While the subjective perception of the circumstances in which one acts may be limited, impaired or flawed, it is the subjective understanding of the circumstances that determines the moral quality of the actor's behaviour.[39] The concept of voluntariness must therefore involve knowledge of the circumstances, indeed

33 *R v Tolson* (1889) 23 QBD 168, 187 (Stephen J.) and set out in Courtney Stanhope Kenny, *A Selection of Cases Illustrative of English Criminal Law* (supplement by E Garth Moore, 8th ed, Cambridge: Cambridge University Press 1935) 19.

34 Robert Ernest Ross and Maxwell Turner, *Archbold's Criminal Pleading: Evidence and Practice* (30th ed, London: Sweet & Maxwell 1938) 11, 13 and 20. Further, as to incapacity in the context of insanity, "Every person at the age of discretion is, unless the contrary is proved, presumed by law to be sane, and be accountable for his actions. But if there is an incapacity, or defect of the understanding, as there can be no consent of the will, the act is not punishable as a crime. This species of non-volition is classified by Coke (Litt. 247) and Hale (1 Hist PC 29) as either natural, accidental, or affected ..." at p 13. While the act of a drunk or person of unsound mind was described in terms on non-volition, Archbold stated that the same principle applied to those who act under compulsion or coercion, "not as a result of an uncontrolled free action proceeding from themselves" p 20.

35 *R v Tolson* (1889) 23 QBD 168, 187 (Stephen J).

36 Robert Ernest Ross and Maxwell Turner, *Archbold's Criminal Pleading: Evidence and Practice* (30th ed, London: Sweet & Maxwell 1938) 20.

37 Which itself accords with Hart's fair opportunity principle.

38 Andrew Ashworth and Jeremy Horder, *Principles of Criminal Law* (7th ed, Oxford: Oxford University Press 2013) 86.

39 *Toppin v Marcus* [1908] 11 KB (Ir) 423 (Palles CB).

"the capacity to commit crime presupposes an act of understanding and an exercise of will".[40]

It is clear, however, that the prominence once afforded the voluntariness doctrine has now declined, having been gradually displaced by an inflated and generalised notion of mens rea, going far beyond its original conception, and this has marked a substantial departure from orthodoxy in the attribution of criminal liability. Mens rea is now considered the hallmark of criminal fault and, as a notion, it is taken to encompass all of the mental states expressed in offence definitions, whether common law or statutory. Although the shift occurred by gradual accretion, rather than orchestration, it has had profound implications for the substantive criminal law and its procedure. Evidence of the emerging conceptual shift can be found in the legal literature of the 1950s. As the primary determinant of criminal fault, and the only element required in statutory offences, it is perhaps surprising that neither practitioner nor student texts published in first half of the 20th century contain any discussion of actus reus concepts or, specifically, "voluntariness".[41] However, by 1958, *Kenny's Outlines of Criminal Law*, edited by Turner, does include a section dedicated to actus reus principles. Voluntariness is also discussed, albeit under the heading of "mens rea",[42] and affirms that any denial of voluntariness, either physical or metaphorical,[43] is still essentially a denial of responsibility for the actus reus of the offence,[44] albeit there is recognition that such pleas were, by then, sometimes alluded to as matters of justification and excuse. In this regard, claims of non-voluntariness were starting to be categorised either as a specific defence, such as mistake or duress, or even as a denial of mens rea.[45] The apparent conceptual confusion was a phenomenon that Turner had himself explained in the following terms. Over time, the criminal law had employed three different criteria of

---

40 Robert Ernest Ross and Maxwell Turner, *Archbold's Criminal Pleading, Evidence and Practice* (30th ed, London: Sweet & Maxwell 1938) 11.

41 Courtney Stanhope Kenny, *A Selection of Cases Illustrative of English Criminal Law* (8th ed, Cambridge: Cambridge University Press 1935); Robert Ernest Ross and Maxwell Turner, *Archbold's Criminal Pleading, Evidence and Practice* (30th ed, London: Sweet & Maxwell 1938); JW Cecil Turner and A LL Armitage, *Cases on Criminal Law* (Cambridge: Cambridge University Press 1953).

42 JW Cecil Turner, *Kenny's Outlines of Criminal Law* (17th ed, Cambridge: Cambridge University Press 1958) 26.

43 JW Cecil Turner, *Kenny's Outlines of Criminal Law* (17th ed, Cambridge University Press 1958) 24, and fn 4 where Turner refers to sleepwalking by way of analogy. See too ibid, 52 and fn 2 where Turner equates involuntariness with mistake and cites 1 Hale PC 42 in support. See also ibid, 61, "In the old authorities statements are to be found to the effect that there may be circumstances in which a man may be excused for deeds which he has done not of his own free volition but under compulsion …, in other words, pleads that his conduct was not voluntary. Compulsion can take other forms than physical force ….", where Turner cites 1 Hale PC 43.

44 JW Cecil Turner, *Kenny's Outlines of Criminal Law* (17th ed, Cambridge: Cambridge University Press 1958) 27.

45 Ibid 16; David Ormerod, *Smith and Hogan's Criminal Law* (13th ed, Oxford: Oxford University Press 2011) 58.

responsibility: strict liability, voluntariness and mens rea. Their simultaneous existence, together with the fact that the common law evolution is gradual and by the accretion of judgments, has meant that old and new doctrines had been employed in courts of the same period according to the inclinations of the judges. The result was inconsistency,[46] vagueness and ambiguity in judicial pronouncements and the legal literature.[47] This problem had been specifically identified by Turner and Jackson, in their 1936 "sister" articles, each explaining that the term "mens rea" had been used loosely in literature and case law to refer to both mental states.[48] Jackson, in particular, provided detailed evidence of the growing tendency to use the term mens rea to refer also to voluntariness. In his analysis of a somnambulist butcher exposing tainted meat for sale, he observes:

> It has become common for judges when dealing with absolute prohibitions to make statements such as "the prisoner had done the thing which was forbidden by the statute and that it was not necessary to prove any further mens rea". That is only another way of saying that the act must be one which can in law be imputed to the accused, and that that imputation is properly made when the accused intended to do what he did. In this use (better described as a misuse) of the expression mens rea, our hypothetical somnambulist butcher would have the defence that mens rea was absent (i.e. that the act was not imputed to him) although the offence does not require mens rea in the usual meaning of that term.[49]

Similarly, the 1933 *Kenny's Outlines of Criminal Law* explains absolute prohibitions such that "ordinary mens rea is still necessary. That is to say, the offender must have actually known that he went through the act [of selling]".[50] As Jackson observes, "the term mens rea is being used in a peculiar sense, not in its common law sense as regards foresight of consequences, but in the "voluntariness" context of the actus reus".[51]

By 1964, Turner was still describing the two mental elements required at common law in the same terms as he had since 1936,[52] the meaning of

46 JW Cecil Turner, *Kenny's Outlines of Criminal Law* (17th ed, Cambridge: Cambridge University Press 1958) 29, 30.

47 Ibid 31.

48 JWC Turner, 'The Mental Element in Crimes at Common Law' (1936–38) 6 CLJ 31, 32; RM Jackson, 'Absolute Prohibition in Statutory Offences' (1936–38) 6 CLJ 83, 91.

49 RM Jackson, 'Absolute Prohibition in Statutory Offences' (1936–38) 6 CLJ 83, 91.

50 Courtney Stanhope Kenny, *Outlines of Criminal Law* (14th ed, Cambridge: Cambridge University Press 1933) 45.

51 RM Jackson, 'Absolute Prohibition in Statutory Offences' (1936–38) 6 CLJ 83, 92.

52 He went on to state that if any definition of actus reus were to be adopted which involves a coincidence of it with either or both of (i) voluntariness or (ii) mens rea, then arguments and conclusions based thereon "would assume a complexity likely to bewilder simple minds", JW Cecil Turner, *Russell on Crime* (12th ed, Stevens & Sons 1964) vol 1, 25, 40.

mens rea restricted to an awareness that specified harmful consequences could follow, these being a matter of law.[53] However, this edition evidences a fundamental change in Turner's analysis of the actus reus/mens rea distinction.[54] At pains to maintain the "sharp" physical/mental contrast suggested by the maxim,[55] the actus reus is defined in terms of the physical result of conduct which keeps it distinct from any mental element that the law may require. In his earlier analysis, illustrated by reference to the *Prince* authority, he had said that if the word "knowingly" could be read into the offence, it would add an extra element to the actus reus, not the mens rea.[56] Now, the mens rea concept was stretched to encompass all mental states, including those expressed in the offence definition.[57] Of note, this departure was at odds with the 1961 Glanville Williams' text which was still providing the orthodox account whereby the actus reus constituted "the whole definition of the crime with the exception of the mental element – and it even includes a mental element in so far as that is contained in the definition of an act".[58] While the Latin maxim, as the classic statement of criminal liability, has remained unchallenged over the centuries,[59] the relative scope and meanings of the actus reus and mens rea concepts have been fluid.[60] Indeed, further evidence of the shifting boundaries is elicited from Williams who observes, "At the present day the exemption from responsibility, such as it is, given by the "act" doctrine could, in respect of the requirement of will, just as well be put on the ground of absence of mens rea",[61] and while acknowledging that an act involved "a willed movement",[62] he seemingly excluded metaphorical non-voluntariness from the

---

53 JW Cecil Turner, *Russell on Crime* (12th ed, London: Stevens & Sons 1964) vol 1, 40.
54 Ibid 25.
55 Ibid.
56 In his 1936 exposition of *R v Prince (1875)* LR 2, CCR 154 Turner had stated that the offender's foresight of the consequences of his incitement was merely that the girl would come with him, and this was not affected by his knowledge of her age, or of the criminal law, or of morality. Writing at that time, it will be recalled that Turner had said that knowledge was not intention and even if the word "knowingly" or the like could be read into the statute, this change would not affect the mens rea of the accused, but that it would merely add another necessary fact to the actus reus, namely the offender's knowledge of the girl's age. JWC Turner, 'The Mental Element in Crimes at Common Law' (1936–38) 6 CLJ 31, 46–7.
57 JW Cecil Turner, *Russell on Crime* (12th ed, London: Stevens & Sons 1964) vol 1; ACE Lynch, 'The Mental Element in the Actus Reus' (1982) 98 LQR 110.
58 JW Cecil Turner, *Russell on Crime* (12th ed, London: Stevens & Sons 1964) vol 1, 25, fn 24; Glanville Williams, *Criminal Law, The General Part* (2nd ed, London: Stevens & Sons 1961) 16; ACE Lynch, 'The Mental Element in the Actus Reus' (1982) 98 LQR 110.
59 JW Cecil Turner, *Russell on Crime* (12th ed, London: Stevens & Sons 1964) vol 1, 22.
60 In 1982, Lynch turned his attention to the construction of crime and concluded that the terms "actus reus" and "mens rea" had been employed ambiguously, ACE Lynch, 'The Mental Element in the Actus Reus' (1982) 98 LQR 109.
61 Glanville Williams, *Criminal Law: The General Part* (2nd ed, London: Stevens & Sons 1961) 12.
62 Ibid 16.

act doctrine.[63] Instead, Williams suggested that voluntariness spliced part of the mental element onto the physical element and asserted that to refer to an absence of will as the absence of an act made the legal distinction between act and state of mind a jagged one.[64] Since the modern interpretation of the Latin maxim requires all the components of an offence to be "pigeon-holed" as either actus reus or mens rea, the inelegant result is evident in the modern texts; involuntariness now bears upon the actus reus whereas non-voluntariness is a denial of mens rea, or a claim of some other excuse or justification.[65] The resulting conceptual confusion, illustrated in the contemporary approach to insane and non-insane automatism, is such that the claim of the exemplary somnambulist may now be either a denial of the actus reus or the mens rea, depending on the cause of the sleepwalking.[66] Given that the common denominator is essentially a denial of voluntariness, it is not surprising that this area of law has been subjected to criticism.[67] Further, although it is agreed that wilfulness, and the notion of the free agent, encompasses a core expectation of criminal responsibility,[68] there is no universal agreement as to whether the voluntariness notion should be considered a basic plank of liability or whether lack of it amounts to an excuse.[69]

By the mid-1960s it is clear that the notion of mens rea has gradually enlarged and the voluntariness doctrine is shrinking. In particular, the principles of metaphorical non-voluntariness are being reconceptualised, either as specific defences, or as a denial of mens rea, depending on the nature of the claim being made. Mens rea is becoming a generic term for any blameworthy mental state, except for voluntariness

---

63 Ibid 12, 18, stating that the act does not suppose "free" will.

64 Glanville Williams, *Criminal Law: The General Part* (2nd ed, London: Stevens & Sons 1961) 12, 14.

65 David Ormerod, *Smith and Hogan's Criminal Law* (13th ed, Oxford: Oxford University Press 2011) 58.

66 An external cause would amount to a claim of automatism whilst an internal cause would come within the insanity principle.

67 See for example David Ormerod, *Smith and Hogan's Criminal Law* (13th ed, Oxford: Oxford University Press 2011) 286, 295, 298; RD Mackay, 'Non-Organic Automatism' [1980] Crim LR 350.

68 KJM Smith and William Wilson, 'Impaired Voluntariness and Criminal Responsibility: Reworking Hart's Theory of Excuses – the English Judicial Response' (1993) 13 OJLS 69.

69 Ibid and see too P H Robinson, 'Should the Criminal Law Abandon the Actus Reus – Mens Rea Distinction?' in Stephen Shute and others (eds.), *Action and Value in Criminal Law* (Oxford: Clarendon Press 1993) 195; Glanville Williams, 'Offences and Defences' (1982) 2 LS 233. It is suggested that in the early 1800s the relationship of defences to concepts of mens rea or involuntariness was of little judicial concern and, later, during the 1870s fault concepts involved the use of terms such as "wilful" which were laden with moralistic tones but confused the distinction between the two, KJM Smith, *Lawyers, Legislators and Theorists* (Oxford: Oxford University Press 1998) 160, 257. Glanville Williams opined that the actus reus should be conceived as including an absence of excuse or justification whereas Janet Dine argues that clarity is promoted by discussing excuse and justification in the distinct context of defences, rather than as part of the actus reus, Glanville Williams, 'Offences and Defences' (1982) 2 LS 233; Janet Dine and others, *Criminal Law, Cases and Materials* (6th ed, Oxford: Oxford University Press 2011) 61.

in its now drastically pruned form, and is no longer confined to the traditionally narrow common law definition. At first blush, while substantive in nature, this reordering appears to be of little practical significance and doubtless neither the architects of the reconstruction, nor the legal commentators, had any inkling of the dramatic effect this would ultimately wreak upon the criminal law.

3.3 Evidential presumptions and their dynamics

Aside from the substantive principles of criminal fault, an integral part of both the voluntariness and mens rea doctrines was the use of evidential presumptions by which those mental states could be imputed to the defendant. The presumptive approach neatly bridged the gap between the external appearance of the act and the internal world of the defendant's mind. As Turner had observed, "It is obvious that it is impossible really to know for certain what was passing in the mind of the accused person; it can only be surmised by a process of inference from what is known of his conduct".[70] In both common law and statutory crimes, liability was founded on the voluntariness of the act and, in this respect, there was an evidential presumption that the defendant had acted voluntarily. By requiring the defendant to raise any claim that his conduct was not voluntary, the law avoided the difficulties that would be associated with the development of a positive conception of voluntariness, particularly since there has never been consensus as to how volition, deliberateness or intentionality of physical movement might be defined.[71] Accordingly, given the broad scope of the voluntariness doctrine, this included a presumption of knowledge[72] and, of note, Lord Diplock's judgment supports this construction in the later case of *Sweet v Parsley* [1970][73]:

> the jury is entitled to presume that the accused acted with knowledge of the facts, unless there is some evidence to the contrary originating from the accused who alone can know on what belief he acted and on what ground the belief, if mistaken, was held.[74]

70 JWC Turner, 'The Mental Element in Crimes at Common Law' (1936–38) 6 CLJ 31. It would seem that Ashworth and Horder describe this in terms of the "normal presumption of free will", Andrew Ashworth and Jeremy Horder, *Principles of Criminal Law* (7th ed, Oxford: Oxford University Press 2013) 24.
71 P H Robinson, 'Should the Criminal Law Abandon the Actus Reus – Mens Rea Distinction?' in Stephen Shute and others (eds.), *Action and Value in Criminal Law* (Oxford: Clarendon Press 1993). 195; *Hill v Baxter* [1958] 1 QB 277. Anthony Duff explores the difficulties surrounding the concept of intention in his seminal work, RA Duff, *Intention, Agency and Criminal Liability: Philosophy of Action and Criminal Law* (Oxford: Basil Blackwell 1990).
72 *Marsh* (1824) 2 B & C 717 [722] (Bayley C.J.) in relation to a carrier's unlawful possession of game; *Sleep* (1861) Le & Ca 44 in relation to the unlawful possession of naval stores. In relation to statutory offences, this can be dispensed with, see *Parker v Alder* [1899] 1 QB 20.
73 *Sweet v Parsley* [1970] AC 132 (HL).
74 *Sweet v Parsley* [1970] AC 132 (HL) 164, (Diplock L.).

As a matter of evidence, the presumptive approach has a procedural efficiency and elegance.[75] While placing an evidential onus on the defendant, it does not disturb the usual burden or standard of proof, which rest on the prosecution, and it does not attract controversy.[76] The presumption of voluntariness, applicable in crimes of both common law and statutory origin, is purely evidential.

In relation to just the common law offences, there was also a presumption of mens rea. In contrast to the presumption of voluntariness, this presumption was not evidential but went to the substance of the law. The orthodox presumption of mens rea imported a tacit element of the offence, in addition to voluntariness, that had to be made out in order to convict, namely the defendant's foresight of the particular harm specified by the law.

In this respect, the prosecution was assisted by a second evidential presumption: that the accused intended the natural consequence of his act.[77] In practice, the determination of fault by reference to "natural consequences" imported an element of objective consideration but, as a presumption of evidential status, it could be rebutted by a defendant. Like the presumption of voluntariness, although the evidential onus was on the defendant to deny the foresight the offence required, the usual burden and standard of proof were unaltered.

As it transpired, it was in the context of the evidential presumptions that the truly devastating effect on the substantive canons of criminal fault was to occur, simply as a result of the tendency to use the language of mens rea in the context of voluntariness.

3.4 The fall of voluntariness and the rise of mens rea

Although earlier statutes had been interpreted to conform to common law principles, during the late 19th century Parliament began the more detailed regulation of social life with the creation of numerous summary offences which imposed relatively light punishment. With this development the courts interpreted the failure to specify a mental element in an offence as a decision to impose strict liability[78] and a proliferation of "public welfare" offences emerged in areas such as health and safety, building, pollution, and the sale and preparation of drugs and food.[79] Of note, the 1870s marked the point

---

75 KJM Smith, *Lawyers, Legislators and Theorists* (Oxford: Oxford University Press 1998) 210.

76 Described elsewhere as the "normal presumption of free will", Andrew Ashworth and Jeremy Horder, *Principles of Criminal Law* (7th ed, Oxford: Oxford University Press 2013) 24.

77 An act foreseen was considered an act intended and the fine distinction between the two states, expressed in the development of the principle of indirect intention, had not yet occurred, see generally Ch 4.

78 JW Cecil Turner, *Kenny's Outlines of Criminal Law* (19th ed, Cambridge: Cambridge University Press 1966) 46 citing, inter alia, *Fowler v Padget* (1798) 101 ER 1103, 7 TR 509, 514; *R v Prince* (1875) LR 2 CCR 154, 163 (Brett J.).

79 Leigh LH, *Strict and Vicarious Liability* (Sweet & Maxwell 1982). See for example, the Factory Act 1878, Liquor Licensing Act 1872, Food and Drugs Act 1875, Public Health Act

at which the judiciary tended away from the presumption of mens rea towards a literal interpretation of statutes,[80] although voluntariness remained essential.[81] However, the tendency to clothe the voluntariness doctrine in the language of mens rea occurred as much in the context of statutory construction as it did in the common law discourse.[82] Although seemingly innocuous, this practice ultimately led to the confusion of the legal presumption with the evidential presumption. Accordingly, where it had been presumed that the defendant had acted voluntarily, it came to be presumed that the prosecution had to prove that the defendant had mens rea. Not only did the voluntariness doctrine become subsumed in the language of mens rea, this operated like an unintended and unnoticed sleight of hand to effect a sea change in the judicial interpretation of statutory offences. The evidential presumption that had assisted the crown was displaced by the legal presumption that, in contrast, now favoured the defendant. The result has unseated the traditional canons of fault, voluntariness and mens rea, altering both the substance of the concepts and the way in which fault is attributed. It has also brought together the previously distinct principles of the common law and statutory offences such that they are now considered in terms of one general jurisprudence of criminal law.

In today's discourse, the presumption of mens rea, devoid of its original meaning, attracts no discussion in the context of common law crimes. Rather, it has become something of a keynote in the interpretation of criminal statutes, an area where it previously had no application. The modern day assertion that there is a presumption of mens rea in a statutory offence is understood to mean

1875, Rivers (Pollution Prevention) Act 1876 and 1893, the Regulation of Railways Act 1868, the Adulteration of Food and Drugs Act 1872. A raft of statutes were enacted in the spirit of public health and safety, others in relation to prohibited behaviour on licensed premises, others to uphold standards of morality. Different policy considerations applied in different contexts. Similarly, the territory covered by strict liability offences spanned across conduct typically performed in a personal capacity and conduct performed in the course of business. The consideration of wrongdoing in the commercial environs necessarily encroached on established principles that have already emerged in that legal environment. Therefore, the criminal law can be seen to have steered a path which often touched on existing principles of master and servant law and that of principal and agent. Accordingly, different influences have shaped the legal response and any search for principles of general application is futile.

80 *R v Prince* (1872–75) LR 2 CCR 154 is the case that is identified as the turning point. According to Turner it is not easy to say what the proper interpretation of Prince was but the commonly accepted defence was wrong, namely bona fide mistake of fact was denied as the accused knew he was doing an immoral act, JW Cecil Turner & A LL Armitage, *Cases on Criminal Law* (Cambridge: Cambridge University Press 1953).

81 JW Cecil Turner, *Kenny's Outlines of Criminal Law* (19th ed, Cambridge: Cambridge University Press 1966) 46.

82 JW Cecil Turner, *Kenny's Outlines of Criminal Law* (17th ed, Cambridge: Cambridge University Press 1958) 44, 50 discussing *R v Wheat and Stocks* (1921) 15 Cr App R 134, 135; *R v Maughan* (1934) 24 Cr App R 130, 132; *Cotterill v Penn* [1936] 1 KB 53; *Nichols v Hall* (1873) LR 8 CP 322 and *Harding v Price* [1948] 1 KB 695.

that Parliament did not intend to create a strict liability crime, lacking any fault requirement, and that a blameworthy state of mind must therefore be read in. This so-called presumption of mens rea is largely associated with the 1969 case of *Sweet v Parsley*[83] which concerned the meaning of the provisions of the Dangerous Drugs Act 1965. However, a close analysis of the judgments in *Sweet v Parsley*[84] reveals that the decision did not mark a sea change in thinking or departure from the orthodox canons of fault. Rather, the decision simply affirmed that in every case the defendant's conduct must be voluntary, albeit this was clothed in what had become the ambiguous language of mens rea. Accordingly, Ms Sweet's defence that she did not have guilty knowledge was not a denial of mens rea, as is now suggested, but simply an orthodox denial of the actus reus[85] which rebutted the presumption of voluntariness. Like the use of the term mens rea in the new generic sense, the effect of this linguistic imprecision appeared innocuous enough in the context of *Sweet v Parsley*,[86] however, the violence done to the voluntariness doctrine in the case[87] does not end there. By a further judicial misinterpretation, of the earlier *Woolmington* judgment,[88] the presumption of voluntariness was subsequently deemed to shift to the defendant not only the evidential burden but the burden of proof itself. On such a view, the continued existence of the presumption of voluntariness went beyond contemplation and could no longer be tolerated in a regime committed to the principle that the crown must prove its case. Not only was the term "voluntariness" sacrificed to the enlarged and generalised notion of "mens rea" but the presumption upon which the orthodox doctrine had operated was also discarded.

3.5 *Sweet v Parsley*: a re-interpretation of the "revitalised presumption"[89]

When the House of Lords were called upon to decide *Sweet v Parsley* [1969][90] the state of the law was such that the concepts of voluntariness and mens rea were still considered distinct. Voluntariness, the universal determinant of fault, continued to be essential in every offence, even the statutory offences now described as "strict liability" for want of expression of any other mental state

---

83 See for example, Dennis J Baker, *Glanville Williams' Textbook of Criminal Law* (3rd ed, London: Sweet & Maxwell 2012) in relation to *Sweet v Parsley* [1970] AC 132 (HL).
84 *Sweet v Parsley* [1970] AC 132 (HL).
85 ACE Lynch, 'The Mental Element in the Actus Reus' (1982) 98 LQR.
86 *Sweet v Parsley* [1970] AC 132 (HL).
87 *Sweet v Parsley* [1970] AC 132 (HL).
88 *Woolmington v DPP* [1935] AC 462 (HL).
89 David Ormerod, *Smith and Hogan's Criminal Law* (13th ed, Oxford: Oxford University Press 2011) 162.
90 *Sweet v Parsley* [1970] AC 132 (HL).

requirement.[91] There was no general principle that mens rea was a constituent in statutory offences,[92] albeit Turner did acknowledge the existence of a much weaker presumption that foresight had to be proved, but observed that it was so weak it was often rebutted by straightforward words of prohibition.[93] Accordingly, in practice, proof of mens rea was frequently taken to have been dispensed with. Notwithstanding the continued clarity of Turner's exposition in relation to the two mental states, the judgments in *Sweet and Parsley*[94] do not refer to voluntariness, exclusively employing the terminology of mens rea to refer to mental blameworthiness.

The facts were that Stephanie Sweet, the non-resident "landlady", did not know that her "beatnik" lodgers were smoking cannabis resin at the house she let to them; nonetheless she was convicted at trial under s. 5(b) of the Dangerous Drugs Act 1965.[95] Section 5(b) created an offence of "being concerned in the management of premises used for the purpose of smoking cannabis". The questions for the House of Lords were:

1   Whether section 5(b) of the Dangerous Drugs Act 1965, creates an absolute offence.
2   What, if any, mental element is involved in the offence; and
3   Whether on the facts found, a reasonable bench of magistrates properly directing their minds to the law could have convicted the appellant.

In reaching its decision, it is of note that the House approved just one case, *R v Tolson* (1889),[96] although it also considered *Warner* [1969][97] which had come to the House just seven months earlier.[98] While the older Tolson authority concerned an altogether different charge of bigamy,[99] *Warner*,[100] like *Sweet*,[101] had been a case requiring the interpretation of the statutory drugs offences.[102] Although

91 Exceptionally this element had been excluded by Parliament, see the controversial cases of *R v Larsonneur* (1933) 24 Cr App R 74 (CCA) and *Winzar v CC Kent* (1983) The Times, 28 March.
92 JW Cecil Turner, *Kenny's Outlines of Criminal Law* (19th ed, Cambridge: Cambridge University Press 1966) 55.
93 Ibid.
94 *Sweet v Parsley* [1970] AC 132 (HL).
95 Dangerous Drugs Act 1965, s. 5, "If a person - (a) being the occupier of any premises, permits those premises to be used for the purpose of smoking ... cannabis resin ... or (b) is concerned in the management of any premises used for any such purpose as aforesaid; he shall be guilty of an offence against this Act."
96 *R v Tolson* (1889) 23 QBD 168.
97 *Warner v MPC* [1969] 2 AC 256 (HL).
98 Common to the judicial panels in both cases were Lords Reid, Morris, Pearce and Wilberforce.
99 Contrary to the Offences Against the Persons Act 1861, s. 57; *R v Tolson* (1889) 23 QBD 168.
100 *Warner v MPC* [1969] 2 AC 256 (HL).
101 *Sweet v Parsley* [1970] AC 132 (HL).
102 Drugs (Prevention of Misuse) Act 1964.

different drugs offences were being considered, both cases concerned the voluntariness doctrine and not mens rea.[103] An odd choice in itself, *Tolson*[104] had given rise to much academic and judicial discussion, indeed Turner examined it in depth in the 1964 edition of Russell on Crime.[105] His explanation of the case is significant, given that a different interpretation has subsequently been attributed to both it and *Sweet v Parsley*.[106] Starting with a statement of general principle, Turner explained that the language of a statute may reject the defence of mistake of fact. Thus, "where the statute excludes a mental element then the presence or absence of that element is irrelevant and the guilt of the accused person is not affected by any mistake of fact which may have led him to suppose that he was not doing the forbidden thing."[107] However, even in these cases, a mistake of fact may be admitted to establish that the act in question is not to be imputed to the

---

103 It was from *Warner* that the following proposition was taken, "The absence of mens rea consists in 'an honest and reasonable belief entertained by the accused of the existence of facts which, if true, would make the act charged against him innocent'", *Warner v MPC* [1969] 2 AC 256 (HL) 276 (L. Reid), quoting from *Bank of New South Wales v Piper* [1897] AC 383, 389–90 (PC) Aus. However, where Lord Reid quoted this statement from *Bank of New South Wales* [1897], a case concerning malicious prosecution, he failed to advert to the preceding sentences in that case and the context in which that assertion was made. In its full expression, Sir Richard Couch in the *Bank of New South Wales* had said, "but the questions whether a particular intent is made an element of the statutory crime, and when that is not the case, whether there was an absence of mens rea in the accused, are questions entirely different, and depend upon different considerations. In cases when the statute requires a motive to be proved as an essential element of the crime, the prosecution must fail if it is not proved. On the other hand, the absence of mens rea really consists in an honest and reasonable belief entertained by the accused of the existence of facts which, if true, would make the act charged against him innocent", 388. Evidently, Sir Richard Couch was alive to both mental states and the difference in the evidential burden. However, by quoting the shortened passage, the result of *Warner* is seemingly to equate mens rea, foresight of specified consequences, with what is clearly the orthodox voluntariness doctrine rather than recognise the distinction between those mental states. That the mental state being identified in *Warner* was voluntariness is supported by the substance of Lord Guest's reasoning which is much along the lines of Jackson's somnambulist butcher example of imputability. He said that there must, "in relation to possession, be some conscious mental element present. The sleeper who has a packet put into his hand during sleep has not got possession of it during sleep, but if when he wakes up he grasps the article, it is then in his possession. If someone surreptitiously puts something into my pocket, I am not in possession of it until I know it is there", 299. Similarly, the other examples provided by Lord Pearce, 303, and Lord Wilberforce can only be identified as illustrations of metaphorical involuntariness.
104 *R v Tolson* (1889) 23 QBD 168.
105 JW Cecil Turner, *Russell on Crime* (12th ed, London: Stevens & Sons 1964) 78.
106 *Sweet v Parsley* [1970] AC 132 (HL).
107 JW Cecil Turner, *Russell on Crime* (12th ed, London: Stevens & Sons 1964) 78 and citing the following cases in support: *R v Bishop* (1880) 5 QBD 259; *R v Wheat & Stocks* (1921) 15 Cr App R 134 (CCA); *R v Maughan* (1934) 24 Cr App R 130 (CC); *Cotterill v Penn* (1936) 1 KB 53, 153 LT 377.

accused. *Tolson*,[108] he observed, could have been dealt with under this principle without further discussion as to the mental element required by the particular section of the statute. Mrs Tolson, believing with good reason that her husband had died, had married again during his lifetime. On appeal, the Court for Crown Cases Reserved had interpreted the provision as not being one of absolute prohibition in the situation where the facts fell within the second proviso of the section and Turner observed that this must mean that belief in the spouse's death, whether arising from seven years' silent absence or from other facts, rendered a second marriage non-felonious. Further, with this belief found as fact, she had been entitled to have her case decided on this fiction; had her husband been dead the second marriage would not have constituted the actus reus of bigamy. Since the trial had to regard the husband as dead, it was immaterial that in addition she was not conscious of doing anything that was wrong.[109] Mrs Tolson's mistake had denied the voluntariness of the act and mens rea was simply not an issue.[110]

Turner's explanation of *Tolson* is borne out by a close reading of the judgments in the case. Cave J., for example, stated that, "Honest and reasonable mistake stands in fact on the same footing as absence of the reasoning faculty, as in infancy ... or lunacy".[111] Similarly, according to Stephen J.

> The full definition of every crime contains expressly or by implication a proposition as to a state of mind ... In all cases whatever, competent age, sanity and some degree of freedom from some kinds of coercion are assumed to be essential to criminality, but I do not believe they are ever introduced into any statute by which any particular crime is defined. ... in every case knowledge of fact is to some extent an element of criminality as much as competent age and sanity.[112]

Given what is known about the extent of the doctrine, these are clear references to voluntariness and the denial of capacity. As the only authority approved in *Sweet v Parsley*,[113] which also involved denial of metaphorical voluntariness, it would appear that the *Sweet* decision simply accorded with the orthodox doctrine of voluntariness. That the term mens rea was being used to

---

108   *R v Tolson* (1889) 23 QBD 168.

109   JW Cecil Turner, *Russell on Crime* (12th ed, London: Stevens & Sons 1964) 78, 79.

110   However, Turner did go on to acknowledge that the court had discussed the issue of mens rea and had concluded that Mrs Tolson did not have it. This discussion, although technically superfluous, would have been expected in 1889 when there was still a judicial leaning to read common law mens rea into statutes, a tendency which was not now present. Turner also pointed to the later case of *R v Wheat and Stocks* [1921] 2 KB 119 in which, 30 years later, the Court of Appeal had interpreted the third proviso of that section in another way, and as an instance of absolute prohibition, refusing the admit the "defence" of mistake.

111   *R v Tolson* (1889) 23 QBD 168, 181 (Cave J).

112   *R v Tolson* (1889) 23 QBD 168, 187–8 (Stephen J.).

113   *Sweet v Parsley* [1970] AC 132 (HL).

describe voluntariness was not unusual, its use as a catch-all term having already been well documented.[114] Indeed, Lord Diplock implicitly recognised as much in his judgment, he observed:

> mens rea itself also lacks precision and calls for closer analysis than is involved in its mere translation into English by Wright J. in *Sherras* … as "evil intention or a knowledge of the wrongfulness of the act" – a definition which suggests a single mental element common to all criminal offences.[115]

Clearly alluding to the orthodox doctrine of voluntariness with reference to insanity, somnambulism, duress and inevitable accident,[116] Lord Diplock also pointed to *Tolson*[117] affirming the general principle that a necessary element of every criminal enactment was the absence of a belief, held honestly and upon reasonable grounds, in the existence of facts which, if true, would make the act innocent.[118]

However, while the use of loose language and the odd choice of *Tolson*[119] as a precedent were otherwise harmless incidents, the decision in *Sweet v Parsley*[120] caused what turned out to be irretrievable damage to the notion of voluntariness. The reasoning that led to the demise of the foundational doctrine turned on the court's analysis of the earlier case of *Sherras v De Rutzen [1895]*[121] which it considered in the light of the erroneous *Woolmington [1935]* decision[122] but not the corrective judgment provided in *Mancini*[123] just seven years later. This over-sight proved fatal to the wide voluntariness doctrine and the evidential

---

114 Jackson RM, 'Absolute Prohibition in Statutory Offences' (1936–38) 6 CLJ 83; JWC Turner, 'The Mental Element in Crimes at Common Law' (1936–38) 6 CLJ 31.

115 *Sweet v Parsley* [1970] AC 132 (HL) 162.

116 "The mere fact that Parliament has made the conduct a criminal offence gives rise to some implication about the mental element of the conduct proscribed. It has, for instance, never been doubted since *M'Naghten's Case* (1843) 10 Cl. & F. 200 that one implication as to the mental element in any statutory offence is that the doer of the prohibited act should be sane within the M'Naghten rules; yet this part of the full definition of the offence is invariably left unexpressed by Parliament. Stephen J. in *R v Tolson (1889) 23 QBD. 168* suggested other circumstances never expressly dealt with in the statute where a mental element to be implied from the mere fact that the doing of an act was made a criminal offence would be absent, such as where it was done in a state of somnambulism or under duress, to which one might add inevitable accident." *Sweet v Parsley* [1970] AC 132 (HL) para 162 and 163.

117 *R v Tolson* (1889) 23 QBD 168.

118 *Sweet v Parsley* [1970] AC 132 (HL) 163 (L. Diplock) referring to the Privy Council in *Bank of New South Wales v Piper* [1897] AC 383 (PC) Aus, 389–90.

119 *R v Tolson* (1889) 23 QBD 168.

120 *Sweet v Parsley* [1970] AC 132 (HL).

121 *Sherras v De Rutzen* [1895] 1 QB 918.

122 *Woolmington v DPP* [1935] AC 462 (HL).

123 *Mancini v DPP* [1942] AC 1 (HL).

presumption upon which it operated. In *Sherras*[124] the conviction of a publican for selling drink to a constable on duty was set aside because the accused had reasonably believed that the officer was not on duty.[125] While a claim of absence of knowledge was effectively a claim of non-voluntariness and voluntariness was an element implicitly required in every offence, Day J. in *Sherras* elaborated on the point because a different subsection of the same act explicitly required that the defendant had acted "knowingly".[126] While acknowledging the existence of the implicit requirement, he went on to pronounce that while the crown had to prove knowledge where it was an element expressed in the offence,[127] the failure to expressly require that the defendant acted knowingly simply had the effect of shifting the "burden of proof" to the accused.[128]

While the presumption of voluntariness operates such a shift, strictly speaking it reverses the evidential burden and not the burden of proof. Although Day J.'s construction had been approved in a number of subsequent cases,[129] the tide turned in 1951 when Devlin J. argued against it in *Roper v Taylor's Central Garages* [1951].[130] The question is whether Day J. meant to refer to the reversal of the burden of proof, which is objectionable, or whether he had the burden of evidence in mind, which is not. What can be observed is that, at the time of his judgment, his choice of words would have made no real difference. Since it was not until 1898 that an accused could give sworn evidence on his own behalf,[131] at the time of *Sherras*[132] the evidential presumptions would have had a force more akin to legal presumption and the distinction was not important.[133]

Indeed, it was in *Woolmington v DPP* [1935][134] that the crucial distinction between the "burden of proof" and the "burden of evidence" was to become a live issue. Having repeatedly used the term mens rea to describe voluntariness,[135] the

---

124 *Sherras v De Rutzen* [1895] 1 QB 918.
125 Licensing Act 1872, s. 16.
126 S 16(1).
127 Under the orthodox analysis it would be considered part of the actus reus of the offence.
128 *Sherras v De Rutzen* [1895] 1 QB 918, 921.
129 *Gaumont British Distributors Ltd v Henry* [1939] 2 KB 711 (Humphreys J.); *Harding v Price* [1948] 1 KB 695 (Singleton J.); *Reynolds v Austin* (GH) & Sons Ltd [1951] 2 KB 135.
130 *Roper v Taylor's Central Garages* [1951] 2 TLR 284, 288, as did the Privy Council in *Lim Chin Aik v The Queen* [1963] AC 160 (PC) Singapore 173.
131 Criminal Evidence Act 1898.
132 *Sherras v De Rutzen* [1895] 1 QB 918.
133 JWC Turner, *Russell on Crime* (12th ed, London: Stevens & Sons 1964) 33. The direction given to juries had the effect of elevating the matter of evidence to a rule of law.
134 *Woolmington v DPP* [1935] AC 462 (HL).
135 For example, Lord Morris of Borth-y-Gest, it has frequently been affirmed and should unhesitatingly be recognised that, "it is a cardinal principle of our law that mens rea, an evil intention or a knowledge of the wrongfulness of the act, is in all ordinary cases an essential ingredient of guilt of a criminal offence. It follows from this that there will not be guilt of an offence created by statute unless there is mens rea or unless Parliament has by the statute enacted that guilt may be established in cases where there is no mens rea." *Sweet v Parsley* [1970] AC 132 (HL) 152.

appellate court in *Sweet v Parsley*[136] then turned its attention to Viscount Sankey in *Woolmington*[137] and his now infamous dicta,

> Throughout the web of the English criminal law one golden thread is always to be seen, that it is the duty of the prosecution to prove the prisoner's guilt, subject to matters as to the defence of insanity and subject also to any statutory exception.[138]

At this point Day J.'s reference to the presumption of voluntariness reversing the burden of proof, rather than evidential onus,[139] became crucial. On the interpretation of Day J.'s expression in *Sherras*[140] in the light of *Woolmington*,[141] it was held in *Sweet v Parsley* that the presumption of voluntariness, seemingly requiring that a defendant had to prove his innocence, could no longer stand.[142] Indeed, some of the passages in *Sweet v Parsley* distinguish authorities decided by reference to a denial of voluntariness on the basis that they were cases preceding the *Woolmington* statement.[143]

Although the language of voluntariness had been subsumed by increasing reference to mens rea, as a catch-all phrase to describe any mental state, the reasoning of the court in *Sweet* now found the substance of the presumption of voluntariness incompatible with a basic tenet of the criminal law. Discredited in this way, the orthodox approach, and hitherto primary determinant of fault, needed to be discarded with haste. As to the resulting lacuna, the advancing language and, indeed, expanding notion of mens rea was the obvious "filler". Where the terminology had for so long been used interchangeably, "the presumption of mens rea" could easily replace "the presumption of voluntariness" in the discourse and do so without drawing attention to what was, in effect, a sea change in the substance of the criminal law. While the language promoted a sense of consistency and coherence with orthodox principles, the effect was to turn a presumption that the defendant had acted voluntarily, and was therefore blameworthy, into the presumption that the crown needed to prove the blameworthy mental state.

Although this profound shift in fundamental doctrine might be explained by the cumulative effect of the use of imprecise terminology in both *Sherras*,[144] regarding the burden of proof, and *Sweet*,[145] in relation to the blurring of mens

---

136 *Sweet v Parsley* [1970] AC 132 (HL).
137 *Woolmington v DPP* [1935] AC 462 (HL).
138 Ibid 469.
139 *Sherras v De Rutzen* [1895] 1 QB 918.
140 Ibid 921.
141 *Woolmington v DPP* [1935] AC 462 (HL).
142 *Sweet v Parsley* [1970] AC 132 (HL) 150 (L. Reid), 158 (L. Pearce).
143 Ibid 158 (L. Pearce).
144 *Sherras v De Rutzen* [1895] 1 QB 918.
145 *Sweet v Parsley* [1970] AC 132 (HL).

rea and voluntariness, there is evidence that this move was more intentional than inadvertent.

In accordance with the orthodox approach, counsel for *Sweet* had argued that although the onus was on the accused to raise the "defence" of lack of guilty knowledge, the burden of proof lay firmly on the prosecution.[146] He cited both *Tolson*[147] and Dixon J. in the Australian High Court case of *Proudman v Dayman* (1941),[148] who pronounced:

> The burden of establishing honest and reasonable mistake is in the first place upon the defendant and he must make it appear that he had reasonable grounds for believing in the existence of the state of facts, which, if true, would take his act outside the operation of the enactment and that on those grounds he did so believe. The burden possibly may not finally rest upon him of satisfying the tribunal in case of doubt.[149]

Given the force of this submission, it is curious that the judgments in *Sweet*[150] relied on *Woolmington* [1935][151] but were silent as to the House of Lords case of *Mancini v DPP* [1942][152] that provided a re-interpretation of it, correcting the point about the shift in the burden of proof.[153] It was a well-known authority, discussed at length in, for example, the 1964 *Russell on Crime* in which Turner had also clarified the manner in which the presumptions operated.[154] Although *Woolmington*[155] had asserted that, "where intent is an

---

146 Ibid 141.
147 *R v Tolson* (1889) 23 QBD 168.
148 *Proudman v Dayman* (1941) 67 CLR.
149 Ibid 536, 551. Thus,"as a general rule an honest and reasonable belief in a state of facts which, if they existed, would make the defendant's act innocent affords an excuse for doing what would otherwise be an offence. The strength of the presumption that the rule applies to a statutory offence newly created varies with the nature of the offence and the scope of the statute. If the purpose of the statute is to add a new crime to the general criminal law, it is natural to suppose that it is to be read subject to the general principles according to which that law is administered ...", *Proudman v Dayman* (1941) 67 CLR 536, 539–40. Further, "There may be no longer any presumption that mens rea, in the sense of the specific state of mind, whether of motive, intention, knowledge or advertence, is an ingredient in an offence created by a modern statute; but to concede that the weakening of the older understanding of the rule of interpretation has left us with no prima facie presumption that some mental element is implied in the definition of any new statutory offence does not mean that the rule that honest and reasonable mistake is prima facie admissible as an exculpation has lost its application also", 551.
150 *Sweet v Parsley* [1970] AC 132 (HL).
151 With the suggestion that the presumptions work to destroy the "golden thread", *Woolmington v DPP* [1935] AC 462 (HL).
152 *Mancini v DPP* [1942] AC 1 (HL).
153 Ibid.
154 JW Cecil Turner, *Russell on Crime* (12th ed, London: Stevens & Sons 1964) 24, 33–6, 73, 102, 123, 453, 494, 508, 510, 684, 849.
155 *Woolmington v DPP* [1935] AC 462 (HL).

ingredient of a crime there is no onus on the defendant to prove that the act alleged was accidental", Turner explained:

> as soon as mens rea had become subjective the burden of proof on the prosecution was a heavy one. It was discharged by relying upon the old assumption of intention, which then became the well-known legal presumption that a man is deemed to have intended the natural consequences of his acts … The result of judges putting the presumption in simple terms to juries was that it gradually moved from a rule of evidence into a rule of law as an objective test of mens rea.[156]

Indeed, such a move had seemingly been observed by Day J. in Sherras[157] and, in this respect, *Woolmington*[158] had operated as a corrective to that[159] but it had been modified subsequently in *Mancini v DPP* [1942],[160] providing a rule of general application to all criminal charges. Viscount Simon L.C. in *Mancini* observed,

> Woolmington's case is concerned with explaining and reinforcing the rule that the prosecution must prove the charge it makes beyond reasonable doubt, and, consequently, that if, on the material before the jury, there is reasonable doubt, the prisoner should have the benefit of it.[161]

The presumption placed no heavier burden on the defence than to put, or to point to, evidence before the court, on which the jury could inform reasonable doubt as to the accused person's guilt.[162] Glanville Williams' seminal text had also concurred with this analysis, specifically that the "defence" of automatism, a classic expression of involuntariness, placed the "evidential burden" on the defendant.[163] Furthermore, as regards the operation of the presumption of voluntariness, he observed:

> The object of placing the evidential burden on the defendant is twofold: (1) to save the prosecution the trouble of meeting the defence unless it is first raised by the defendant, with sufficient evidence in support of it to be left to a jury, and (2) (particularly where the matter relates to the

---

156 JW Cecil Turner, *Russell on Crime* (12th ed, London: Stevens & Sons 1964) 34.
157 *Sherras v De Rutzen* [1895] 1 QB 918.
158 *Woolmington v DPP* [1935] AC 462.
159 JW Cecil Turner, *Russell on Crime* (12th ed, Stevens & Sons 1964) 34.
160 Ibid 35, citing *Mancini v DPP* [1942] AC 1 (HL).
161 *Mancini v DPP* [1942] AC 1 (HL) 11.
162 JW Cecil Turner, *Russell on Crime* (12th ed, London: Stevens & Sons 1964) 36.
163 Glanville Williams, *Criminal Law, The General Part* (2nd ed, Stevens & Sons 1961) 886.

defendant's state of mind) to force the defendant to go into the witness box and give evidence. By giving evidence, he subjects himself to cross-examination.[164]

Although Lord Diplock in *Sweet* had clearly alluded to the voluntariness doctrine[165] and was clear as to the true effect of *Woolmington*,[166] *Sweet v Parsley*[167] was nonetheless to be identified as the modern revitalisation of the presumption of mens rea[168] and not as a simple restatement of orthodox principle. Where voluntariness once formed the central plank of criminal liability in all cases, it was now displaced in favour of the modern notion of mens rea. While the criminal law continues to be analysed by reference to the maxim *"actus non facit reum nisi mens sit rea"* today, Turner's modified analysis now represents the established position whereby offence elements are typically categorised by reference to either their physical or mental qualities,[169] and each element is considered in isolation.[170] In contrast to its restrictive common law meaning, mens rea is now taken to denote all of the mental elements expressed in the offence definition, previously considered to be actus

---

164 Ibid 887, see too his discussion at 891.
165 "It is a general principle of construction of any enactment which creates a criminal offence that, even where the words used to describe the prohibited conduct would not in any other context connote the necessity for any particular mental element, they are nevertheless to be read as subject to the implication that a necessary element in the offence is the absence of a belief, held honestly and on reasonable grounds, in the existence of facts which, if true, would make the act innocent" *Sweet v Parsley* [1970] AC 132 (HL) 163.
166 *Woolmington v DPP* [1935] AC 462 (HL), Lord Diplock recognised that it "did not decide anything so irrational as that the prosecution must call evidence to prove the absence of a mistaken belief by the accused in the existence of facts which, if true, would make the act innocent, any more than it decided that the prosecution must call evidence to prove the absence of any claim of right in a charge of larceny". He observed that, "the jury is entitled to presume that the accused acted with knowledge of the facts, unless there is some evidence to the contrary originating from the accused who alone can know on what belief he acted and on what ground the belief, if mistaken, was held. What Woolmington's case did decide is that where there is any such evidence the jury after considering it and also any relevant evidence called by the prosecution on the issue of the existence of the alleged mistaken belief should acquit the accused unless they feel sure that he did not hold the belief or that there were no reasonable grounds upon which he could have done so", *Sweet v Parsley* [1970] AC 132 (HL) 164 (L. Diplock).
167 *Sweet v Parsley* [1970] AC 132 (HL).
168 David Ormerod, *Smith and Hogan's Criminal Law* (13th ed, Oxford: Oxford University Press 2011) 162.
169 Andrew Ashworth and Jeremy Horder, *Principles of Criminal Law* (7th ed, Oxford: Oxford University Press 2013).
170 *Lawrence v MPC* [1972] AC 626 (HL), (Megaw LJ); *DPP v Gomez* [1993] AC 442 (HL) 495 (Browne-Wilkinson L.); *R v Hinks* [2001] 2 AC 241 (HL). Alternatively, criminal liability is constructed by reference to the addition of the actus reus and mens rea and, further, the absence of a defence.

reus requirements, encompassing, for example, "intention", "knowledge", "belief", "recklessness" and "dishonesty".[171] The distinction between common law and statutory principles of criminal law has disappeared and the two mental states, voluntariness and mens rea as traditionally conceived, simply have no frame of reference. The actus reus of an offence is defined by default, taken to refer to any non-mental element[172] and a typical exposition of the doctrine in modern learning and practitioner texts includes discussion of circumstances, consequences and principles of liability in relation to omissions and causation.[173] Voluntariness, formerly the primary determinant of fault, now tends to attract little more than a passing glance and usually only does so in the limited context of the automatism "defence".[174] What remains is a shadow of the traditional doctrine, now conceptualised in the form of various specific defences.

The examination of the orthodox doctrine of voluntariness has, however, provided a fruitful line of enquiry as to a central plank of criminal fault that might be reconstructed and applied to the corporate actor. A return to the explicit recognition of voluntariness as the hallmark of criminal fault in all cases would not only restate the law as traditionally conceived, it would also provide a step towards the facilitation of a general model of corporate liability. Voluntariness as a concept is still a satisfactory determinant of fault and the return to a fully acknowledged presumption of voluntariness continues to have practical application as regards evidential matters in the corporate context. Without the need for the prosecution to prove specific mental states, it would be open for a representative of the organisation to raise evidence of any denial that the corporate conduct was voluntary. Since voluntariness, conceived in its wider sense, is indicative of the capacity of the actor, it would provide the means by which the corporation could be recognised as a responsibility-bearing entity in its own right. Further, since the orthodox doctrine imports a rebuttable presumption of knowledge of the circumstances surrounding the act, the knowledge element required by the false representation mode may also be presumed.[175] Of significance, a return to this analysis would not cause any change or detriment in cases alleging the criminal conduct of individuals.

171 Andrew Ashworth and Jeremy Horder, *Principles of Criminal Law* (7th ed, Oxford: Oxford University Press 2013) 83. Ormerod also includes "wilfully" in his list of mens rea expressions, David Ormerod, *Smith and Hogan's Criminal Law* (13th ed, Oxford: Oxford University Press 2011).

172 Janet Dine and others, *Criminal Law: Cases and Materials* (6th ed, Oxford: Oxford University Press 2011) 61.

173 David Ormerod, *Smith and Hogan's Criminal Law* (13th ed, Oxford: Oxford University Press 2011) 46 ff.

174 Ibid 59.

175 Fraud Act 2006, s 2(2)(b).

Bibliography

Books

Ashworth A and Horder J, *Principles of Criminal Law* (7th ed, Oxford: Oxford University Press 2013)

Austin J and Campbell R (eds.), *Lectures on Jurisprudence* (orig pub 1874, Montana: Kissinger Legacy 2010)

Baker DJ, *Glanville Williams' Textbook of Criminal Law* (3rd ed, London: Sweet & Maxwell 2012)

Coke E, *The Third Part of the Institutes of the Laws of England* (London: first printed by M Flesher for W Lee & D Pakeman 1644)

Dine J and others, *Criminal Law, Cases and Materials* (6th ed, Oxford: Oxford University Press 2011)

Duff RA, *Intention, Agency and Criminal Liability: Philosophy of Action and Criminal Law* (Oxford: Basil Blackwell 1990).

Hart HLA, *Punishment and Responsibility* (Oxford: Clarendon Press 1968)

Kenny CS, *A Selection of Cases Illustrative of English Criminal Law* (8th ed, Cambridge: Cambridge University Press 1935)

Kenny CS, *Outlines of Criminal Law* (14th ed, Cambridge: Cambridge University Press 1933)

Leigh LH, *Strict and Vicarious Liability* (London: Sweet & Maxwell 1982)

Ormerod D, *Smith and Hogan's Criminal Law* (13th ed, Oxford: Oxford University Press 2011)

Radzinowicz L and Turner JWC (eds.), *The Modern Approach to Criminal Law* (2nd ed, London: Macmillan 1948)

Ross RE and Turner M, *Archbold's Criminal Pleading, Evidence and Practice* (30th ed, London: Sweet & Maxwell 1938)

Shute S and others (eds.), *Action and Value in Criminal Law* (Oxford: Clarendon Press 1993)

Smith KJM, *Lawyers, Legislators and Theorists* (Oxford: Oxford University Press 1998)

Turner JWC, *Kenny's Outlines of Criminal Law* (17th ed, Cambridge: Cambridge University Press 1958)

Turner JWC, *Russell on Crime* (12th ed, London: Stevens & Sons 1964)

Turner JWC and Armitage A LL, *Cases on Criminal Law* (Cambridge: Cambridge University Press 1953)

Turner JWC, *Kenny's Outlines of Criminal Law* (19th ed, Cambridge: Cambridge University Press 1966)

Williams G, *Criminal Law, The General Part* (2nd ed, London: Stevens & Sons 1961)

Journal articles

Jackson RM, '*Absolute Prohibition in Statutory Offences*' (1936–38) 6 CLJ 83

Lacey N, '*In Search of the Responsible Subject: History, Philosophy and Criminal Law Theory*' (2001) 64 MLR 350–371

Lacey N, '*Responsibility and Modernity in Criminal Law*' (2001) 9 Journal of Political Philosophy 249–277

Lacey N, '*Space, Time and Function: Intersecting Principles of Responsibility across the Terrain of Criminal Justice*' (2007) 1 Criminal Law and Philosophy 233–250

Lynch ACE, '*The Mental Element in the Actus Reus*' (1982) 98 LQR 110.
Mackay RD, '*Non-Organic Automatism*' [1980] Crim LR 350
Smith KJM and Wilson W, '*Impaired Voluntariness and Criminal Responsibility: Reworking Hart's Theory of Excuses – the English Judicial Response*' (1993) 13 OJLS 69
Turner JWC, '*The Mental Element in Crimes at Common Law*' (1936–38) 6 CLJ 31
Williams G, '*Offences and Defences*' (1982) 2 LS 233

Official materials

Criminal Law Commission Fourth Report of Her Majesty's Commissioners on Criminal Law 1839 (168) XIX
Law Commission, *Criminal Liability: Insanity and Automatism*, discussion paper, 23 July 2013

4 Mens rea, metaphysics and the manifest assessment of fault

4.1 Subjective individualism and the presumption of intention

The way in which the law has developed in relation to fault attribution has had a profound effect in relation to the development of theories of corporate criminality. The combined effect of the demise of the presumption of voluntariness and the expanded concept of mens rea has led to the primary enquiry focusing on the defendant's state of mind, a metaphysical mind that the fictional corporate entity simply cannot possess. However, given that the need to prove mens rea has been the real hurdle to corporate prosecution, typical academic accounts of the law's approach to corporate criminality fail to acknowledge that "mens rea" has not been constant in terms of either its substantive meaning or the way in which it is attributed to the defendant and proved. While Chapter 3 addressed the former dynamic and the presumption relating to the voluntariness doctrine, this chapter addresses that lacuna in the context of other mental states.

It will be recalled that proof of the orthodox canons of liability turned upon the operation of two evidential presumptions. Chapter 3 identified the combination of factors which led to the demise of the presumption of voluntariness and this chapter will reveal how the presumption of intention suffered a similar fate. According to this presumption, a defendant was presumed to have intended the natural consequences of his act. This conclusion was based on the assumption that an act foreseen was an act intended and, further, that the defendant had the mental capacity of a reasonable man such that he would have foreseen what were deemed its natural consequences. The presumption of intention of natural consequences, like that of voluntariness, presupposed that an initial consideration of the appearance of the conduct had taken place. The act and its consequences were inferential of the defendant's state of mind, namely that the conduct was both voluntary and that the resulting harm was intended. In this respect it might be said that if the appearance is outwardly or "manifestly" criminal, the presumptive mechanism then affords the defendant an opportunity to refute the inference by giving evidence of his own mental state.

However, when this evidential presumption came to be mistaken for a presumption of law, this mode of fault assessment became uncomfortably objective in nature. Thus, while the presumption of voluntariness had seemed to offend one basic tenet of criminal law, reversing the burden of proof, the presumption of intention seemingly offended the whole principle of subjective individualism.

Although s. 8 of the Criminal Justice Act 1967 was enacted to remedy any remaining misperception,[1] and placed the factual presumption on a statutory footing,[2] the language it perpetuated was subsequently subjected to a fierce judicial onslaught in the context of murder and the requisite intention for this particular offence.[3] That a jury could infer a murderous intent if the defendant had foreseen serious bodily harm or death as a natural consequence of his action was considered "unsafe and misleading".[4] Although the legal territory attracting such heightened interest was narrow, the silencing of the language of natural consequences, and its associated presumption, was more general in effect. Further, as explicit references to the two presumptions of fault progressively diminished in the narrative of the criminal law, the term "mens rea" assumed greater prominence in the discourse. Used in its enlarged catch-all sense, the notion of mens rea began to encompass the idea that the blameworthy mental state needed to be positively proved. Although the presumption of innocence and the burden of proof had not been in doubt,[5] the practical effect was a gradual move from a position in which fault was presumed by reference to the appearance of the act, subject to the defendant's rebuttal, to a position in which it was presumed that the culpable mental state needed to be examined and specifically proved. Thus, the diminution in the use of the presumptions resulted in a further conceptual shift in the nature of the enquiry, from the manifest and the directly observable to the internal and the unobservable. It was arguably this conceptual re-ordering and the disappearance of the evidential presumptions that necessitated a mechanism by which the corporate mind could be identified.

This chapter will expose the way in which this evidential mechanism shrank from the discourse and the various influences on its disappearance. Accordingly, it charts the shift away from the objective and manifest approaches to fault attribution to the subjective model and the evidential problems this incurred. Having demonstrated how the presumptions bridged the evidential gap, it will reveal the fatal confusion between the evidential issue of the presumption of intention and the nature of intention itself. The case for the full re-acknowledgment of the presumption of intention will be made.

There are two narratives relevant to this conceptual shift. The first is the transition from the manifest assessment of blameworthiness, by reference to the

---

1 The provision made it clear that the presumption of intention should not operate to exclude regard to the totality of the evidence.
2 David Ormerod, *Blackstone's Criminal Practice* (Oxford: Oxford University Press 2015) F3.63
3 See for example *Hyam v DPP* [1975] AC 55 (HL); *R v Moloney* [1985] AC 905 (HL); *R v Hancock and Shankland* [1986] AC 455 (HL); *R v Woollin* [1999] 1 AC 82(HL).
4 *R v Hancock and Shankland* [1986] AC 455 (HL), 473 (L. Scarman).
5 Described as "the most important of the disputable presumptions of law in criminal cases", William Feilden Craies and Henry Delacombe Roome, *Archbold's Criminal Pleading, Evidence and Practice* (24th ed, London: Sweet & Maxwell 1910) 404.

defendant's overt conduct and his known character. The second is the move from the objective consideration of the foreseeability of the consequences, by reference to an external standard, to the subjective enquiry of the defendant's own mental state. Both strands are inevitably interwoven, influenced by the fact that an accused could not give evidence on his own behalf at trial until the enactment of the Criminal Evidence Act 1898. Consequently, until this time, the actual intention with which a suspect had done the act in question could only be established as a matter of inference arising from the evidence of other witnesses as to what the accused had said or done. Further, in drawing any inference, it was necessary to presume that the accused had the mental capacity of a "reasonable man" such that he could be said to have intended everything that was the probable consequence of his act. Thus, although the modern criminal law institution was concerned with the mental attitude of the accused himself, and whether he attracted moral oppro-brium by virtue of his capacity and foresight of potential harm, in practice this enquiry necessitated the employment of both the manifest assessment of the conduct and the objective consideration of foreseeability.

The former approach to the determination of fault had been a longstanding feature of the criminal law institution. The Prisoners' Counsel Act 1836 had entitled a defendant to be represented by lawyers at every stage of his trial but, prior to the 18th century, fault was determined through what has been described as "manifest assessment".[6] Manifest liability, in this sense, looked first to the overt conduct of the suspect and then considered the outward appearance of the act by reference to his known character and standing in the community.[7] This process was called "character-vouching" and was thus indicative of a criminal regime that was largely arbitrary in nature.[8] There was little professional policing prior to 1830 and, even until the late 1800s, criminal prosecution was generally a private matter with little involvement of lawyers.[9] Accordingly, most crimes were

---

6 Manifest liability therefore seems to mean that it took account of all the evidence save for that of the defendant himself, Lucia Zedner, *Criminal Justice* (Oxford: Oxford University Press 2004); Gerry Johnstone and Tony Ward, *Key Approaches to Criminology: Law and Crime* (London: Sage 2010).

7 Lucia Zedner, *Criminal Justice* (Oxford: Oxford University Press 2004); Gerry Johnstone and Tony Ward, *Key Approaches to Criminology: Law and Crime* (London: Sage 2010).

8 The criminal law, as we would recognise it today, was still of marginal importance at this time because of the lack of public agencies to enforce and prosecute, WR Cornish and G Clark, *Law and Society in England 1750-1950* (London: Sweet & Maxwell 1989).

9 WR Cornish and G Clark, *Law and Society in England: 1750-1950* (London: Sweet & Maxwell 1989). If a formal prosecution was sought, the expenses involved in both the criminal investiga-tion and the prosecution were borne by the victim himself which meant that the availability of the criminal justice system was limited to the wealthier classes or at least those who could subscribe to a private prosecution association, see Allen Steinberg, 'The Spirit of Litigation; Private Prosecution and Criminal Justice in 19th Century Philadelphia' (1986) 20 Journal of Social History 243; Les Johnston, *The Rebirth of Private Policing* (London: Routledge 1992). See also the accounts given in Douglas Hay, 'Property, Authority and Criminal Law' in Douglas Hay and others (eds.), *Albions Fatal Tree, Crime and Society in 18th Century England* (London: Penguin 1975); Michael Foucault, *Discipline and Punish: The Birth of A Prison* (London:

dealt with locally by informal processes which were dependent upon hierarchical social relations and the authority of the local landowners to maintain order and settle disputes.[10] This informal arrangement facilitated discretion and encouraged settlements between victim and offender in less serious cases.[11] However, whereas informal penal sanctions included dismissal or chastisement by employer, pressure from priest or land-owner, arbitration or ostracism,[12] the formal criminal justice institution was maintained through the threat of violence tempered by the discretionary use of mercy.[13] In these circumstances character-vouching was important, involving reliance on character evidence provided by those higher in the social scale. This might be followed by the use of pardon[14] or, if mercy was not to be shown, the infliction of public degradation, violence or the public killing of the offender in a carnival-type atmosphere.[15] This pre-modern institution, infamous for its "bloody, penal code", lasted into the 19th century.[16]

Penguin 1977); A Schubert, 'Private Initiative in Law Enforcement: Associations for the Prosecution of Felons' in Victor Bailey (ed.), *Policing and Punishment in 19th Century Britain* (London: Croom Helm 1981); B King, 'Prosecution Associations and Their Impact in 18th Century Essex' in Douglas Hay and Frances G Snyder (eds.), *Policing and Prosecution in Britain 1750–1850* (Oxford: Clarendon 1989); Marcus D Dubber and Lindsay Farmer, *New Trends In the History of Criminal Law* (Stanford: Stanford University Press 2007).

10 Lucia Zedner, *Criminal Justice* (Oxford: Oxford University Press 2004).

11 Les Johnston, *The Rebirth of Private Policing* (London: Routledge 1992).

12 Ibid.

13 The early view of crime was that it constituted a sin and this had a number of consequences, imbuing the law with a moral significance, and deliberate disobedience invited God's wrath. Wrongdoing of this nature demanded a response that would reclaim the offender's spirituality and this involved the making of amends to the injured party and also some form of penance. In turn came the idea of purging by pain and the pre-modern institution, which lasted into the 19th century. Although England had abolished absolutism in the 17th century, it was replaced by a political and social regime termed "Old Corruption", and the Whig oligarchy of 18th century England operated the criminal law institution as if absolutism still existed such that the bloodiness of the law increased substantially in this period, Gerry Johnstone and Tony Ward, *Key Approaches to Criminology, Law and Crime* (London: Sage 2010).

14 Alan Norrie, *Crime, Reason and History* (2nd ed, London: Butterworths 2001) justice was dispensed by the ruling class, reinforcing the social hierarchy and old feudal ties.

15 Deportation was also a method of dealing with offenders from the mid-17th century. Historical accounts are given by Leon Radzinowicz, *The History of the English Criminal Law* (London: Stevens 1948) vol 1; Douglas Hay, 'Property, Authority and the Criminal Law' in D Hay and others (eds.), *Albion's Fatal Tree, Crime and Society in 18th Century England* (London: Penguin 1975); Michael Foucault, *Discipline and Punish: The Birth of A Prison* (London: Penguin 1977); Harold J Berman, *Law and Revolution: The Formation of the Western Legal Tradition* (Cambridge, Massachusetts: Harvard University Press 1983); Philip Corrigan and Derek Sayer, *The Great Arch: State Formation, Cultural Revolution and the Rise of Capitalism* (Oxford: Blackwell 1985) 87; Alan Norrie, *Crime, Reason and History* (2nd ed, London: Butterworths 2001); Lucia Zedner, *Criminal Justice* (Oxford: Oxford University Press 2004); Gerry Johnstone and Tony Ward, *Key Approaches to Criminology, Law and Crime* (London: Sage 2010).

16 Gerry Johnstone and Tony Ward, *Key Approaches to Criminology, Law and Crime* (London: Sage 2010).

Condemnation of this barbarity is said to be linked to the Enlightenment philosophy that was starting to emerge in the 18th century. This began to focus on principles of liability and also the notion of the autonomous individual capable of rational calculation.[17] At the same time new problems of crime were emerging, consequent on the then novel conditions created by urbanisation and industrialisation. For the first time a mobile and anonymous society had come into existence and as a result of this, and the associated poor living conditions,[18] there was an increase in crime in an environment where crime was easier to commit.[19] The growth of industry and the market economy had

17 For the development of the shift from manifest to the individualist account of criminal liability see Jeremy Bentham, 'An Introduction to the Principles of Morals and Legislation' in John Bowring (ed.) *Collected Works of Jeremy Bentham* (New York: Russell 1962) vol 1; CB MacPherson, *The Political Theory of Possessive Individualism* (Oxford: Oxford University Press 1962); JWC Turner, *Kenny's Outlines of Criminal Law* (18th ed, Cambridge: Cambridge University Press 1962); Heath J, *18th Century Penal Theory* (Oxford: Oxford University Press 1963); Cesare Beccaria, *On Crimes and Punishments* (Indianapolis: Bobs Merrill 1966); Harold Perkin, *The Origins of Modern English Society 1780-1880* (London: Routledge 1969); David J Rothman, *The Discovery of the Asylum* (Boston: Little Brown and Co 1971); Jeremy Bentham, *Theory of Legislation* (New York: Oceana 1975); D Philips, 'A New Engine of Power and Authority: The Institutionalisation of Law Enforcement in England 1780–1830' in VAC Gattrell and others (eds.), *Crime and the Law: The Social History of Crime in Western Europe Since 1500* (London: Europa 1980); A Schubert, 'Private Initiative in Law Enforcement: Associations for the Prosecution of Felons' in Victor Bailey (ed), *Policing and Punishment in 19th Century Britain* (London: Croom Helm 1981); S Spritzer, 'The Rationalisations of Crime Control in Capitalist Societies' in Stanley Cohen and Andrew Scull (eds.), *Social Control and the State: Historical and Comparative Essays* (Oxford: Basil Blackwell 1983); JA Sharpe, *Crime in Early Modern England 1550-1750* (London: Longman 1984); B King, 'Prosecution Associations and Their Impact in 18th Century Essex' in Douglas Hay and Francis G Snyder (eds.), *Policing and Prosecution in Britain 1750–1850* (Oxford: Clarendon 1989); Les Johnston, *The Rebirth of Private Policing* (London: Routledge 1992); Lindsay Farmer, 'The Obsession With Definition: The Nature of Crime and Critical Legal Theory' (1996) S & SL 5, 57; Lindsay Farmer, *Criminal Law, Tradition and Legal Order: Crime and the Genius of Scots Law: 1747 to Present* (Cambridge: Cambridge University Press 1997) Ch. 4; Jonathan Simon, 'Governing Through Crime' in Friedman and Fisher (eds), *The Crime Conundrum: Essays on Criminal Justice* (New York: Westview Press 1997) 174; George P Fletcher, *Basic Concepts of Criminal Law* (Oxford: Oxford University Press 1998); Robert Reiner, *The Politics of the Police* (3rd ed, Oxford: Oxford University Press 2000); Alan Norrie, *Crime, Reason and History* (2nd ed, London: Butterworths 2001); Lucia Zedner, *Criminal Justice* (Oxford: Oxford University Press 2004); Celia Wells, *Corporations and Criminal Responsibility* (2nd ed, Oxford: Oxford University Press 2001); Charles de Montesquieu, *The Spirit of the Laws* (London: Forgotten Books 2010).

18 Alan Norrie, *Crime, Reason and History* (2nd ed, London: Butterworths 2001).

19 The Victorians believed that one of the reasons for the increase in crime was that, "the restraints of character, relationship and vicinity are … lo st in the crowd … multitudes remove responsibility without weakening passion", Anon, 'Causes of the Increase of Crime' (Jul–Dec 1844) 56 Blackwood's Edinburgh Magazine 7–8; Gerry Johnstone and Tony Ward, *Key Approaches to Criminology, Law and Crime* (London: Sage 2010).

undermined the traditional informal controls.[20] Significantly, local knowledge of individual character was lost within this new community and, consequently, the hitherto central role of character-vouching was largely extinguished.[21] It also became apparent that deterrence through terror would not work where there was little chance of being detected. Consequently, the criminal justice system became the primary tool for maintaining social order.[22] Indeed, Parliament's first Report on criminal law in 1834 expressed the new-felt chaos of the common law and recognised that a new methodology was required for identifying criminal conduct.[23] It was recognised that an effective institution demanded professional policing[24] with a higher detection rate and a system that was transparent, systematic and humane.[25] This brought changes to the trial procedure and the law of evidence with the origination of the adversarial criminal trial.[26]

At the same time, cognitive and volitional capacity theories were emerging with the growth of the psychological and social science disciplines, and this was

---

20 Martin J Weiner, *Reconstructing the Criminal, Culture: Law and Policy in England 1830–1914* (Cambridge: Cambridge University Press 1990).

21 See too Nicola Lacey, 'In Search of the Responsible Subject: History, Philosophy and Social Sciences in Criminal Law Theory' (2001) 64 MLR 350–71

22 David J Rothman, *The Discovery of the Asylum* (Boston: Little Brown and Co 1971). In order to process the increased numbers of cases, a more expeditious mode of summary trial was introduced with little adversarial lawyerly involvement, little concern for rules of evidence and, of significance, scant concern as to whether the suspect had what we would now call mens rea, see Lindsay Farmer 'The Obsession With Definition: The Nature of Crime and Critical Legal Theory' (1996) S & LS 5, 57; Lindsay Farmer, *Criminal Law, Tradition and Legal Order: Crime and the Genius of Scots Law: 1747 to Present* (Cambridge: Cambridge University Press 1997) Ch. 4.

23 George P Fletcher, *Rethinking Criminal Law* (Boston: Little Brown and Co 1978)

24 Charles Reith, *A Short History of the British Police* (Oxford: Oxford University Press 1948); Les Johnston, *The Rebirth of Private Policing* (London: Routledge 1992), public policing came to dominance from 1880–1950. The formation of new police forces after 1829 signalled a shift from private to public enforcement. See too David Philips 'Good Men to Associate and Bad Men to Conspire: Associations for the Prosecution of Felons in England 1760–1860' in Douglas Hay and Francis G Snyder (eds.), *Policing and Prosecution in Britain 1750-1850* (Oxford: Clarendon Press 1989); Barry Godfrey and Paul Lawrence, *Crime and Justice 1750-1950* (Cullompton: Willan 2005).

25 Robert Reiner, *The Politics of the Police* (3rd ed, Oxford: Oxford University Press 2000). However, it was only when the formal police forces were established in the mid-19th century that the state assumed responsibility as the primary provider of crime control. There is evidence of organised and uniformed private policing from the 16th century when wealthy Londoners paid retainers to watch over their property, see Hilary Draper, *Private Police* (Hassocks: Harvester 1978) and a number of voluntary and subscription forces, see Robert Storch, 'Policing Rural Southern England Before the Police: Opinion and Practice 1830- 56' in Douglas Hay and Francis G Snyder (eds.), *Policing and Prosecution in Britain 1750–1850* (Oxford: Clarendon Press 1989)

26 David J A Cairns, *Advocacy and the Making of the Adversarial Criminal Trial* (Oxford: Clarendon 1998); John H Langbein, *The Origins of Adversary Criminal Trial* (Oxford: Oxford University Press 2003).

conducive to the development of a subjective theory of mens rea.[27] The utilitarian system was thus conceived on the basis of certainty of law and punishment and the underlying ideology that individuals, as rational calculators, would determine that the cost of punishment would outweigh the benefit of crime.[28] Furthermore, the ascription of criminal responsibility to mental states was consistent with both the dualistic philosophy of Descartes and also the idea that the interior world of the human individual could be proved as a matter of fact at trial, on the basis of the evidence of the accused himself.[29] Culpability therefore came to be based on this different form of knowledge which could be found within the mind of the individual.[30] Accordingly, the doctrine of mens rea, in the wide catch-all sense, and the gradual recognition of associated defences,[31]

27 At the same time came the idea that if the function of the criminal law institution was to protect social interests, was futile to wait until harm or damage had occurred. Thus, the 18th Century theorists also emphasised prevention of harm and the first cases recognising a doctrine of attempts emerged later that century. This development was in itself influential in the gradual move from manifest criminality to a pattern of subjective liability. See e.g. W Blackstone, *Commentaries on the Laws of England 1765–69* (Chicago: University of Chicago Press 1979) 4, 251; Douglas Hay, 'Property, Authority and the Criminal Law' in Douglas Hay and others (eds.), *Albion's Fatal Tree, Crime and Society in 18th Century England* (London: Penguin 1975); George P Fletcher, 'The Metamorphosis of Larceny' (Jan 1976) 89 Harv L Rev 3; JKN Smith, *Lawyers, Legislators and Theorists* (Oxford: Oxford University Press 1998); Alan Norrie, *Crime, Reason and History* (2nd ed, London: Butterworths 2001).

28 See Jeremy Bentham, 'An Introduction to the Principles of Morals and Legislation' in John Bowring (ed.), *Collected Works of Jeremy Bentham* (New York: Russell 1962) vol 1; Cesare Becarria, *On Crimes and Punishment* (Indianapolis: Bobs Merrill 1966); Charles de Montesquieu, *The Spirit of the Laws* (London: Forgotten Books 2010) 108–10. In addition, the Victorians used the law to educate the lower orders in standards of behaviour and provide guidance, e.g. contract law was also developed in this period as a means of imposing important rules of behaviour. The utilitarian theories were popularised by for example by Bentham and Beccaria: Jeremy Bentham, 'An Introduction to the Principles of Morals and Legislation' in John Bowring (ed.), *Collected Works of Jeremy Bentham* (New York: Russell 1962) vol 1; Cesare Beccaria, *On Crimes and Punishment* (Indianapolis: Bobs Merrill 1996). Expressed in Bentham's words, "men calculate some with less exactness, indeed some with more: but all men calculate", Jeremy Bentham, *Economic Writings* (For the Royal Economic Society, London: Allen and Unwin 1952–54) III, 434.

29 Nicola Lacey, 'Responsibility and Modernity in Criminal Law' Journal of Political Philosophy (2001) 9, 249–77.

30 Nicola Lacey, 'The Resurgence of Character: Responsibility in the Context of Criminalization' in Duff RA and Stuart P Green (eds.), *Philosophical Foundations of Criminal Law* (Oxford: Oxford University Press 2011).

31 Nicola Lacey, 'The Resurgence of Character: Responsibility in the Context of Criminalization' in Duff RA and Stuart P Green (eds.), *Philosophical Foundations of Criminal Law* (Oxford: Oxford University Press 2011); Lindsay Farmer, *Tradition and Legal Order: Crime and the Genius of the Scots Law: 1747 to Present* (Cambridge: Cambridge University Press 1997); Nicola Lacey, 'Contingency and Conceptualism: Reflections on an Encounter Between Critique and Philosophical Analysis of Criminal Law' in RA Duff (ed.), *Philosophy and Criminal Law; Principle and Critique* (Cambridge University Press 1998); Nicola Lacey, 'Space, Time and Function: Intersecting Principles of Responsibility Across the Terrain of Criminal Justice', (2007) 1 Criminal Law and Philosophy (2007) 233, 235.

met both the contemporary practical challenges and the need to legitimise the basis of criminal culpability.[32]

As the notion of individual responsibility became established, the doctrine of mens rea necessitated enquiry of the defendant's mind and the problem of proof arose. The criminal law responded with the use of the evidential presumption which held that a man must have intended the necessary consequence of his acts. The linking of the observable outcome with the internal mental state was, in practice, well established and longstanding and for example, reference to this approach can be found in the institutional texts as early as the 1700s,[33] although it was not until the enactment of the 1898 Act that a defendant was permitted to give sworn evidence on his own behalf to refute the appearance of blameworthiness.[34] Previously, a defendant had been neither a competent nor a compellable witness at any stage in the proceedings because of the maxim, *nemo tenetur seipsum prodere*, which protected both him and all witnesses from having to answer incriminating questions.[35] However, even after the enactment of

---

32 Zedner suggests that by reference to historical contingency, it can be demonstrated that individualism is "simply an artifice constructed in order to legitimate holding individuals to account" Lucia Zedner, *Criminal Justice* (Oxford: Oxford University Press 2004). Similarly, Lacey opines that the development of ideas of individual responsibility are responses to problems of co-ordination and legitimation of the law, Nicola Lacey, 'In Search of the Responsible Subject: History, Philosophy and Social Sciences in Criminal Law Theory' (2001) 64 MLR 350–71. In the same paper she states that these problems change according to the environment and in the light of political interests, economic power, and, inter alia, the cultural and intellectual environment. Weiner also suggests that the ideology of the responsible individual, exercising free choice, is the central myth of the criminal law institution. The individual, as constructed by the Enlightenment reformers, was an ideal one, Martin J Weiner, *Reconstructing the Criminal: Culture, Law and Policy in England 1830–1914* (Cambridge: Cambridge University Press 1990). Norrie describes, "an abstract juridical individual, existing in a universe of equally responsible individuals, regarded in isolation from the real world and their social and moral contexts", Alan Norrie, *Crime, Reason and History* (2nd ed, London: Butterworths 2001). He suggests that the logic, and arguably the genius, of abstract individualism, introduced in the concept of subjective mens rea, was that it masked the reality that the judges and those seeking the protection of the criminal law were of a different social class from the offenders.

33 E.g. Sir Michael Foster, *Foster's Crown Law* (2nd ed, 1776) 255, "In every charge of murder, the fact of killing being first proved, all the circumstances of accident, necessity, or infirmity are to be satisfactorily proved by the prisoner, unless they arise out of the evidence produced against him; for the law presumeth the fact to have been founded in malice, until the contrary appeareth". See too the expression used in *R v William Farrington* (1811) Russell & Ryan 207; 168 All ER 763.

34 David Bentley, *English Criminal Justice in the Nineteenth Century* (London: Hambledon 1998) referred to by Lindsay Farmer 'Criminal Responsibility In the Proof of Guilt' in Marcus D Dubber and Lindsay Farmer (eds.), *Modern Histories of Crime and Punishment* (Stanford: Stanford University Press 2007) Ch. 2. It is said that one consequence was to facilitate the task of securing conviction on the basis of circumstantial evidence and the defendant would then need to give evidence to try to give an innocent explanation. Criminal Evidence Act 1898, s. 1 also set out what would now be described as bad character provisions.

35 William Feilden Craies & Henry Delacombe Roome, *Archbold's Criminal Pleading, Evidence and Practice* (24th ed, London: Sweet & Maxwell 1910) 457.

the Criminal Evidence Act, the inescapable truth remained, in that although the defendant might give evidence, his mental state was still not directly observable. Turner articulated the problem in this way:

> A great difficulty arises ... We cannot enter a prisoner's mind, and therefore we can only surmise the state of it by inference from his acts, i.e. through his declarations, or other conduct of his own. That is to say, the test of whether a man's state of mind be one of intention, or recklessness ... must necessarily be objective.[36]

Thus, while the separation of the physical and mental enquiry was philosophically appealing to both individualism and Cartesian dualism, which sharply distinguished mind and body, it was still the case that the defendant's state of mind was a matter of manifest assessment.[37] The result of enactment of the Criminal Evidence Act was therefore to add the defendant's demeanour and behaviour at trial to the other available evidence as regards his capacity to commit crime. In this respect, publications such as Gross's Manual on Criminal Psychology tutored legal professionals on topics such as how to interpret mental states from the outward appearances of witnesses and suspects.[38] Notwithstanding the irrevocable changes made to the trial itself, the presumption that the accused must have intended the natural consequences of his act remained central to the process.

The presumption was therefore of fundamental importance in that it provided the crucial bridge between the new subjective conception of mens rea and the old manifest approach which had been premised on the assumption that one would recognise crime when one saw it.[39] The presumption of intention was itself premised on another presumption, namely that the individual was endowed with the mental capacity of a reasonable man. Accordingly, he was taken to have foreseen as a possible consequence anything which, in the ordinary course of events, might result from his act. The inference thus provided the infrastructure for the operation of the presumption of intention and, of itself, clearly resonated

---

36 JWC Turner, 'The Mental Element in Crimes at Common Law', in L Radzinowicz and JWC Turner (eds.), *The Modern Approach to Criminal Law* (2nd ed, London Macmillan 1948) 208.
37 Anthony Duff, *Intention, Agency and Criminal Liability: Philosophy of Action and Criminal Law* (Basil Blackwell 1990) 28.
38 Hans Gross, *Criminal Psychology: A Manual for Judges, Practitioners and Students* (Translated into English in 1911, Boston: Little Brown 1911) referred to by Lindsay Farmer 'Criminal Responsibility In the Proof of Guilt' in Marcus D Dubber and Lindsay Farmer (eds.), *Modern Histories of Crime and Punishment* (Stanford: Stanford University Press 2007) Ch. 2. See also Hugo Munsterberg, *On the Witness Stand: Essays on Psychology and Crime* (New York: Doubleday 1909); George Frederick Arnold, *Psychology Applied to Legal Evidence and other Constructions of Law* (2nd ed, Calcutta: Thacker, Spink 1913).
39 Nicola Lacey, 'Responsibility and Modernity in Criminal Law' (2001) 9 Journal of Political Philosophy (2001) 249–77; Nicola Lacey, 'In Search of the Responsible Subject' (2001) 64 MLR 350–71.

with the assumptions of individualism – namely that the actor was possessed of the capacity for rational calculation. However, while being seen to provide the necessary gateway to the subjective mental state, the use of the presumptions brought implications that were inconsistent with the prevailing theory. Since the defendant was disqualified from giving sworn evidence at his own criminal trial until the end of the 19th century, the reality of the presumption in practice may well have been that it was closer to an irrebuttable, fixed rule of law.[40] Accordingly, the presumption would have blurred the conceptual distinction between subjective and objective principles of mens rea[41] although, in most cases, the individual's foresight would correspond with what was objectively foreseeable such that it could be described as the natural or probable consequence. That being so, it was then presumed that a natural consequence was an intended one and this thought process effectively upgraded instances in which a defendant was objectively reckless to instances of intentionality. Although the distinctions between objective and subjective fault, intention and recklessness, are crucial to the modern construction of criminal liability, earlier notions of responsibility were not so finely delineated.[42] With its status tantamount to a rule of law, it was almost inevitable that continued reliance upon the presumption in this form would pose conceptual problems as the modern distinctions became ever more refined. Indeed, even after the confusion between the substantive and evidential issues had been tackled by the House of Lords in *Woolmington* [1935],[43] a decade later Turner was still observing that:

> once the actus reus is proved ... the accused can only escape if the evidence shows ... that he did not foresee the possibility of harm [which] he will be unable to do ... if the facts show either that he clearly did foresee it or that an ordinary person in the circumstances could not ... fail to foresee it.[44]

Since the main purpose of the criminal law was to protect innocent persons from harm caused by others, their protection was seen to be equally necessary against those who were reckless or indifferent as to the harm they may cause, as against those who intended that harm. Accordingly, the law at this time was not overly

---

40 KJM Smith, *Lawyers, Legislators and Theorists* (Oxford: Oxford University Press 1998) 160. This was seemingly the case in relation to the presumption of voluntariness discussed in Ch. 3.

41 The distinction between intention and subjective recklessness was not significant, see for example the Fourth Report of Her Majesty's Commissioners on Criminal Law 1839 (168) XIX; Nicola Lacey, 'Responsibility and Modernity in Criminal Law' (2001) 9 Journal of Political Philosophy 249–77.

42 Aside from the application of this presumption, the early institutional texts reveal that notions of culpability had often rested on various interpretations of concepts such as "malice" and other heavily moralistic language.

43 *Woolmington v DPP* [1935] AC 462 (HL) and in the light of *Mancini v DPP* [1942] AC 1 (HL). See JW Cecil Turner, *Russell on Crime* (12th ed, London: Stevens & Sons 1964) 34.

44 JWC Turner, 'Mens Rea and Motorists' in L Radzinowicz and JWC Turner (eds.), *The Modern Approach to Criminal Law* (London: Macmillan 1945) 298.

concerned to distinguish between subjective and objective mental states.[45] That being said, the fact that defences gradually developed to rebut the presumption of intention are indicative of the fact that, in most cases, it came to be regarded as a rebuttable evidential inference. Similarly, the 1938 edition of *Archbold's*, having given due consideration to the basic tenets upon which the modern criminal law rested, expressed the position on presumptions generally in the following way:

> Presumptive or (as it is usually termed) circumstantial evidence is receivable in criminal as well as in civil cases; and, indeed, the necessity of admitting such evidence is more obvious in the former than the latter; for, in criminal cases, the possibility of proving the matter charged in the pleading by the direct and positive testimony of eye-witnesses or by conclusive documents is much more rare than in civil cases; and where such testimony is not available the jury are permitted to infer from the facts proved other facts necessary to complete the elements of guilt or establish innocence. It has been said that although presumptive evidence must, from necessity, be admitted, yet it should be admitted cautiously.[46]

More specifically, presumptions of law were categorised as either disputable or conclusive and the most important of the disputable presumptions was the presumption that the accused was innocent, expressed in the maxim *semper praesumitur pro negate*. However, the presumption was said to be easily rebutted by proof of acts tending to show guilt, and, "when these acts are wrongful and not accidental a presumption of malice or criminal intent arises ... the evidence of guilt must not be a mere balance of probabilities, but must satisfy the jury beyond reasonable doubt that the accused is guilty".[47]

However, the formulation of the presumption of intention varied between different authorities[48] and it was not until the 1960's that the last vestige of the objective assessment of mens rea can be found. Indeed, in *DPP v Smith* [1961][49] marks the high water mark when its status was recognised as an irrebuttable presumption of law, encompassing an objective test of mens rea. To quote Viscount Kilmuir L.C.:

> It is immaterial what the accused in fact contemplated as the probable result of his actions, provided he is in law responsible for them in that he is capable of forming an intent, is not insane within the M'Naghten Rules and cannot

---

45 JWC Turner, 'The Mental Element in Crimes at Common Law', in L Radzinowicz and JWC Turner (eds.), *The Modern Approach to Criminal Law* (2nd ed, London: Macmillan 1948) 208, citing e.g. *R v Welch* (1875) 1 QBD 23.

46 Robert Ernest Ross and Maxwell Turner, *Archbold's Criminal Pleading, Evidence and Practice* (London: Sweet & Maxwell 1938) 404.

47 Ibid 408–9.

48 See for example *R v Philpot* (1912) 7 Cr App R 140 (CCA); *Stoddart* (1909) 2 Cr App R 217, 233.

49 *DPP v Smith* [1961] AC 290 (HL).

establish diminished responsibility. On that assumption, the sole question is whether the unlawful and voluntary act was of such a kind that grievous bodily harm was the natural and probable result, and the only test of this is what the ordinary responsible man would, in all the circumstances of the case, have contemplated as the natural and probable result.[50]

However, given the gravity of the offence under consideration, namely murder, the *Smith* judgment attracted considerable criticism, which sparked a renewed interest in the nature of the presumption. Glanville Williams, for example, described it as the expression of a psychological theory. He said that since it is impossible to delve into a man's mind, he must be judged on his outward acts although, in addition to the supposed uniformity of human nature, there were also confessions, denials, demeanour in the witness box and circumstantial evidence that could be taken into account.[51] Turner, in the 1966 edition of *Kenny's Outlines*, also continued to recognise it as an evidential presumption, "rebuttable" by the accused through the raising of reasonable doubt, "on the balance of probabilities".[52] Similarly, he approved Denning L.J.'s dicta in *Hosegood* (1950)[53] in which he had stated that:

The presumption of intention is not a proposition of law but a proposition of ordinary good sense. It means this: that a man is usually able to foresee what are the natural consequences of his acts, so it is, as a rule, reasonable to infer that he did foresee them and intend them. But, while that is an inference which may be drawn, it is not one that must be drawn. If on all of the facts of the case it is not the correct inference, then it should not be drawn.[54]

4.2 Virtual certainty and the silencing of the presumption

In the event, *DPP v Smith*[55] had raised sufficient uncertainty that Parliament felt obliged to enact s. 8 of the Criminal Justice Act 1967 to provide clarification. The provision finally put the status of the presumption beyond doubt and placed the common law factual presumption on a statutory basis, such that:

50 *DPP v Smith* [1961] AC 290 (HL) 327.
51 Glanville Williams, *Criminal Law, The General Part* (London: Stevens & Sons 1961) 89 commented that if the presumption was accepted it would destroy the subjective definition of intention and efface the line between intention and negligence.
52 JW Cecil Turner, *Kenny's Outlines of Criminal Law* (19th ed, Cambridge: Cambridge University Press 1966) 39.
53 *Hosegood v Hosegood* (1950) 66 TLR 735.
54 JWC Turner, *Kenny's Outlines of Criminal Law* (19th ed, Cambridge: Cambridge University Press 1966).
55 *DPP v Smith* [1961] AC 290 (HL) and see Richard Buxton, 'The Retreat from Smith' (1966) Crim LR 196.

A court or jury, in determining whether a person has committed an offence, (a) shall not be bound in law to infer that he intended or foresaw a result of his actions by reason only of its being a natural and probable consequence of those actions; but (b) shall decide whether he did intend or foresee that result by reference to all the evidence, drawing such inferences from the evidence as appear proper in the circumstances.

While confirming that the presumption did not constitute a legal rule or import an objective standard of fault, s. 8 acknowledges that a person may be presumed to have intended or foreseen the natural and probable consequence of his act, but that the presumption may be refuted by other evidence raising contrary inferences. However, although the provision has remained unchanged, a string of high-profile appeals against murder convictions[56] went on to provide the test bed for a refined understanding of how evidence of intention may be found.[57] After successive definitions emanating from successive cases over successive decades, the position was finally settled in *Woollin* [1999] and expressed in this way:

In the rare cases where the direction that it is for the jury simply to decide whether the defendant intended to kill or to do serious bodily harm is not enough, the jury should be directed that they are not entitled to find the necessary intention, unless they feel sure that death or serious bodily harm was a virtual certainty (barring some unforeseen intervention) as a result of the defendant's actions and that the defendant appreciated that such was the case.[58]

Thus, although s. 8 puts the common law presumption of fact on a statutory basis and continues to refer to inferences of intention and foresight that may be drawn by reference to the terminology of "natural and probable consequences",[59] the now infamous jury direction in *Woollin* emphasises subjective foresight amounting to the vastly higher standard of "virtual certainty" if a finding of intention is to be made.[60] The relevant authorities, as are typically rehearsed in academic texts dealing with intention, now tend to omit or overshadow the statutory articulation contained in s. 8 and the language of natural and probable results appears long since rejected. Thus, in

---

56 See *Hyam v DPP* [1975] AC 55 (HL); *R v Moloney* [1985] AC 905 (HL); *R v Hancock and Shankland* [1986] AC 455(HL); *R v Nedrick* [1986] 1 WLR 1025 (CA); *R v Woollin* [1999] 1 AC 82 (HL).

57 *R v Woollin* [1999] 1 AC 82 (HL) and see *R v Matthews and Alleyne* [2003] EWCA Crim 192, 2 Cr App R 30.

58 *R v Woollin* [1999] 1 AC 82 (HL) (Lord Steyn).

59 Reversing the decision that had elevated its status in *DPP v Smith [1961] AC 290.*

60 David Ormerod, *Blackstone's Criminal Practice* (Oxford: Oxford University Press 2015) sets out the presumption at F3.63 whilst directing the reader to section A2.4 as regards jury directions on intention.

Hyam v DPP [1975], Lord Diplock endorsed the view that an actor intended a result if, although it was not his purpose, he knew that it was a highly probable, or perhaps a merely probable, result.[61] Whereas this was sufficient mens rea for murder at that time, in the following decade the link between probability, foresight and intention was refined and given a more nuanced explanation.[62] However, the current law, deriving from *Nedrick* [1986][63] and *Woollin* [1999][64] articulates the finding of intention exclusively by reference to virtual certainty and the language of natural and probable consequences is absent.[65]

Similarly, contemporary academic texts explain intention by reference to an actor's purpose or desire and, where this is denied, by reference to indirect or "oblique" intention in which a discussion of the test of "virtual certainty" typically takes centre stage.[66] As far as the legal landscape is concerned, the evidential presumption that a man intends the natural consequences of his act has been effectively silenced by the academic thrall surrounding the notion of virtual certainty as the level of foresight required to find intention.

It is disconcerting that s. 8 Criminal Justice Act and case law are apparently at odds. Of note, Lord Steyn in *Woollin* explicitly referred to s. 8 in his judgment and he dealt with it in this way. In his opinion, s. 8(a), the subsection which includes the phraseology of natural and probable consequences, is simply an instruction to the trial judge. In contrast, it is subsection 8(b) that sets out the legislative instruction to the jury, namely that they must take account of all relevant evidence. That being so, the case law, and in particular *Nedrick*, did "not prevent a jury from considering all the evidence: it merely stated what state of mind (in the absence of a purpose to kill or to cause serious harm) is sufficient for murder."[67] Lord Steyn's interpretation of the applicability of the relevant subsections is, however, to be doubted. Read in its entirety, "a court or jury" is to have regard of both subsections, (a) and (b), and the intention of the Law Commission, the architect of s. 8, was simply to require that intention and

61 *Hyam v DPP* [1975] AC 55 (HL).
62 For example, *R v Hancock and Shankland* [1986] AC 455 (HL), 473, "the greater the probability of a consequence the more likely it is that the consequence was foreseen and ... if that consequence was foreseen the greater the probability is that the consequence was also intended", (Lord Scarman).
63 *R v Nedrick* [1986] 1 WLR 1025 (CA).
64 *R v Woollin* [1999] 1 AC 82 (HL).
65 Although the test bed for a "definition" of intention is confined to cases dealing with murder allegations, it is thought that the means to find intention should be consistent across the criminal law, see David Ormerod and Anthony Hooper, *Blackstone's Criminal Practice* (Oxford: Oxford University Press 2014) A2. 4.
66 E.g. David Ormerod, *Smith and Hogan's Criminal Law* (13th ed, Oxford: Oxford University Press 2011) 106ff.
67 *R v Woollin* [1999] 1 AC 82 (HL) 93 (Lord Steyn) quoting *R v Nedrick* [1986] 1 WLR 1025 (CA) 1028 (Lord Lane C.J.).

foresight were subjectively proved.[68] However, the message emanating from Lord Steyn's dicta is that a jury is not to be directed in terms of foresight of natural and probable consequences and, as far the jury are concerned, the finding of intention rests on foresight that the result was a virtually certain one. This silencing of the language of natural and probable consequences is not confined to the judicial discourse and it is clear that the presumption of intention of natural and probable consequences is disappearing from the criminal law narrative generally. It is of note that academic texts, which inevitably focus on intention in the context of the murder offence, also tend to omit this articulation in favour of a detailed exposition of the test of virtual certainty where intention may be indirect.[69]

As was the case with the demise of the voluntariness doctrine, the linguistic and resulting conceptual shift away from "natural and probable consequences" to the paradigm of "virtual certainty" has had far-reaching implications. At one level, the extent of subjective foresight required has been elevated such that the outcome has gone from a probable one to a point of near certainty, at least in the context of murder. In this respect, given the gravity of the offence, the "higher" test of fault is salutary. However, by rejecting the language of natural consequences, together with the objective stance it was erroneously taken to import, it is submitted that the metaphorical baby was, yet again, thrown out with the bathwater. Whereas the presumption of voluntariness became subsumed within the general doctrine of mens rea, effectively displacing the first fault presumption, the notion of virtual certainty effectively swamped its sister, the presumption of intention. Where a man was once presumed to have intended the natural and probable result of his act, subject to his evidence in denial, the onus has subtly shifted onto the prosecution to positively prove the defendant's state of mind. Again, the practical and theoretical implication is to divert the primary focus from the appearance of the act to the internal mental state. As has been observed in the context of voluntariness, it is this reconception that has proved particularly problematic in the case of corporate wrongdoing.

4.3 Intention, dishonesty and the corporate actor

While reference to the presumption that a person intends the natural and probable consequences of his act has largely slipped from the legal narrative, both case law and academic texts, its demise is not yet final. Indeed, in contrast to the academic and judicial preoccupation with the subjective test of "virtual certainty" of foresight, it is of note that passing, but explicit, reference was made

---

68 JC Smith and Brian Hogan, *Criminal Law: Cases and Materials* (3rd ed, London: Butterworths 1986) 43.
69 For example, David Ormerod and Karl Laird, *Smith and Hogan's Text, Cases and Materials on Criminal Law* (11th ed, Oxford: Oxford University Press 2014) 98.

to the orthodox presumption in the Criminal Justice and Courts Act 2015[70] and Blackstone's Criminal Practice continues to recognise the presumption of intention in its original form.[71] As is expected of a practitioner text, it provides a detailed exposition as regards all of the potential evidential inferences that may be drawn in the trial process. Unsurprisingly, the offence of murder provides the context of the rehearsal, with reference to the controversial decision in *Smith* [1961][72] and the corrective provisions of s. 8 Criminal Justice Act 1967.[73] Although, on its face, s. 8 does not appear to be confined to evidence of a murderous intent, Blackstone interprets the effects of *Moloney*,[74] *Nedrick*[75] and *Woollin*,[76] cases on this area of law, on the statutory provision. It proceeds on the basis that where death or grievous bodily harm is the natural and probable result of an act, the logical processes available to the jury appear to be threefold.[77] First, the jury may infer that death or grievous bodily harm was intended. Second, they may infer that such an outcome was foreseen and, from this, they may then infer that the death or grievous bodily harm was intended. Finally, a jury might decide not to draw either of the above inferences. However, while s. 8 addresses the concepts of intention and foresight together and their relationship with natural consequences, it is of note that the practitioner text separates the concepts. Accordingly, it provides an explanation of the difference between the first two propositions such that, in the first instance, the inference of intention is made directly and, while needing to consider all the evidence, this can be by reference to the natural and probable consequences of the act. It is only in the second case that the inference of intention is made indirectly via foresight of a virtually certain outcome. The first process applies where the jury conclude from all the evidence that the accused intended the result in the sense that he desired it, the second where they may conclude that the accused intended the result, even though he did not desire it.

The requirement of a higher standard of foresight for a finding of murderous intent is doubtless a laudable development in the common law. However, it is regrettable that it has consequently put a seemingly complex spin on a

70 Criminal Justice and Courts Act 2015, s. 33(8). This section relates to the new offence of disclosing private sexual photographs and films with intent to cause distress and this subsection states that a person is not to be taken to have such an intent merely because that was a natural and probable consequence of the disclosure.

71 David Ormerod and Anthony Hooper, *Blackstone's Criminal Practice* (Oxford: Oxford University Press 2014).

72 *DPP v Smith* [1961] AC 290 (HL).

73 David Ormerod and Anthony Hooper, *Blackstone's Criminal Practice* (Oxford: Oxford University Press 2014) F3.63 in which s.8 is quoted with the observation that this section placed the presumption of intention on a statutory footing.

74 *R v Moloney* [1985] AC 905 (HL).

75 *R v Nedrick* [1986] 1 WLR 1025 (CA).

76 *R v Woollin* [1999] 1 AC 82 (HL).

77 David Ormerod and Anthony Hooper, *Blackstone's Criminal Practice* (Oxford: Oxford University Press 2014) B1.13.

plainly-drafted statutory provision of general application.[78] What a jury may take as evidence of desire is a matter of conjecture, the difference between direct and oblique (indirect) intention not necessarily that great, and the choice of evidential principle applied might well turn on the finest of distinctions.

However, since the "virtual certainty" direction as regards foresight is only given in the rarest case, what can be said with confidence is that in the vast majority of trials the orthodox presumption of intention, as expressed at s. 8, is applicable.[79] That almost the entirety of the academic discourse on intention goes to foresight of virtually certain consequences is, therefore, inversely proportionate to its application in practice. Furthermore, although the evidential presumption of intention is applicable in almost all cases, it fails to attract explicit judicial reference since the question of intention is usually left to the jury without any further elaboration.[80] Accordingly, the presumption of intention, and that an inference can be drawn from the natural and probable consequences of an act, is unlikely ever to be articulated in plain terms.[81] The absence of any judicial articulation of the presumption is a fact supported by reference to the judicial *Compendium* on jury directions. Although mentioning s. 8 and the relationship between intention and natural and probable consequences, the specimen directions confirm that elaboration of the meaning of intention will be required only in an exceptional case.[82] Thus, while the academic narrative lacks reference to the evidential presumption, explicit reference to it is also rare in practice and this status quo has an apparently self-perpetuating quality. However, whatever the collective academic and judicial voices imply,[83] the judicial and

---

78 According to Lord Steyn in *R v Woollin* [1999] 1 AC 82 (HL), 96 "it does not follow that 'intent' necessarily has precisely the same meaning in every context in the criminal law". It remains possible, therefore, that lower levels of foresight could still be a sufficient basis for a legitimate inference in relation to other offences requiring intention.

79 I.e. those not turning on the finding of an oblique intent. The Judicial College, The Crown Court Compendium, Feb 2017 – compiled by Maddison, Ormerod, Tonking and Wait – states that the direction on virtual certainty will be given "only in an exceptional case ... where D denies his purpose", at 8.4 and quoting *Allen* [2005] EWCA CRIM 1344. See also David Ormerod and Anthony Hooper, *Blackstone's Criminal Practice* (Oxford: Oxford University Press 2014) B.13; Andrew Ashworth and Jeremy Horder, *Principles of Criminal Law* (7th ed, Oxford: Oxford University Press 2013) 172.

80 David Ormerod and Anthony Hooper, *Blackstone's Criminal Practice* (Oxford: Oxford University Press 2014) A.2.

81 David Ormerod and Anthony Hooper, *Blackstone's Criminal Practice* (Oxford: Oxford University Press 2014) A.2.

82 Judicial College, The Crown Court Compendium, Feb 2017 – compiled by Maddison, Ormerod, Tonking and Wait.

83 Lacey, for example, refers to the presumption in the past tense opining that it is surprising that the presumption operated well into the 20th century, notwithstanding it remained founded on an objective approach to culpabilty. She asserts that it is a modified version of Fletcher's manifest liability model, Nicola Lacey 'In Search of the Responsible Subject: History, Philosophy and Social Sciences in Criminal Law Theory' (2001) 64 MLR 350–71 referring to George

practitioner materials at least demonstrate that the presumption of intention is alive and is still a fundamental evidential factor, albeit enjoying a somewhat tacit existence.[84]

The fact that the observable consequences of an act may be taken as indicative of intention has important application for a theory of corporate criminality. In the context of fraud particularly, the offence requires that the conduct is accompanied by a specific intention to make a gain or to cause a loss to another or expose another to a risk of loss.[85] Accordingly, it is submitted that in cases where, having considered all the evidence, the requisite intention can be presumed by reference to the consequences of the corporate conduct, the need to attribute fault via the fictional "identification" mechanism is obviated. The presumption effectively averts the primary enquiry to the visible consequences of the act and away from metaphysical mental states, while affording the defendant organisation the opportunity to challenge the inference. Arguably this "common sense" approach, considered so obvious that it requires no elaboration, is intrinsic to jury deliberations. Accordingly, practice and theory appear to have fallen out of step; while practice has quietly tended to a manifest assessment of fault, by reference to the appearance of the conduct, the highly-vocalised doctrine of subjective mens rea has been the predominant ideology and focus of attention.

Having concluded that the manifest assessment of conduct more closely reflects the reality of fault attribution at trial, the extent to which the doctrine of mens rea truly departs from this approach must be considered. Arguably, this question is at the heart of this book and it raises the perennial problem: how to determine the internal mental state of a defendant? While *Smith* erroneously upgraded the evidential presumption to a rule of law,[86] effectively importing an objective test of intention, s. 8 affirmed the subjective nature of intention as the determinant of criminal fault.[87] That being said, if a defendant does not give evidence in his own trial, the objective test facilitated by the presumption is the only one available.[88] Otherwise, in cases where the accused does testify, the assessment of his subjective state must be

P Fletcher, 'The Metamorphosis of Larceny' (Jan 1976) 89 Harv L Rev 3; George P Fletcher, *Rethinking Criminal Law* (Boston: Little Brown and Co 1978).

84 For example, David Ormerod and Anthony Hooper, *Blackstone's Criminal Practice* (Oxford: Oxford University Press 2014) F3.63; Judicial College, The Crown Court Compendium, Feb 2017 – compiled by Maddison, Ormerod, Tonking and Wait.

85 Fraud Act 2006, ss. 2(1)(b)(i) and (ii); 3(b)(i) and (ii) and 4(1)(c)(i) and (ii).

86 *DPP v Smith* [1961] AC 290 (HL).

87 Criminal Justice Act 1967.

88 Richard Buxton, 'The Retreat From Smith' (1966) Crim LR 196. Blackstone's confirms that in the absence of an explanation, a jury will doubtless infer that a defendant intended the natural and probable result of his action and that, as a purely factual inference, this is unexceptional. Apart from admissions made, this is the most obvious way to ascertain the defendant's state of mind. David Ormerod and Anthony Hooper, *Blackstone's Criminal Practice* (Oxford: Oxford University Press 2014) A2.34.

effected objectively, or manifestly, since external evidence is the only available evidence.[89] Accordingly, although foresight and intention have, as legal concepts, attracted considerable debate and increasingly refined definitions in cases where the defendant denies desire, the requisite mental state must still be determined as a matter of fact.[90]

Considered in this light, it would appear that the shift from the objective assessment of fault to the subjective approach amounted to little more in substance than the procedural change, brought about by the Criminal Evidence Act 1898, and the opportunity it provided for a defendant to give evidence in his own trial. Before its enactment, the presumption of intention of natural consequences was needed to operate as an objective assessment of fault but, with the passing of the act, the defendant could now testify as regards his subjective state of mind. However, the distinction between the objective test of fault and the objective or manifest assessment of conduct is paramount. As a matter of practice, it is clear that juries still infer intention, in the sense of desire, on the common sense basis that the outcome was the natural and probable consequence of the act in question. The presumption of intention, considered with all of the other evidence, means that a jury may make the inference on the basis of everything relevant that they have observed. Since the totality of the evidence includes that of the defendant himself, the presumption is naturally rebuttable. Accordingly, the theoretical weight placed on the mens rea doctrine is an apparently artificial construct, the inescapable fact being that whatever the subjective mental state, its determination can only be made objectively. It is thus submitted that the shift from the examination of the overt and physical to the consideration of the internal and metaphysical amounts to an ideological sleight of hand, altering nothing more than mere perception. The prominence given to the expanded doctrine of mens rea in the criminal narrative therefore effectively masks the continued existence of the evidential presumptions of fault which continue, albeit tacitly, to provide the structural basis for the determination of liability.

A corrective refocusing, and restatement, of the orthodox presumptions of fault would realign theory with the evidential practicalities of both prosecution and defence. Furthermore, an acknowledged return to such an approach generally would accommodate the prosecution of the corporate entity and would do so with no effect, detrimental or otherwise, to the position of individual defendants. As far as corporate culpability is concerned, the

89 As regards this indirect knowledge of the internal state, Bentham, for example, said that the factors which should be considered are the act itself; the accompanying circumstances; the intention of the perpetrator; his degree of understanding or perceptive faculties which are to be inferred from the nature of the act or from circumstances peculiar to it; the particular motive or motives at its root and the general disposition of which it is indicative, JW Cecil Turner, *Kenny's Outlines of Criminal Law* (19th ed, Cambridge: Cambridge University Press 1966) 32 citing Jeremy Bentham's, *Principles of Morals and Legislation*.

90 In this respect a man's thoughts are said to be "as much facts as are his bodily movements", JW Cecil Turner, *Russell On Crime* (12th ed, London: Stevens & Sons 1964) 23.

absence of a metaphysical "mind" would not be fatal to the finding of criminal fault, nor would it involve the necessary inculpation of an associated individual. The explicit employment of the evidential presumptions would simply acknowledge the continuing need to infer fault through the observance of the manifest. In appropriate circumstances, the observable conduct of the defendant organisation would move directly into the focal point of relevant enquiry and relatively inconsequential issues, such as those relating to the management structure, seniority and individual responsibility or culpability of its individual officers, would cease to serve as distractions from the real issues.

The practicability of this approach to the specific problem of corporate fraud is readily demonstrable. The generic fraud offence can be perpetrated through the dishonest making of a false representation,[91] failure to disclose information[92] or abuse of a position[93] intending, by so doing, to make a gain for himself or another, or to cause loss to another or to expose another to a risk of loss.[94] Taking by way of example the widespread practice of mis-selling of personal protection insurance alongside other financial products, assuming that this conduct might be considered dishonest, the current approach turns on the successful application of the identification principle. This means that a corporation can only be convicted of fraud if a sufficiently senior director was personally guilty of the same offence such that his culpable state of mind can be considered that of the company. In this context, given the distance between the personnel at top level management and those who carry out the day to day corporate functions, and for various other reasons, a corporate conviction on this basis could be difficult to sustain. However, leaving aside the issue of establishing dishonesty for the moment, by applying the evidential presumption of intention, a corporate intention might be readily ascertained by the inference that the organisation intended to make a gain, through such sales activity, since this is the natural and probable result of such activity. It is clear that both the presumption of voluntariness and the presumption of intention can serve equally in the context of corporate action as in that of individual action. Furthermore, the defendant organisation is as capable as the accused individual of calling witnesses to refute either or both presumptions in its defence.

While it is clear that organisational capacity and intention may be attributed by application of the orthodox evidential presumptions, the generic fraud offence also requires proof of dishonesty. As regards fraudulent intent, in the context of obtaining by false pretences,[95] the 1938 edition of *Archbold's* stated that where

---

91 Fraud Act 2006, s. 2(1)(a).
92 Ibid s. 3(a).
93 Ibid s. 4(1)(a).
94 Ibid s. 2(1)(b)(i) and (ii); s. 3(b)(i) and (ii); s. 4(1)(c)(i) and (ii).
95 E.g. at Larceny Act 1916, s. 32(1).

money was obtained by pretences that were false, there was a prima facie intent to defraud.[96] Similarly, the use of false statements or documents to obtain money amounted to evidence from which an intent to defraud could be inferred, even if the money might have been obtained without them.[97] At this time there was also, of course, explicit recognition that "prima facie everyone must be taken to intend the consequences of his acts".[98] Of note, contemporary analysis evidences a continued reliance on the inferential approach to fraudulent intents. For example, as regards the fraudulent trading offence:

> Whether there has been intent to defraud is a question of fact to be determined in every case and a person's intent usually has to be inferred from what the person did. The courts have said that there is some behaviour will usually give rise to an inference that there has been an intent to defraud.[99]

The Fraud Act 2006 is somewhat different in that it does not articulate liability in terms of fraudulent intent, employing instead the concept of "dishonesty" that was introduced in the deception offences contained in the Theft Act 1968. These provisions replaced the offence of obtaining by false pretences which was set out in the Larceny Act 1916 and, of note, the Court of Appeal, in *R v Wright* [1960],[100] affirmed that an intent to defraud was synonymous with dishonesty. Final clarification to that effect was later provided in the Court of Appeal case of *Ghosh* [1982][101] which set out both objective

---

96 RE Ross and MJH Turner, *Archbold's Criminal Pleading: Evidence and Practice* (London: Sweet & Maxwell 1938) 724 citing *R v Hammerson* (1914) 10 Cr App R 121 (CCA). This comment was made as regards Larceny Act 1916, s. 32(1) which was the statutory forerunner of the 1968 and 1978 Theft Act deception offences. These were then replaced by the generic offence contained in the Fraud Act 2006.

97 *R v Hopley* (1916) 11 Cr App R 248 (CCA).

98 Robert Ernest Ross and Maxwell Turner, *Archbold's Criminal Pleading: Evidence and Practice* (London: Sweet & Maxwell 1938) 725 citing *R v Williams* (1836) 7 C & P 354.

99 Stephen Mayson and others, *Company Law* (27th ed, Oxford: Oxford University Press 2010–11) 693.

100 *R v Wright* [1960] Crim LR 366 and see JWC Turner, *Kenny's Outlines of Criminal Law* (19th ed, Cambridge: Cambridge University Press 1966) 365.

101 *R v Ghosh* [1982] QB 1053 (CCA), 2 All ER 689, 692. Lord Lane observed that in *Scott v Comr of Police for the Metropolis* [1975] AC 819 (HL) Viscount Dilhorne traced the meaning of the words "fraud", "fraudulently" and "defraud" in relation to simple larceny, as well as the common law offence of conspiracy to defraud. After referring to *Stephen's History of the Criminal Law of England* (London: Macmillan 1883) vol 2, 121–2 and *East's Pleas of the Crown* (1803) vol 2, 553 he continued as follows at [1975] AC 819, 836–7: "The Criminal Law Revision Committee in their eighth report on 'Theft and Related Offences' (Cmnd 2977 (1966)) in para 33 expressed the view that the important element of larceny, embezzlement and fraudulent conversion was 'undoubtedly the dishonest appropriation of another person's property'; in para 35 that the words 'dishonestly appropriates' meant the same as 'fraudulently converts to his own use or benefit, or the use or benefit of any other person', and in para 39 that 'dishonestly' seemed to them a better word than 'fraudulently'. Parliament endorsed these views in the Theft Act 1968".

and subjective elements that are required to establish dishonesty. In cases where a jury direction is necessary, Lord Lane held that the first question is:

> whether according to the ordinary standards of reasonable and honest people what was done was dishonest. If it was not dishonest by those standards, that is the end of the matter and the prosecution fails. If (but only if) D's conduct was dishonest by those standards, the jury must consider the second question, namely: ... whether the defendant himself must have realised that what he was doing was [by the standards of reasonable and honest people] dishonest.[102]

However, although the second question constitutes the subjective element, the Court of Appeal provided further elucidation when it said, "In most cases, where the actions are obviously dishonest by ordinary standards, there will be no doubt about it. It will be obvious that the defendant himself knew that he was acting dishonestly".[103] Accordingly, in the majority of cases dishonesty is so obvious (or manifest)[104] that the *Ghosh* direction is not required and it is not given.[105] The wording of the Fraud Act 2006 encourages focus on the honesty or dishonesty of the defendant's methods, rather than that of his ulterior purpose[106] and dishonesty may, for example, be presumed from the conduct such that the making of the false representation is itself evidence of dishonesty. Similarly, this approach accords with the view that where there has been "an apparent abuse of position ... there is likely to be a whiff of dishonesty in most cases".[107] Furthermore, if dishonesty is synonymous with intent to defraud and the latter notion was subject to the evidential presumption of intention, proof of dishonesty is also the appropriate subject of such an approach. Indeed, this accords with the Supreme Court's judgment in *Ivey v Genting* [2017] which strongly disapproves the second limb of Ghosh and advocates the criminal law's adoption of the civil, objective, test for dishonesty.[108] That test looks at the individual's knowledge or belief as to the facts and whether the conduct was honest or dishonest is determined by applying the objective standards of ordinary decent people.[109]

---

102 *R v Ghosh* [1982] QB 1053 (CCA), 2 All ER 689, 692.
103 *R v Ghosh* [1982] QB 1053 (CCA), 2 All ER 689, 692 (L. Lane).
104 See also Dennis J Baker, *Glanville Williams' Textbook of Criminal Law* (3rd ed, London: Sweet & Maxwell 2012) 1190.
105 David Ormerod and Anthony Hooper, *Blackstone's Criminal Practice* (Oxford: Oxford University Press 2014) B4.55.
106 David Perry and David Ormerod, *Blackstone's Criminal Practice* (Oxford: Oxford University Press 2017) B5.9.
107 Andrew Ashworth and Jeremy Horder, *Principles of Criminal Law* (7th ed, Oxford: Oxford University Press 2013).
108 *Ivey v Genting Casinos (UK) Ltd t/a Crockfords* [2017] UKSC 67.
109 *Royal Airlines Sdn Bhd v Tan* [1995] 2 AC 378 per L. Nicholls.

It is submitted that findings of organisational voluntariness and intention can be facilitated via the mechanism of the evidential presumptions and the manifest assessment of conduct. Further, a finding of corporate dishonesty can be inferred in the same way. As with the presumptive approach to voluntariness and intention, where the conduct in question is manifestly dishonest such that the inference could be drawn, it would be open to a defendant organisation to bring evidence to refute that appearance. It can be concluded that as between the external act and the requisite mental state, albeit framed in subjectivist terms, the essential bridge continues to be made by the evidential, behavioural presumptions based on the objective perception of manifest appearance.[110] A renewed commitment to the presumptive approach to evidence would facilitate corporate convictions for fraud where there is an appearance of misconduct of a dishonest nature.

Bibliography

Books

Arnold GF, *Psychology Applied to Legal Evidence and other Constructions of Law* (2nd ed, Calcutta: Thacker, Spink 1913)

Ashworth A and Horder J, *Principles of Criminal Law* (7th ed, Oxford: Oxford University Press 2013)

Bailey V (ed.), *Policing and Punishment in 19th Century Britain* (London: Croom Helm 1981)

Baker DJ, *Glanville Williams' Textbook of Criminal Law* (3rd ed, London: Sweet & Maxwell 2012)

Beccaria C, *On Crimes and Punishments* (Indianapolis: Bobs Merrill 1966)

Bentham J, *Economic Writings* (For the Royal Economic Society, London: Allen and Unwin 1952–54)

Bentham J, *Theory of Legislation* (New York: Oceana 1975)

Bentley D, *English Criminal Justice in the Nineteenth Century* (London: Hambledon 1998)

Berman HJ, *Law and Revolution: The Formation of the Western Legal Tradition* (Cambridge, Massachusetts: Harvard University Press 1983)

Blackstone W, *Commentaries on the Laws of England 1765–69* (Chicago: University of Chicago Press 1979)

Bowring J (ed.), *Collected Works of Jeremy Bentham* (New York: Russell 1962)

Cairns DJA, *Advocacy and the Making of the Adversarial Criminal Trial* (Oxford: Clarendon 1998)

Cohen S and Scull A (eds.), *Social Control and the State: Historical and Comparative Essays* (Oxford: Basil Blackwell 1983)

---

110 Indeed, a revival of interest in the idea that criminal responsibility is and should be founded on an evaluative assessment of moral character, displayed in putatively criminal conduct, has been identified by Nicola Lacey, 'Character, Capacity, Outcome' in Marcus Dubber and Lindsay Farmer (eds.), *Modern Histories of Crime and Punishment* (Stanford: Stanford University Press 2007).

Cornish WR and Clark G, *Law and Society in England 1750–1950* (London: Sweet & Maxwell 1989)

Corrigan P and Sayer D, *The Great Arch: State Formation, Cultural Revolution and the Rise of Capitalism* (Oxford: Blackwell 1985)

Craies WF and Roome HD, *Archbold's Criminal Pleading, Evidence and Practice* (24th ed, London: Sweet & Maxwell 1910)

Draper H, *Private Police* (Hassocks: Harvester 1978)

Dubber MD and Farmer L (eds.), *Modern Histories of Crime and Punishment* (Stanford: Stanford University Press 2007)

Dubber MD and Farmer L, *New Trends In the History of Criminal Law* (Stanford: Stanford University Press 2007)

Duff RA, *Intention, Agency and Criminal Liability: Philosophy of Action and Criminal Law* (Oxford: Basil Blackwell 1990)

Duff RA (ed.), *Philosophy and Criminal Law; Principle and Critique* (Cambridge: Cambridge University Press 1998)

Duff RA and Green SP (eds.), *Philosophical Foundations of Criminal Law* (Oxford: Oxford University Press 2011)

Farmer L, *Criminal Law, Tradition and Legal Order: Crime and the Genius of Scots Law: 1747 to Present* (Cambridge: Cambridge University Press 1997)

Fletcher GP, *Basic Concepts of Criminal Law* (Oxford: Oxford University Press 1998)

Fletcher GP, *Rethinking Criminal Law* (Boston: Little Brown and Co 1978)

Foster M, *Foster's Crown* Law (2nd ed, 1776)

Friedman and Fisher (eds.), *The Crime Conundrum: Essays on Criminal Justice* (New York: Westview Press 1997)

Foucault M, *Discipline and Punish: The Birth of A Prison* (London: Penguin 1977)

Gattrell VAC and others (eds.), *Crime and the Law: The Social History of Crime in Western Europe Since 1500* (London: Europa 1980)

Godfrey B and Lawrence P, *Crime and Justice 1750–1950* (Cullompton: Willan 2005)

Gross H, *Criminal Psychology: A Manual for Judges, Practitioners and Students* (Translated into English in 1911, Boston: Little Brown 1911)

Hay D and Snyder FG (eds.), *Policing and Prosecution in Britain 1750–1850* (Oxford: Clarendon 1989)

Hay D and others (eds.), *Albion's Fatal Tree, Crime and Society in 18th Century England* (London: Penguin 1975)

Heath J, *18th Century Penal Theory* (Oxford: Oxford University Press 1963)

Johnstone G and Ward A, *Key Approaches to Criminology: Law and Crime* (London: Sage 2010)

Johnston L, *The Rebirth of Private Policing* (London: Routledge 1992)

Judicial College, *The Crown Court Compendium* (Feb 2017) compiled by Maddison, Ormerod, Tonking and Wait

Langbein JH, *The Origins of Adversary Criminal Trial* (Oxford: Oxford University Press 2003)

MacPherson CB, *The Political Theory of Possessive Individualism* (Oxford: Oxford University Press 1962)

Mayson S and others, *Company Law* (27th ed, Oxford: Oxford University Press 2010–11)

Montesquieu C D, *The Spirit of the Laws* (London: Forgotten Books 2010)

Munsterberg M, *On the Witness Stand: Essays on Psychology and Crime* (New York: Doubleday 1909)

Norrie A, *Crime, Reason and History* (2nd ed, London: Butterworths 2001)

Ormerod D, *Blackstone's Criminal Practice* (Oxford: Oxford University Press 2015)

Ormerod D, *Smith and Hogan's Criminal Law* (13th ed, Oxford: Oxford University Press 2011)

Ormerod D and Hooper A, *Blackstone's Criminal Practice* (Oxford: Oxford University Press 2014)

Ormerod D and Laird K, *Smith and Hogan's Text, Cases and Materials on Criminal Law* (11th ed, Oxford: Oxford University Press 2014)

Perkin H, *The Origins of Modern English Society 1780–1880* (London: Routledge 1969)

Perry D and Ormerod D, *Blackstone's Criminal Practice* (Oxford: Oxford University Press 2017)

Radzinowicz L, *The History of the English Criminal Law* (London: Stevens 1948)

Radzinowicz L and Turner JWC (eds.), *The Modern Approach to Criminal Law* (London: Macmillan 1945)

Radzinowicz L and Turner JWC (eds.), *The Modern Approach to Criminal Law* (2nd ed, London: Macmillan 1948)

Reiner R, *The Politics of the Police* (3rd ed, Oxford: Oxford University Press 2000)

Reith C, *A Short History of the British Police* (Oxford: Oxford University Press 1948)

Ross RE and Turner M, *Archbold's Criminal Pleading, Evidence and Practice* (London: Sweet & Maxwell 1938)

Rothman DJ, *The Discovery of the Asylum* (Boston: Little Brown and Co 1971)

Sharpe JA, *Crime in Early Modern England 1550–1750* (London: Longman 1984)

Smith JC and Hogan B, *Criminal Law: Cases and Materials* (3rd ed, London: Butterworths 1986)

Smith JKN, *Lawyers, Legislators and Theorists* (Oxford: Oxford University Press 1998)

Turner JWC, *Kenny's Outlines of Criminal Law* (18th ed, Cambridge: Cambridge University Press 1962)

Turner JWC, *Kenny's Outlines of Criminal Law* (19th ed, Cambridge: Cambridge University Press 1966)

Turner JWC, *Russell on Crime* (12th ed, London: Stevens & Sons 1964)

Wells C, *Corporations and Criminal Responsibility* (2nd ed, Oxford: Oxford University Press 2001)

Weiner MJ, *Reconstructing the Criminal, Culture: Law and Policy in England 1830–1914* (Cambridge: Cambridge University Press 1990)

Williams G, *Criminal Law, The General Part* (London: Stevens & Sons 1961)

Zedner L, *Criminal Justice* (Oxford: Oxford University Press 2004)

Journal articles

Anon, '*Causes of the Increase of Crime*' (Jul–Dec 1844) 56 Blackwood's Edinburgh Magazine 7

Buxton R, '*The Retreat from Smith*' (1966) Crim LR 196

Farmer L, '*The Obsession With Definition: The Nature of Crime and Critical Legal Theory*' (1996) 5 S & SL 57

Fletcher GP, '*The Metamorphosis of Larceny*' (Jan 1976) 89 Harv L Rev 3

Lacey N, '*In Search of the Responsible Subject: History, Philosophy and Social Science in Criminal Law Theory*' (2001) 64 MLR 350–371

Lacey N, '*Responsibility and Modernity in Criminal Law*' (2001) 9 Journal of Political Philosophy 249

Lacey N, '*Space, Time and Function: Intersecting Principles of Responsibility Across the Terrain of Criminal Justice*' (2007) 1 Criminal Law and Philosophy 233

Steinberg A, '*The Spirit of Litigation: Private Prosecution and Criminal Justice in 19th Century Philadelphia*' (1986) 20 Journal of Social History 243

Official materials

Fourth Report of Her Majesty's Commissioners on Criminal Law 1839 (168) XIX

5 Modern philosophy: mirror neurons and the manifest approach

Although the respective scope of the notions of actus reus and mens rea have not remained static, the modern understanding of the Latin maxim *actus non facit reum nisi mens sit rea*, has generally involved the idea that the physical and the mental elements of an offence should be distinguished. Although this construct of criminal liability accorded with Cartesian dualism, it is widely agreed that act and intent are not ontologically distinct. Accordingly, this chapter provides a basic examination of contemporary philosophy, in particular "mind/action" theory, with some important contributions in this area having already been made in the context of the criminal law.[1] The philosophical case for the dismantling of the rigid actus reus/mens rea construct reveals a much more nuanced understanding of action such that contemporary philosophy and criminal law doctrine are demonstrably out of step. Departing from the dualist assumptions, it will be shown that the physical and mental are neither separate nor severable and, accordingly, a more holistic and contextual approach to fault attribution is desirable. This recognition removes the perceived need to distinguish finely delineated mental states that are currently considered in isolation from the physical act.

This chapter goes on to consider the advancements made in scientific understanding of the workings of mirror neurons in the brain. These disclose that the observer acquires more than an objective direct knowledge of the conduct of the observed and transforms visual information into subjective knowledge involving a direct appreciation of purpose. This provides further support for the re-establishment of the orthodox evidential presumptions and the manifest model of fault attribution, affirming the notion that criminal behaviour is readily recognisable as such. That being so, it is proposed that, in our individual capacity as actors within the organised groups typical of modern life, subjective direct knowledge of organisational action is also possible through the observation of it. It will be shown that these discoveries afford a retreat from the predominance of the inflated mens rea doctrine in its current form such that corporate fault might now be attributed directly, without the need to identify an associated individual's metaphysical mind.

---

1 RA Duff, *Intention, Agency and Criminal Liability: Philosophy of Action and Criminal Law* (Oxford: Basil Blackwell 1990).

While this book argues the case for capacity-based liability, founded primarily on the orthodox voluntariness doctrine, it is also of note that contemporary philosophy recognises group agency, albeit of an institutional rather than biological form. No longer explained in terms of emergentism, which holds that properties can combine to amount to something *sui generis*, that exceeds and is different from the sum of the parts, organisational agency is theorised by reference to the performative capacity to make normative judgements about its options and the accompanying control necessary to make those choices.[2] The clear implication for a theory of corporate culpability is that organisations can and do become personalities that are distinct from their members and can be recognised as responsibility-bearing actors. Accordingly, where corporate misconduct is the result of systemic and pervasive behaviour, not reducible to identifiable individuals, there is a case for inculpating the organisation directly, obviating the need to employ the artificial "identification theory" where it is inappropriate.

Accordingly, this chapter briefly charts the developing theories of mind and action, which, taken together with neuroscientific advances, underpin the case for a return to a realist account of organisations and a presumptive approach to the attribution of fault.

5.1 Cartesian dualism: the root of the actus reus/mens rea divide

The basis of criminal fault, expressed in the maxim *actus non facit reum nisi mens sit rea* with its characteristic demarcation of physical and mental elements, is still understood and constructed in accordance with what is called philosophy's "official doctrine".[3] The force behind the distinction was driven by the doctrine of dualism which separates the non-physical mind from the tangible body,[4] hailing chiefly from the thinking of Descartes nearly four centuries ago.[5] The dualist assumption holds that human beings have both a mind and a body which, although mutually exclusive ontological categories, are somehow harnessed together.[6] Accordingly, this thinking assumes two different kinds of existence, the physical which is composed of matter and the mental comprising

2 Christian List and Philip Pettit, *Group Agency* (Oxford: Oxford University Press 2011) 176.
3 Gilbert Ryle, *The Concept of Mind* (London: Penguin 2000).
4 See e.g. RA Duff, *Intention, Agency and Criminal Liability: Philosophy of Action and Criminal Law* (Oxford: Basil Blackwell 1990).
5 Scholastic and reformation theology was also influential. Platonic and Aristotelian theories of the intellect shaped the orthodox doctrines of the soul's immortality.
6 Plato opined that we each have a soul which is divine and immutable and before birth we pre-existed in a pure and disembodied state. The body is the vehicle for existence in the earthly world which is a transitory stage in the soul's eternal journey. It would seem that Descartes' interest in maintaining the dualist approach to the mind was partly motivated by his religious desire to allow for the survival of the soul after physical death such that after the death of the body, the mind may continue to exist and function.

consciousness. The physical body exists spacially, subject to mechanical laws, and is observable whereas the workings of the mind are private and can only be observed, internally, by the individual himself. Although comprising distinct substances, there is causal interaction such that by a mental act of will, the individual can cause his physical body to move and, conversely, physical phenomena can cause a mental sensation of pain. However, the laws of physics fail to explain the causal relationship between the mechanical animate and the inanimate.[7]

While the respective disciplines of philosophy and science have struggled to provide an explanation for this mind-body relationship, the criminal law has continued to labour under the influence of 17th century Cartesian dualist philosophy. This has ultimately led to an approach whereby the making out of a criminal offence typically involves a "step by step" accumulation of the requisite physical and mental elements, each apparently considered in isolation.[8] In addition, the Cartesian view of the mental process is that it is staged in the "private theatre" of the mind of the individual and this view has endured such that it has been generally accepted that the state of a man's mind cannot be observed by anyone but the individual himself. Hence, although the moral attribution of fault has come to demand a subjective approach to criminality, the evidential implication of the philosophy rejects an objective or manifest assessment of the defendant's state of mind. The necessary bridges between the internal and the external, and thus the subjective and objective, have been constructed using the evidential presumptions of both voluntariness and that the accused must have intended the natural consequences of his actions. Although the presumptions are no longer openly acknowledged, the dualist philosophy has never been displaced as the theoretical underpinning of the criminal law.

Although substance dualism is not widely accepted in philosophy today,[9] the problem of explaining consciousness and the mind-body relationship remains. However, faith that science would ultimately provide the link may well be borne out in the attention now being given to recent neuroscientific research.[10] For

---

7 Various theories have been put forward, for example Descartes himself thought that a fluid of "animal spirits" flowing in the pineal gland provided the solution as to the interface between the mental and physical; others have suggested that God is the medium, for example Berkeley, Malebranche and Geulinext; that there is a pre-established harmony, Leibniz; or that there is only one underlying substance which is neither material nor mental, Spinoza.

8 *R v Hinks* [2001] 2 AC 241 (HL).

9 See e.g. Jaegwon Kim, *Philosophy of Mind* (3rd ed, Boulder, CO: Westview Press 2011); Ryle infamously referred to it as the dogma of the "ghost in the machine", Gilbert Ryle, *The Concept of Mind* (London: Penguin 2000) 17; Vadim V Vasilyev, 'Philosophy of Mind, Past and Present' (2013) 44, 1–2 Metaphilosophy 15. This dualist dilemma is avoided in monist thinking which holds that the world exists of a substance of just one kind. Thus the mental version of monism, idealism, holds that the mind constitutes the primary reality in that material things are simply the creation of our thoughts and mental experiences, whereas materialist monism perceives mental states as physical states, see e.g. Thomas Hobbes, Richard Rorty, Daniel Dennett.

10 Gilbert Ryle, *The Concept of Mind* (London: Penguin 2000).

example, sophisticated brain imaging techniques have demonstrated correlations between mental phenomena and neural brain states and that there is a physical brain state accompanying every mental event, the physical brain being identified as the determinant of mental activity.[11] Even so, the problem of explaining how a mental phenomenon can correlate with a physical one remains.[12] Various theories have been put forward, for example that of psychoneural identity[13] and, thereafter, functionalism which has become the orthodox philosophy of cognitive science.[14] However, while functionalism provides a holistic conception of

11 This follows scientific analysis of the psychoneural correlations. The mind-brain correlation thesis holds that for each type of mental event (M) that occurs to an organism (O), there exists a brain state of kind (B) (which is M's neural correlate or substrate) such that M occurs to O at time T if, and only if, B occurs to O at T, Jaegwon Kim, *Philosophy of Mind* (3rd ed, Boulder, CO: Westview Press 2011) Ch. 4.

12 If C-fibre stimulation correlates to the feeling of pain this still leaves the problem of explaining how a mental phenomenon (pain) can correlate with a physical one (C-fibre stimulation), Jaegwon Kim, *Philosophy of Mind* (3rd ed, Boulder, CO: Westview Press 2011) Ch. 4.

13 Explained in this way, i.e. replacing the "pain occurs if there is C-fibre stimulation" theory with the notion that "pain equals C-fibre stimulation", pain and C-fibre stimulation is but one phenomenon, not two phenomena whose correlation needs to be explained. According to the phsychoneural identity theory first advanced in the late 1950s, the mental state is identified with the physical processes of the brain. Although "C-fibre activation" and "pain" do not have the same dictionary meaning, they are one and the same, see Jaegwon Kim, *Philosophy of Mind* (3rd ed, Boulder, CO: Westview Press 2011). In the same way bolts of lightning can be also described as atmospheric electrical discharges; they are not synonymous but the two expressions, "lightning" and "atmospheric electrical discharge", refer to the same phenomenon. The claim that the mind is produced by the brain and the naturalistic approach to the interaction of the mind and body has become mainstream opinion during the past few decades, see Vadim V Vasilyev, 'Philosophy of Mind, Past and Present' (2013) 44, 1–2 Metaphilosophy 15. Identifying the mental with the physical brought the hypothesis within the ambit of physical theory which could then provide a complete framework to explain all aspects of the natural world. However, it is argued that psychoneural identities are no more reducible to basic physical/biological laws than the psychoneural correlations are, so they must also be viewed as fundamental and ineliminable postulates about how things are in the world. For the non-reductivist, mental properties, along with other higher level properties of the special sciences like biology, geology and the social sciences, resist reduction to the basic physical domain.

14 Hilary Putnam, 'Psychological Predicates' in WH Capitan and DD Merrill (eds.), *Art, Mind and Religion* (Pittsburgh: University of Pittsburgh Press 1967) reprinted as 'The Nature of Mental States' in Hilary Putnam, *Mind, Language and Reality: Philosophical Papers* (Cambridge: Cambridge University Press 1975) vol 2. The core of the functionalist conception of the mind is that organisms which are different, biologically and physically, can have the same psychology and, conversely, organisms with the same physical structure can have different psychological capacities and functions, depending on the way the physical stucture is causally embedded in a larger system. Most neurons are alike and are largely interchangeable. According to functionalism, a mental kind is a functional kind or a causal–functional kind and, therefore, the feeling of pain accords with the concept of the tissue damage detector, a functional concept, specified by the job description. Thus, what makes something a mousetrap, for example, is its ability to perform that function rather than being composed of a specific psycho-chemical structure. Accordingly, pain is defined by reference to its function, that being to serve as a causal intermediary between pain inputs and pain outputs. Moreover, the causal

mentality,[15] it de-substantialises the mind and, therefore, encompasses the view that mental processes depend on, and are realised in, the physical make-up of the organism, although they are not reducible to it.[16] That being so, the mind must be a "non-physical" thing and this still leaves the need to explain how the mind can cause something physical, such as a bodily movement.[17] In an attempt to avoid a return to the dualist dilemma, Vicari has argued that both monist and dualist theories are implicitly based on the same rationally unjustified assumptions.[18] The main assumption is the exclusion principle which perceives the mental and physical as independent and exclusive ontological realms. However, scientific theories can explain the existence of the mind without reducing it or eliminating it such that it is compatible with the physical. Searle, for example, refers to this as biological naturalism, the theory being that consciousness is a state or a process realised in the brain whose causal base is at the lower, microstructural level of organisation of the brain itself.[19] Conscious states are therefore created in the physical structure of the brain and consciousness is causally explained by the interactions between the elements composing the brain as an organic system. It is realised at a level of the same system which is higher than that of the basic elements. Consciousness is therefore a causally emergent property of the brain in that it is a feature of the entire system but not of its basic elements. It is causally explained not as the simple addition of the parts but from the causal interactions at the level of the basic components of the system itself. For example, liquidity is an emergent property of water although no individual water molecule is in a liquid state, unlike the system as a whole. In the same way Searle argues that consciousness is the emergent of certain systems of neurons

conditions that activate the pain mechanism can include other mental states and the outputs of the pain mechanism can include mental states as well, for example the sense of distress or desire to be pain-free. The functionalist holds that mental states are real internal states with causal powers; pain is thus an internal neurobiological state typically caused by tissue damage that might, in turn, cause groans and avoidance behaviour. Mental states form a complex causal network which is anchored to the external world at various contact points. Here interaction takes place with the outside world, receiving sensory inputs and admitting behaviour outputs. The identity of a given mental kind depends solely on the place it occupies in the causal network. That is, what makes a mental event the kind of mental event that it is, is the way it is causally linked to other mental event kinds and input–output conditions. The identity of each mental kind therefore depends ultimately on the whole system – its internal structure and the way it causally links to the external world via sensory inputs and behaviour outputs.

15 The mind is seen as a set of powers, abilities and processes which perform a causal role in the management of organism–environment transactions.

16 What makes them irreducible is the fact that they are multiply realisable in different physical systems, Giuseppe Vicari, 'Beyond Conceptual Dualism: Ontology of Consciousness, Mental Causation, and Holism' in John R Searle (ed.), *Philosophy of Mind* (Value Enquiry Book Series 2008).

17 Jaegwon Kim, *Philosophy of Mind* (3rd ed, Boulder, CO: Westview Press 2011).

18 Giuseppe Vicari, 'Beyond Conceptual Dualism: Ontology of Consciousness, Mental Causation, and Holism' in John R Searle (ed.), *Philosophy of Mind* (Value Enquiry Book Series 2008) 60.

19 John R Searle (ed.), *Philosophy of Mind* (Value Enquiry Book Series 2008).

and that although no individual neuron can think or speak or feel, the system as a whole has this capacity. Thus, consciousness cannot be deduced or calculated from the sheer physical structure of the neurons without some additional account of the causal relations between them. The failure of ontological reduction can be explained by reference to other phenomena, for example, money and musical performances which are, in principle, reducible to molecular structures or sound waves, but a redefinition of the concepts in these terms would lose the sense of the concepts themselves.[20]

By abandoning the disconnected Cartesian categories of the mental and the physical, the problem of mental causation disappears. Furthermore, scientific research provides an explanatory structure which accounts for the emergence of ontologically "new" levels, with properties that are non-existent at the lower levels but which emerge from the lower-level interactions as system macrofeatures. The reverse approach is reductionism, with which science has been successful in reducing various organic matters into atomic states.[21] However, reductionist analysis moves from wholes down into parts and, by so doing, moves in the opposite direction from the way that matters arise. To understand how matters arise, the process must be run in reverse, for example from the sub atom to the atom to the amino acids to the protein to the polymer to the cell to the muscle to the contraction.[22] As scientists have undertaken such upwards projects, they have discovered that the whole is not something greater or something more, but something altogether different. Indeed, this something else can, in turn, participate in generating a new something else at a different level of organisation.[23] Thus, although the water molecule comprises hydrogen and oxygen atoms, the molecule also possesses unprecedented attributes because the joining of the atoms has distorted the shapes of each, producing a composite shape with its own intrinsic properties. Further, different outcomes are possible when water molecules interact together. Ice forms when the kinetic energy of the average molecule is low and the molecules' stickiness overcomes their movement; liquid water forms when their movement is sufficient to overcome that stickiness; and steam forms when their relative velocities are high enough that collisions seldom allow stickiness.[24] Thus, emergentism suggests that human characteristics are constructed bottom-up and are then deeply influenced by environmental contexts. Accordingly, human evolution has entailed the co-evolution of three emergent modalities – brain, symbolic

20 Giuseppe Vicari, 'Beyond Conceptual Dualism: Ontology of Consciousness, Mental Causation, and Holism' in John R Searle (ed.), *Philosophy of Mind* (Value Enquiry Book Series 2008) 60.
21 Ursula Goodenough and Terrence W Deacon, 'The Sacred Emergence of Nature' in Philip Clayton (ed.), *The Oxford Handbook of Religions and Science* (Oxford University Press 2006) Ch. 50.
22 Ibid.
23 Ibid.
24 Ibid.

language and culture – each feeding into and responding to the other two, thereby generating particular complex patterns and outcomes. This identification of a naturalistic and non-reductive ontology of mind is exciting in that it can now dialogue with scientific research to address the traditional philosophical problems.[25]

5.2 Mind-action, mirror neurons and understanding action

While this thinking provides one of any number of possible answers that might respond to the dualist dilemma, at the very least the scientific research demonstrates that the notions of mind and body, mental and physical, are inextricably interwoven and, in contrast to the traditional model of criminality, defy any simplistic separation. Although this book in no way professes to be a contribution to disciplines of either philosophy or science, there is evidently no bright-line distinction to be made between an act and its accompanying mental state and the modern bifurcation of actus reus and mens rea concepts labours under a fundamental misconception. Thus, any attempt to demarcate the territory of the mental from the physical is naturally predisposed to difficulty. Arguably, a more satisfactory basis for criminal liability would be established if the Latin maxim, on which it was based, was analysed holistically, avoiding the faux distinctions between the physical and mental elements. Indeed, the early understanding of the terms actus reus and mens rea more readily accords with today's scientific findings, the actus reus encompassing both the physical and mental elements of criminality, the mens rea specifying with exactness the awareness of risk required before moral opprobrium could attach to the defendant. For example, the 1966 edition of *Kenny's Outlines* explained the meaning of actus reus in this way:

> such result of human conduct as the law seeks to prevent. This may include legally essential facts and included amongst them there may be one or more which are personal to the accused himself, including even his own thoughts. Thus, in burglary the prosecution must prove that the prisoner (1) broke and entered, (2) the dwelling house of another, (3) in the night, (4) *with intent to commit a felony therein*. Elements (2) and (3) are objective facts so the subjective mental attitude of the prisoner is irrelevant; that is to say, whether or not the prisoner believed it to be a dwelling house, or belonging to another, or that it was in the night can make no difference to his liability to conviction if the other facts are established. But (4) is subjective and the prosecution must establish beyond reasonable doubt that he had the specified intention, however, although this is a subjective matter it has nothing to do with the *mens rea* of the crime of

---

25 Giuseppe Vicari, 'Beyond Conceptual Dualism: Ontology of Consciousness, Mental Causation, and Holism' in John R Searle (ed.), *Philosophy of Mind* (Value Enquiry Book Series 2008).

burglary but is simply one of the facts which together constitute the *actus reus*, since a man's thoughts are as much facts as are his bodily movements.[26]

Notwithstanding the current interpretation of the maxim, the orthodox understanding of the actus reus and mens rea notions was not of a strict separation of the physical and mental elements. That the modern interpretation makes for an uncomfortable fit in the overall conceptual scheme is clearly demonstrated by some obvious theoretical problems that arise through the attempt of such an exercise. One example of this can be seen in the controversial judicial approach to dishonest appropriation in the context of the theft offence, whereby the elements of dishonesty and appropriation are considered as distinct elements.[27] The contrary effect of this approach is that the recipient of a gift can be convicted of theft even if the transfer of the property is otherwise indefeasible at civil law[28] since "appropriation" considered in isolation has been simply defined as the assumption of any right of the owner.[29] Similarly, some actus reus elements inhere a particular mental aspect of their own, for example, the fact of being in possession.[30] Troublesome examples of this nature come as no surprise when considered more generally in the light of science-led philosophy. To accord with the scientific advances made in this field, the criminal law will need to abandon the physical/mental bright-line distinction and accept that the blameworthy state of mind does not accompany the act, it is an elemental aspect of it.

Additional to the difficulties encountered in attempting to demarcate the mental and the physical constituents of an offence, conceptual problems arise in regard to the orthodox distinction between the mental states, voluntariness and foresight of consequences.[31] Where metaphorical voluntariness presumes that the actor has knowledge of the circumstances in which he acts, the requirement of mens rea, namely that the actor has foreseen its consequence, also depends upon his subjective knowledge of the facts in which he decides to act.[32] Although Turner remained committed to the distinction between the two mental states, it is at this juncture that the modern approaches to fault attribution can be seen at their most problematic. It is widely accepted that the development of the

---

26 JW Cecil Turner, *Kenny's Outlines of Criminal Law* (19th ed, Cambridge: Cambridge University Press 1966) 17 and referring to JWC Turner, *Russell on Crime* (12th ed, London: Stevens & Sons 1964) 23.
27 Theft Act 1968, s. 1.
28 *R v Hinks* [2001] 2 AC 241 (HL).
29 Theft Act 1968, s. 3.
30 See above Ch. 4 and *Warner v MPC* [1969] 2 AC 256 (HL).
31 Mens rea in its original sense. That such fine mental distinctions cannot be made is hinted at by the points of tension identified in Ch. 3. For example, the curious co-existence of insane and non-insane automatism, and the "defence" of mistake, which can go either to deny the actus reus or mens rea, depending on their nature in the context of the modern construct.
32 JW Cecil Turner, *Kenny's Outlines of Criminal Law* (17th ed, Cambridge: Cambridge University Press 1958) 28 and fn 1.

concepts of criminal fault was a gradual process and that the doctrine of voluntariness began in the narrow sense to temper the harshness of a criminal law where fault had previously been attributable on the basis of simple causation. Thus, an early refinement added the requirement that the actor was the author of his act in the sense that literal involuntariness would negate liability. The doctrine was subsequently extended to encompass metaphorical non-voluntariness, as is now expressed in concepts such as duress and mistake. While voluntariness was the mental element required in every offence, the common law evolved further such that an accused would not attract criminal culpability if he had not foreseen whatever consequence of his act was specified. Although this came to be particularised as "mens rea", it is plausible that this later requirement may have constituted a further refinement of the voluntariness doctrine, in common law offences, rather than the identification of an additional and distinct mental state.

The notions of voluntariness and mens rea are not capable of segregation. Capacity-based responsibility, underpinned by the theory of the individual as a "rational calculator", must capture the notion that the choice expressed is not only freely made (and autonomous) but that it is also an informed choice. Implicit in the very language of "rational calculation" is the inference that the accused has calculated, weighed up the circumstances, at least as far as he himself knows or perceives them. Put another way, it is simply the gradual refinement to the doctrine as it recognised metaphorical involuntariness.[33] Indeed, the presumption of voluntariness encompasses a presumption of knowledge of circumstances.[34] If the actor is possessed of this knowledge, and is not acting under a mistake, there must remain only the finest of distinctions between this state of mind and that of mens rea in the sense of foresight of particular consequences. If the rational actor is making choices in the context of the surrounding circumstances, he is almost certainly doing so with some insight or allusion as to the possible outcome of his choice. It is only on the basis of his personal "knowledge" or belief of the circumstances that consequences can be foreseen; like the rational calculator making his choices as regards the action itself, consequences cannot be predicted in a vacuum. Inevitably, such mental states cannot be artificially separated when they are integral to one process.[35] Accordingly, mens rea, defined as foresight of consequences, and voluntariness, encompassing the notion of free action in

---

33 That the fault doctrines evolved gradually is consistent with the gradual transition from objective to subjective fault assessment and also the emergence of various defences which did not originate at the same time.

34 See the discussion in Ch. 4.

35 Ashworth identifies the relationship between voluntariness and the capacity of the individual for rational choice and says that since choice can only be exercised in the context of awareness of surrounding circumstances, belief as to what one is doing at the time of the act is central to the attribution of moral responsibility. This is what he calls the "belief principle", Andrew Ashworth and Jeremy Horder, *Principles of Criminal Law* (7th ed, Oxford: Oxford University Press 2013) 156.

knowledge of the circumstances, are better considered as points across a spectrum of awareness rather than distinct mental states since knowledge, or perception of the circumstances in which the act is done, must bear directly on the issue of foresight. Thus, it is entirely possible that the apparent enlargement of the criminal law's orthodox mens rea concept, and its use as a catch-all term for all mental blameworthy states, is symptomatic of the fact that the mental fault elements cannot be divided.[36]

On the strength of scientific developments in the understanding of action, the evidential presumptions of fault, which were deemed to provide the essential link to the subjective mental state, beg comment in two respects. First, it is clear that the mental and physical realms defy identification as distinct notions. Accordingly, the perception of the evidential presumptions as bridges providing access from the external world to the individual's internal mind was misconceived. However, it is also the case that the manifest approach, implicitly adopted by the presumptions, more readily accords with today's more sophisticated and holistic understanding of action. Since the mental and physical are not severable, the observance of the outward conduct provides a perspective of the conduct in its totality, not just its mechanics. Indeed, advances in neuroscience support such a proposition and provide tantalising evidence that the manifest approach to fault attribution provides the knowledge required to establish culpability and does so according to the criminal law's subjectivist ideal.

5.3 The paradox of the manifest approach

The orthodox presumptions of fault, first that the act was presumed to be voluntary and, second, that the actor was presumed to have intended its natural consequences, implicitly recognise that the blameworthy "mental state" was generally discernible by reference to the appearance of the defendant's physical behaviour.[37] This approach is not inconsistent with the modern, scientific understanding of action which fundamentally challenges the bifurcated actus reus/mens rea construct of crime. Indeed, discoveries

---

36 Scientific theories provide an explanatory device that can account for the existence of mind without reducing or eliminating it, effectively making the mind compatible with the physical. In accordance with emergentism, the mental is explained as a feature, at the system level, of the physical structure of the brain, and, causally speaking, there are not two independent phenomena comprising conscious effort and unconscious neuron firings. Rather, there is just the "brain system" which has one level of description when neuron firings are occurring and another level of description, the level of the system, where the system is conscious and indeed consciously trying to effect physical movement, Introduction to Giuseppe Vicari, 'Beyond Conceptual Dualism: Ontology of Consciousness, Mental Causation, and Holism' in John R Searle (ed.), *Philosophy of Mind* (Value Enquiry Books Series 2008) 71.

37 It must not be forgotten that evidential presumptions are capable of rebuttal by the defendant.

from the discipline of neuroscience bring exciting implications for the criminal law. In particular, advancements in the context of mirror neurons have considerable potential to redefine the way in which an individual's action is understood by others. The science now emerging is startling in that it suggests that the manifest observance of another's act provides the observer with knowledge of it, not indirectly as had been thought, but a direct knowledge.

While the dualist challenge was always to access the internal theatre of the actor's mind, neuroscience now shows that sophisticated human cognitive abilities have their roots in a pre-linguistic, pre-conceptual and pragmatic understanding of the intentions and actions of other people.[38] It is precisely this human ability to infer other people's mental states, such as intentions, emotions or desires, that provides an essential basis for successful social interaction by enabling the prediction of others' most probable future acts.[39] This primitive ability is embodied in particular areas of the prefrontal motor cortex where the same neurons that fire when a subject performs an intentional action also fire when the subject observes the same action performed by another.[40] The implications are startling – what was considered objective knowledge, and offensive to the criminal law's subjectivist ideal, turns out, after all, to be subjective knowledge. The mirror neuron system is the mechanism by which people re-use their own mental states, or processes represented in bodily format, to functionally attribute it, the mental state, to others. In this way it enables a direct appreciation of purpose without relying

38 G Rizzolatti et al, 'Neurophysiological Mechanisms Underlying the Understanding and Imitation of Action' (2001) 2 Nature Reviews Neuroscience 661–70; Giacoma Rizzolatti and Corrado Sinigaglia, *Mirrors in the Brain* (Oxford University Press 2008); G Rizzolatti and C Sinigaglia, 'The Functional Role of the Parieto-frontal Mirror Circuit: Interpretations and Misinterpretations' (2010) 11 Nature Reviews Neuroscience (2010) 264–74.

39 Maren E Bodden et al, 'Comparing the Neural Correlates of Affective and Cognitive Theory of Mind using fMRI: Involvement of the Basal Ganglia in Effective Theory of Mind' (2013) 9(1) Advances in Cognitive Psychology 32–43.

40 Rizzolatti and Sinigaglia discovered the involvement of the parietal cortex during theory of mind processing, specified the fronto-parietal mirror circuit. Initially observed in the monkey pre-motor cortex, research into the human mirror neuron system is now providing results. The identification of mirror neurons not only enforces the thesis that action is not the result of pure perception and cognition, they have also been interpreted as the expression of a direct form of action understanding via embodied simulation, providing a unitary account of basic aspects of intersubjectivity, Giuseppe Vicari, 'Beyond Conceptual Dualism: Ontology of Consciousness, Mental Causation, and Holism' in John R Searle (ed.), *Philosophy of Mind* (Value Enquiry Books Series 2008), referring to Vittorio Gallese, 'Mirror Neurons, Embodied Simulation and a Second-Person Approach to Mind Reading' (2013) 49(10) Cortex 2954–6. The existence of the mirror mechanism is now firmly established in the human brain, see Kilner et al, 'Evidence of Mirror Neurons in Human Inferior Frontal Gyrus' (2009) 29 (32) 10 Journal of Neuroscience153–9; Mukamel et al, 'Single Neuron Responses in Humans During Execution and Observation of Actions' (2010) 20(8) Current Biology 750–6.

on explicit propositional inference[41] and the internal simulation of others' experiences by observation[42] transforms visual information into knowledge.[43]

Although the systematic investigation of affective and cognitive theory of mind has only begun relatively recently,[44] it is also suggested that there is a distinction of the level of processing that differentiates between a mirror and a mentalising system.[45] This means that the ability can be further subdivided into affective and cognitive subcomponents, each of which can be affected individually or in combination. The affective component recognises the feelings of another person[46] and the cognitive infers the other's mental states, for example his desires, beliefs, or intentions. The mirror system[47] engages when perceiving biological motion to ascertain the underlying intentions of the observed movement while the mentalising system[48] provides a more abstract inference of goals. The mentalising system operates when there is no observable action of body parts and when intentions need to be inferred from abstract cues such as eye gaze, semantic information, facial expression, or knowledge about the situation. Mentalising and mirroring are thus the processes used to access the mental states of others[49] and, since multiple actions may be effected to achieve a specific result, it

41 V Gallese, 'The Manifold Nature of Interpersonal Relations: The Quest for a Common Mechanism' (2003) 358 Philosophical Transactions of the Royal Society of London B, 517–28; V Gallese and C Sinigaglia, 'What is So Special with Embodied Simulation' (2011) 15 Trends in Cognitive Sciences 512–19.

42 G Rizzolatti et al, 'Neurophysiological Mechanisms Underlying the Understanding and Imitation of Action' (2001) 2 Nature Reviews Neuroscience 661.

43 G Rizzolatti and C Sinigaglia, 'The Functional Role of the Parieto-frontal Mirror Circuit: Interpretations and Misinterpretations' (2010) 11 Nature Reviews Neuroscience 264–74, 269. Neuroscientists suggest that the affective and cognitive theory of mind abilities recruit a network of brain structures, irrespective of the differentiation between its affective and cognitive subcomponents.

44 Only a few functional imaging studies have compared both components to date, Maren E Bodden et al, 'Comparing the Neural Correlates of Affective and Cognitive Theory of Mind using fMRI: Involvement of the Basal Ganglia in Effective Theory of Mind' (2013) 9(1) Advances in Cognitive Psychology 32–43.

45 Van Overwalle F and Baetens K, 'Understanding Others' Actions and Goals by Mirror and Mentalizing Systems: A Meta-analysis' (2009) 48 Neuralimage 564–84.

46 M Schaefer et al, 'Mirror like Brain Responses to Observed Touch and Personality Dimensions' 29th May 2013 Front Hum Neurosci 7:227.doi10.3389/fnhum.2013.00227 citing Bufalari et al, 'Empathy for Pain and Touch in the Human Somatosensory Cortex' (2007) 17 Cereb Cortex 2553–61 who reported that somatosensory evoked potentials were modulated by the observation of a touched hand with increased P 45 amplitudes during pain observation and decreased P 45 amplitudes during touch observation. Studies employing fMRI, magnetoencephalography, or TMS, transcranialmagnetic stimulation, support the results of vicarious somatosensory activation when observing touch.

47 This consists of the anterior intraparietal sulcus and the premotor cortex.

48 This comprises the temporoparietal junction, the medial prefrontal cortex, and the precuneus.

49 It is recognised that there is a continuum from concrete to highly abstract goals and intentions and there is no a priori way to make a clear-cut and objective contrast between action means and action ends or goals. Similarly, multiple actions can be effected to achieve a specific result, therefore in order to drink one might grasp a cup, order a beer or open the tap. Consequently it

is suggested that the process is not a simple one-to-one map between action and goal but a sophisticated process of many-to-many mapping. Furthermore, it is recognised that goals are also context dependent such that a different context leads to a different interpretation of the observed act.[50]

The advancements in neuroscience explicitly support the reliability of an observer's assessment of another's action and the manifest approach to fault determination. Furthermore, the actions to which the corresponding knowledge can relate are not confined to the direct observance of the act in question but would clearly extend to the reconstruction of the act at trial, in addition to the act of the giving of evidence generally. While this is supportive of the manifest approach to criminality, which is readily accommodated with the use of the orthodox fault presumptions, the discoveries relating to mirror neurons also have particularly interesting implications for a theory of intentionality in the specific context of collective action.[51] It is suggested that this research confirms that collective intentionality is the biologically primitive and pre-linguistic condition of the possibility of collective and cooperative behaviour which cannot be reduced or eliminated in favour of something else.[52] We are, it seems, innately "programmed" to have direct knowledge not just of individual behaviour, but of collective behaviour too. Indeed, this particular discovery has led to the new discipline called "social neuroscience" in which the mirror neuron system provides an explanation of the emergence of sharedness and collectiveness from a biological perspective.[53] Further, while mirroring provides

   is suggested that the process is not a one-to-one map between action and goal but many-to-many mapping, S Uithol, 'What Do Mirror Neurons Mirror?' Philosophical Psychology (2011) Oct 24, 5, 607–23.

50 S Uithol, 'What Do Mirror Neurons Mirror?' (Oct 2011) 24(5) Philosophical Psychology 607–23 where Uithol suggests that there are reasons to believe that no simple mechanism can support a general capacity for making context-sensitive goal inferences. Inferring goals from action is a form of abduction, also called "inference to best explanation"; C Baker et al, 'Theory-based Social Goal Inference', (2008) Proceedings of the 30th Annual Conference of the Cognitive Science Society, Washington, 1447–52.

51 Giuseppe Vicari, 'Beyond Conceptual Dualism: Ontology of Consciousness, Mental Causation, and Holism' in John R Searle (ed.), *Philosophy of Mind* (Value Enquiry Book Series 2008) 120.

52 Giuseppe Vicari, 'Beyond Conceptual Dualism: Ontology of Consciousness, Mental Causation, and Holism' in John R Searle (ed.), *Philosophy of Mind* (Value Enquiry Book Series 2008) 120.

53 Jan Treur, 'Biological and Computational Perspectives on the Emergence of Social Phenomena: Shared Understanding and Collective Power' (2012) 8 Transactions on Computational Collective Intelligence 168–91; Cacioppo JT and Berntson GG: *Social Neuroscience* (Hove: Psychology Press 2005); Cacioppo JT et al, *Social Neuroscience: People Thinking about Thinking People* (Cambridge, MA: MIT Press 2006); Decety J and Cacioppo JT (eds.), *Handbook of Social Neuroscience* (Oxford: Oxford University Press 2010); Decety J and Ickes W, *The Social Neuroscience of Empathy* (Cambridge, MA: MIT Press 2009); Harmon-Jones E and Winkielman P (eds.), *Social neuroscience: Integrating Biological and Psychological Explanations of Social Behavior* (New York: Guilford 2007).

the means by which collective action is understood, it goes further still to explain how collective power,[54] encompassing collective intention,[55] arises. Accordingly, neuroscience now provides clear scientific support for the proposition that a distinct organisational personality can and does emerge from its collective members. It is suggested that to result in a collective power, the individual momenta simply converge to a similar direction and in so doing create a collective momentum.[56] More specifically, the collective action occurs as a result of a sophisticated mutual "tuning process" via the mirroring process. Mirror neurons therefore play an important role in producing joint action as well as understanding it.[57] These findings put beyond doubt the fact that organisational fault, like individual fault, can be attributed by the manifest assessment of the behaviour of the collective, and that this observation of the group conduct provides direct knowledge of it in the observer.

It is evident that philosophy and science are now finding common ground through advancements in neuroscience and the discovery of the mirror neuron system in the brain. Where philosophy has struggled to answer the dualist dilemma of the so-called mind/body divide, scientific endeavour is providing potential answers. However, the criminal law's dogged commitment to the mental and physical distinction, articulated in the twin concepts of actus reus and mens rea (as they are now understood), is indicative of an institution which has thus far refused to contemplate a more sophisticated theory of mind and action. Since it is now accepted that action is not a thing capable of sub-division into mental and physical elements, the criminal law's continued attempt to construct liability on this basis is increasingly outdated. A holistic approach to the assessment of conduct is more conducive to the modern understanding of the unified nature of the body, brain and mental processes and the orthodox presumptions of fault, which explicitly link the overt appearance of behaviour with the internal state, are readily accommodated. Paradoxically, the manifest approach is not manifest at all; as it transpires, the operation of the mirror neuron system satisfies the subjectivist ideology. As such, this discovery has exciting implications for a theory of corporate criminality in which the presumptions

---

54 Jan Treur, 'Biological and Computational Perspectives on the Emergence of Social Phenomena: Shared Understanding and Collective Power' (2012) 8 Transactions on Computational Collective Intelligence 168–91.
55 Elisabeth Pacherie and Jerome Dokic, 'From mirror neurons to joint actions' (2006) 7(2–3) June Cognitive Systems Research 101–12; Cristina Becchioa and Cesare Bertoneb, 'Wittgenstein Running: Neural Mechanisms of Collective Intentionality and We-mode' (2004) 13 Consciousness and Cognition 123–33.
56 This is what happens in the universe when, for example, comets or planets are formed out of smaller particles, based on mutual attraction based on gravitation, Jan Treur, 'Biological and Computational Perspectives on the Emergence of Social Phenomena: Shared Understanding and Collective Power' (2012) 8 Transactions on Computational Collective Intelligence 168–91.
57 Elisabeth Pacherie and Jerome Dokic, 'From Mirror Neurons to Joint Actions' (2006) 7(2–3) June Cognitive Systems Research 101–12.

provide a process for fault attribution which does not involve enquiry and emphasis on a metaphysical mental state.

Bibliography

Books

Ashworth A and Horder J, *Principles of Criminal Law* (7th ed, Oxford: Oxford University Press 2013)
Cacioppo JT and Berntson GG: *Social Neuroscience* (Hove: Psychology Press 2005)
Cacioppo JT et al, *Social Neuroscience: People Thinking about Thinking People* (Cambridge, MA: MIT Press 2006)
Clayton P (ed.), *The Oxford Handbook of Religions and Science* (Oxford: Oxford University Press 2006)
Decety J and Cacioppo JT (eds.), *Handbook of Social Neuroscience* (Oxford: Oxford University Press 2010)
Decety J and Ickes W, *The Social Neuroscience of Empathy* (Cambridge, MA: MIT Press 2009)
Duff RA, *Intention, Agency and Criminal Liability: Philosophy of Action and Criminal Law* (Oxford: Basil Blackwell 1990)
Harmon-Jones E and Winkielman P (eds.), *Social Neuroscience: Integrating Biological and Psychological Explanations of Social Behavior* (New York: Guilford 2007)
Kim J, *Philosophy of Mind* (3rd ed, Boulder, CO: Westview Press 2011)
List C and Pettit P, *Group Agency* (Oxford: Oxford University Press 2011)
Putnam H, *Mind, Language and Reality: Philosophical Papers* (Cambridge: Cambridge University Press 1975)
Rizzolatti G and Sinigaglia C, *Mirrors in the Brain* (Oxford: Oxford University Press 2008)
Ryle G, *The Concept of Mind* (London: Penguin 2000)
Searle JR (ed.), *Philosophy of Mind* (Value Enquiry Book Series 2008)
Turner JWC, *Kenny's Outlines of Criminal Law* (17th ed, Cambridge: Cambridge University Press 1958)
Turner JWC, *Kenny's Outlines of Criminal Law* (19th ed, Cambridge: Cambridge University Press 1966)
Turner JWC, *Russell on Crime* (12th ed, London: Stevens & Sons 1964)

Journal articles

Baker C et al, '*Theory-based Social Goal Inference*' (2008) Proceedings of the 30th Annual Conference of the Cognitive Science Society, Washington, 1447
Becchioa C and Bertoneb C, '*Wittgenstein Running: Neural Mechanisms of Collective Intentionality and We-mode*', (2004) 13 Consciousness and Cognition 123
Bodden ME et al, '*Comparing the Neural Correlates of Affective and Cognitive Theory of Mind using fMRI: Involvement of the Basal Ganglia in Effective Theory of Mind*' (2013) 9(1) Advances in Cognitive Psychology 32
Bufalari et al, '*Empathy for Pain and Touch in the Human Somatosensory Cortex*' (2007) 17 Cereb Cortex 2553
Gallese V, '*The Manifold Nature of Interpersonal Relations: The Quest for a Common Mechanism*' (2003) 358 Philosophical Transactions of the Royal Society of London B, 517

Gallese V, '*Mirror Neurons, Embodied Simulation and a Second-Person Approach to Mind Reading*' (2013) 49(10) Cortex 2954

Gallese V and Sinigaglia C, '*What is So Special with Embodied Simulation*' (2011) 15 Trends in Cognitive Sciences 512

Kilner et al '*Evidence of Mirror Neurons in Human Inferior Frontal Gyrus*' (2009) 29(32) 10 Journal of Neuroscience 153

Mukamel et al, '*Single Neuron Responses in Humans During Execution and Observation of Actions*' (2010) 20(8) Current Biology 750

Pacherie E and Dokic J, '*From Mirror Neurons to Joint Actions*' (2006) 7(2–3) June Cognitive Systems Research 101

Rizzolatti G and Sinigaglia C, '*The Functional Role of the Parieto-frontal Mirror Circuit: Interpretations and Misinterpretations*' (2010) 11 Nature Reviews Neuroscience 264

Rizzolatti G et al, '*Neurophysiological Mechanisms Underlying the Understanding and Imitation of Action*' (2001) 2 Nature Reviews Neuroscience 661

Schaefer M et al, '*Mirror like Brain Responses to Observed Touch and Personality Dimensions*', 29th May 2013 Front Hum Neurosci 7:227.doi10.3389/fnhum. 2013. 00227

Treur J, '*Biological and Computational Perspectives on the Emergence of Social Phenomena: Shared Understanding and Collective Power*' (2012) 8 Transactions on Computational Collective Intelligence 168

Uithol S, '*What Do Mirror Neurons Mirror?*' (2011) 25(5) Oct Philosophical Psychology 607

Van Overwalle F and Baetens K, '*Understanding Others' Actions and Goals by Mirror and Mentalizing Systems: A Meta-analysis*', (2009) 48 Neuralimage 564

Vasilyev VV, '*Philosophy of Mind, Past and Present*' (2013) 44 (1–2) Metaphilosophy 15

6   Realism: back to the future?

6.1 Realist theory

While neuroscience now supports the recognition of a distinct collective entity, the realist theory of organisations is not new. Indeed, what neuroscience would ultimately demonstrate, other disciplines had long envisaged. However, it is a matter of some irony that what is now considered the landmark legal authority for the emergence of the contrary fiction theory of corporations was actually a case decided in the midst of prevailing realist ideology, albeit the theory was then based on the now discredited emergentist account.[1] The first articulation of the fictionist approach, the so-called "identification principle" of corporate liability which equates corporate liability with the criminal fault of a person who is deemed to be the organisation's "directing mind and will", is attributed to Viscount Haldane L.C. in *Lennards' Carrying Company* [1915].[2] What makes this authority particularly surprising is that Viscount Haldane was seemingly not bound by any earlier authority and, with a keen interest in philosophy, he was very much a proponent of the realist theory, as was fashionable in the early 20th century.[3] This chapter therefore sets out the philosophical and legal context in which the landmark *Lennard's* case[4] was decided. The first narrative deals broadly with the realist thinking of the time which indicated a shift from individualist theory to the consideration of the significance and ontology of collective groups. The second narrative addresses specifically the common law of the period, demonstrating a judicial readiness

---

1 Christian List and Philip Pettit, *Group Agency* (Oxford: Oxford University Press 2011) 8.
2 *Lennard's Carrying Co Ltd v Asiatic Petroleum Ltd* [1915] AC 705 (HL).
3 In 1883, he published *Essays in Philosophical Criticism*, and in the same year, his translation of Schopenhauer's *The World as Will and Idea*. Other philosophical works include *Pathway to Reality* (1903), *Reign of Relativity* (1921), *The Philosophy of Humanism* (1922) and *Selected Addresses and Essays* (1928), see David Kahan's introduction to Richard Burdon Haldane's 1902–1904 Gifford Lectures: The Pathway to Reality at www.giffordlectures.org/Browse.asp?PubID=TPTPTR&Volume=O&Issue=O&ArticleID=6 accessed 15 May 2014. Richard Burdon Haldane, *The Pathway to Reality: Being the Gifford Lectures Delivered in the University of St Andrews in the Session 1902–1904* (Ulan Press 2012).
4 *Lennard's Carrying Co Ltd v Asiatic Petroleum Ltd* [1915] AC 705 (HL).

to attribute corporate criminal liability on the existing legal principles derived from master and servant law and agency doctrines.

As regards the philosophical context, it is suggested that here were two defining moments in Western political and scientific thought, the first being the 17th century birth of individualism, the second being the 20th century rise of holism in the life and human sciences.[5] These have been viewed as a conceptual pair, since for individualism to exist, individuals had to accept a supreme state that would protect individual property and thus transcend the rights and powers of the individual.[6] During this evolution, the first broad approach to realism has been described as the authorisation theory, explicitly articulated by Thomas Hobbes in *Leviathan* (1651) and it was endorsed by the end of the 17th century by John Locke and, a century later, by Jean-Jacques Rousseau.[7] In essence, this account was based on the theory that the group agent was the majoritarian, or aggregate, reflection of its individual member's minds. Accordingly, what this recognition entailed was already expressible in the language of individualism.[8] The alternative animation theory emerged later and this held that the group agent was an emergent entity over and above the individual members.[9] In the last decade of the 19th century, for example, Durkheim,[10] asserted that society was created when individual consciences interacted and fused together to create a synthetic reality that is completely new and greater than the sum of its parts.[11] With what he called the "collective consciousness", by which he meant a set of shared beliefs, he opined that collective groups "can be considered to possess agential capabilities: to think, judge, decide, act, reform; to conceptualise self and others as well as self's actions and interactions; and to reflect".[12] The Durkheimian view of organisational culture was that

5 Tom Otto and Nils Bubandt, *Experiments in Holism, Theory and Practice in Contemporary Anthropology* (Oxford: Wiley-Blackwell 2010).
6 Ibid.
7 Christian List and Philip Pettit, *Group Agency* (Oxford: Oxford University Press 2011) 7.
8 Ibid.
9 Ibid 8.
10 E Durkheim (1858–1917).
11 www.iep.utm.edu/durkheim/internet accessed 15 May 2014, encyclopaedia of philosophy. Society, conceived as a collection of ideas, beliefs and sentiments of all sorts that are realised to individuals indicates a reality that is produced through the interaction of individuals, resulting in the fusion of consciences.
12 Tom R Burns and Erik Engdahl, 'The Social Construction of Consciousness, Part 1: Collective Consciousness and its Socio-Cultural Foundations' (1998) 5(1) Journal of Consciousness Studies 72. The authors further their argument by reference to national behaviours during the Second World War in which different nations behaved differently towards their Jewish populations, according to their different collective consciousness, 77. Of note, writing in 1912, Durkheim was not blind to the forces driving social disintegration which had been brought about by modernity, he observed "the old gods are aging or are already dead, and others are not yet born", Emile Durkheim, *The Elementary Forms of the Religious Life* (Originally published 1912, Oxford: Oxford University Press 2008). Society as a whole had

all consciousness of necessity resides in individual minds ... [but] ... it converges and coalesces to a dynamic process of interaction and so becomes exterior and constraining in the incontrovertible sense that individuals find themselves enmeshed in thick and unyielding webs of social pressure that leave little recourse but to join the crowd.[13]

Heralding the 20th century rise in holism, this thinking emphasised notions of wholeness or collectiveness[14] and, specifically, that the state, comprising the individuals who are its subjects, was more than the sum of its parts.[15] The philosophy was extended beyond Durkheim's social realism, for example, Smuts[16] published his "holist" analysis in 1907 and he focused on the biological realm and the tendency in nature to form wholes that are greater than the sum of the parts through creative evolution.[17] According to his theory, the whole is in charge and all development and activity can only be properly understood when being viewed as a holistic character rather than as separate activities of special organs, or the separate products of special mental functions.[18] Although framed in language strongly resonant of emergentism,[19]

lost its former unity and cohesiveness and this rendered former beliefs and practices irrelevant. The institutions of the past, for example the institutions animating mediaeval life, which had previously brought unity and cohesiveness, were now lost. The big things of the past, the political, economic, social, and especially religious institutions, no longer inspired the enthusiasm they once did. Belief in God weakened and this brought a rejection of other elements of Christian doctrine, such as Christian morality and metaphysics which were being replaced by modern notions of justice and modern science. But no new gods were created to replace the old ones. This loss made way for what he called the new cult of the individual, the abstract conception of the autonomous actor endowed with rationality and born free and equal to all other individuals.

13 J Lincoln and D Guillot, 'A Durkheimian View of Organisational Cultures' in M Korczynski and others (eds.), *Social Theory at Work* (Oxford: Oxford University Press 2006).
14 The term 'holism' is attributable to the South African statesman Jan Christiaan Smuts. Jan Christiaan Smuts, *Holism and Evolution* (orig. pub. 1926, Greenwood Press 1973).
15 Tom Otto and Nils Bubandt, *Experiments in Holism: Theory and Practice in Contemporary Anthropology* (Oxford: Wiley-Blackwell 2010). However, in recognising that the analysis of social groups and structures needed to begin at the level of society or culture as a whole, the metaphor of the machine as a model for knowledge of life, mind and society was increasingly used. This metaphor provoked a particularly strong reaction from those, especially in the German speaking countries, who considered society a *sui generis* reality, unique to itself and irreducible to its component elements, Emile Durkheim, De La Division Du Travail Social (1893), *The Division Of Labour in Society* (trans WD Halls, The Free Press 1984).
16 J Smuts (1870–1950).
17 He observed that small units inevitably developed into bigger wholes, and they, in their turn, inevitably grew into ever larger structures without cessation. Jan Christiaan Smuts, *Holism and Evolution* (Originally published 1926, Greenwood Press 1973).
18 Ibid 284.
19 Ursula Goodenough and Terrence W Deacon, 'The Sacred Emergence of Nature' in Philip Clayton (ed.), *The Oxford Handbook of Religions and Science* (Oxford: Oxford University Press 2006) Ch. 50.

his theory also applied to human associations such as the state.[20] As regards social realism, Smuts observed that:

> while the wholes may be mutually exclusive, their fields overlap and pene-
> trate and reinforce each other, and thus create an entirely new situation.
> Thus we speak of the atmosphere of ideas, the spirit of a class, or the soul of
> a people. The social individuals as such remain unaltered, but the social
> environment or field undergoes a complete change. There is a multiplication
> of force in the society or group owing to this mutual penetration of the
> conjoint fields, which creates the appearance and much of the reality of a
> new organism. Hence we speak of social or group or national organisms.[21]

6.2 Legal theory: the really fictitious fiction

Notwithstanding Durkheim's identification of the new cult of the individual, the abstract conception of the autonomous actor endowed with rationality and born free and equal to all other individuals,[22] juristic thinking of the same period was also influenced by realist philosophy. It is suggested that this was to some extent shaped by Otto von Gierke's[23] *Das Deutsche Genossenschaftsrecht*[24] in which he asserted that legal personality developed as recognition of real social fact as opposed to legal fiction.[25] Thus, espousing the realist view,[26] Maitland[27] translated von Gierke's work under the title *Political Theories of the Middle Age*.[28] Similarly, a collection of essays published in a 1911 edition of the prestigious Law Quarterly Review agreed that the corporation was a creature of social fact, which preceded the creation of legal recognition and regulation. Indeed, it was observed that the fiction theory of organisations had never been received into the common law[29] and, recognising the *sui generis* nature of collective groups, Dicey[30] observed that,

20 Jan Christiaan Smuts, *Holism and Evolution* (orig. pub. 1926, Greenwood Press 1973) Ch. 5.
21 Ibid 339, Ch. 12.
22 Emile Durkheim, *The Elemental Forms of Religious Life* (orig. pub. 1912, Oxford: Oxford University Press 2008).
23 Otto Von Gierke (1841–1921).
24 Berlin 1868–81. This is translated as the German law of associations.
25 David Foxton, 'Corporate Personality in the Great War' (2002) 118 LQR (July) 428–57.
26 Frederic William Maitland, 'Moral Personality and Legal Personality' and 'Trust and Corpora-
    tion' in HAL Fisher (ed.), *The Collected Papers of Frederick William Maitland* (Cambridge:
    Cambridge University Press 1911) vol 3 at 210–319, 321–440; William Martin Geldart, 'Legal
    Personality' (1911) 27 LQR 90; Frederick Pollock, 'Theories of Corporations in Common
    Law' (1911) LQR 219.
27 FW Maitland (1850–1906).
28 Otto Friedrich von Gierke, *Political Theories of the Middle Age* (trans Frederic William Mait-
    land, Cambridge: Cambridge University Press 1913).
29 David Foxton, 'Corporate Personality in the Great War' LQR (2002) 118 LQR (July) 428–57.
30 AV Dicey (1835–1922).

when a body of 20, or 2000, or 200,000 men bind themselves together to act in a particular way for some common purpose, they create a body, which by no fiction of law, but by the very nature of things, differs from the individuals of whom it is constituted.[31]

Indeed, in 1905, just a decade before the landmark *Lennard's* judgment,[32] CT Carr had produced an encyclopaedic work on the topic of the law of corporations. This was the result of Maitland's request for a detailed exposition of English Group-life[33] to match the German equivalent written by Dr von Gierke.[34] This comprehensive work drew together much of Maitland's earlier material to demonstrate the nature and attributes of the corporation and the steps by which it had reached its legal form at that time.[35] While acknowledging that the origin of corporate liability was vicarious in nature, grounded in the laws of master and servant and agency,[36] Carr emphatically endorsed the prevailing realist philosophy. Remarking that, "it may be worthwhile to reflect that the morality of all is not always identical with the morality of its constituent members: collectiveness has its effect upon conduct",[37] he went on to say:

> in dealing with the Corporation, we are, after all, dealing with a body of men of flesh and blood, and a body which has a recognised personality, capacity, and will of its own. The will is hardly less real because it is the group will; the person hardly less real because it is a group person ... there comes a time when the fictions fail to satisfy.[38]

Carr rehearsed the wide field that had been long occupied by various forms of corporations[39] which included different:

> churches, universities, village communities, the manor, the township, the counties and hundreds, the chartered boroughs, the gild, the inns of court, the merchant adventurers, the militant "companies" of English condottieri,

---

31 Quoted by Frederic William Maitland in, 'Moral Personality and Legal Personality' in HAL Fisher (ed.), *The Collected Papers of Frederick William Maitland* (Cambridge: Cambridge University Press 1911) vol 3, 304 referring to the Sidgwick lecture 1910.

32 *Lennard's Carrying Co Ltd v Asiatic Petroleum Ltd* [1915] AC 705 (HL).

33 Cecil Thomas Carr, *The General Principles of the Law of Corporations* (Yorke prize essay 1902, Cambridge: Cambridge University Press 1905).

34 Otto Friedrich Von Gierke, *Das Deutsche Genossenschaftsrecht* (1866).

35 Cecil Thomas Carr, *The General Principles of the Law of Corporations* (Cambridge: Cambridge University Press 1905).

36 The principle derives from a time when the servant was a slave with no persona, the relationship between master and servant was therefore not distinguished from that of principal and agent.

37 Cecil Thomas Carr, *The General Principles of the Law of Corporations* (Cambridge: Cambridge University Press 1905) 105.

38 Ibid 180.

39 Described as the English "Fellowship" and association.

the trading companies, the companies that become colonies, the companies that make war, the friendly societies, the trade unions, the clubs, the group that meets at Lloyd's coffeehouse, the group that becomes the stock exchange, and so on even to the one-man company, the Standard Oil Trust and the South Australian statutes for communistic villages.[40]

The corporate form had been a longstanding and intrinsic part of the architecture of English society since the Middle Ages[41] and it was recognised in two forms, the corporation sole and the corporation aggregate.[42] Carr also included a detailed analysis of the development of both the civil and criminal liability of corporations. Of note, it was within the civil law context that the issue of attributing liability to a corporation, and whether "malice" could be imputed, had been argued.[43] The submissions made in a line of

40 Otto Friedrich von Gierke, *Political Theories in the Middle Age*, (trans Frederic William Maitland, Cambridge: Cambridge University Press 1913) translator's Introduction, xxvii.
41 HAL Fisher (ed.), *The Collected Papers of Frederick William Maitland* (Cambridge: Cambridge University Press 1911) vol 3. This was the result of the influence of Roman law towards the end of the Middle Ages.
42 The corporation thus constituted the official character of the holder for the time being of the same office or the common interest of the persons who for the time being were adventurers in the same undertaking, into an artificial person or ideal subject of legal capacities and duties, HAL Fisher (ed.), *The Collected Papers of Frederick William Maitland* (Cambridge: Cambridge University Press 1911) vol 3, referring to Sir F Pollock's explanation in his book on Contract.
43 As regards the potential for civil liability, the earliest view had been articulated in the religious context and at the first Council of Lyons (1245) Pope Innocent III issued a decree in which he forbade the excommunication of corporations on the basis that "they have neither minds nor souls: they cannot sin", see Cecil Thomas Carr, *The General Principles of the Law of Corporations* (Yorke prize essay 1902, Cambridge: Cambridge University Press, 1905) 73. It was from this ecclesiastical context that lawyers were later to set out the general proposition that corporations were incapable of malice or intention. Later, in the 15th century, a year-book of Henry VI stated that a dean and chapter "cannot have predecessor nor successor, they cannot commit treason, be outlawed or excommunicated, for they have no soul", X Rep 32b. A further expression of the sinlessness and soullessness of corporations can be found in the classic passage in Coke's Report of the case of *Sutton's Hospital* in 1612, [1558–1774] All ER Rep 11 at 13, see Cecil Thomas Carr, *The General Principles of the Law of Corporations* (Yorke prize essay 1902, Cambridge: Cambridge University Press 1905) 76. This case involved the validity of a bequest to this charitable corporation, in which Coke said, "The Corporation is only *in abstracto*, and rests only in intendment and consideration of the law. It is invisible and immortal." However, this view was not settled and, in dissent, Lord Blackburn responded, "I quite agree that a corporation cannot, in one sense, commit a crime – a corporation cannot be imprisoned, if imprisonment be the sentence for the crime; a corporation cannot be hanged or put to death, if that be punishment for the crime; and so, in those senses a corporation cannot commit a crime. But a corporation may be fined; and a corporation may pay damages", *Pharmaceutical Society v The London and Provincial Supply Association* [1874–80] 5 App Cas 857 (HL), 869. Thereafter, it took a series of cases between 1880 and 1904 to finally develop the principle of corporate liability in civil actions, *Eastern Counties Rly Co v Broom* (1851) 6 Ex 314; *Whitfield v SE Rly Co* (1858) 27 LT QB 229; *Green v London General Omnibus Company*

cases culminated in judicial acceptance that malice could be imputed[44] to a corporation. This was based on reasoning such as that of Chief Baron Kelly in 1871 who said, "If they [corporations] are not to be liable for the abuse of this power, they are given a power to commit acts of oppression to an extension of the nature really fearful to contemplate".[45] Similarly, in 1886, Lord Fitzgerald had expressed his opinion in this way, "I shall only say of corporations, and of these trading corporations especially, that I have often heard it observed that they certainly are very frequently without conscience and sometimes very malicious".[46] Darling J. in the 1899 case of *Cornford v Carlton Bank* held that:

> If malice in law were synonymous with malice in French – a sort of esprit tinged with ill nature – I should entirely agree [with L. Bramwell]. In such a sense a Corporation would be as incapable of malice as wit. But of malice – actual malice – in a legal sense, I think a corporation is capable.[47]

Indeed, according to Carr, the 1901 *Taff Vale Railway* case provided evidence that, in accordance with realist theory, the law recognised the unincorporated association as a legal entity.[48] The now infamous case involved an action by the Railway Company against the unincorporated trade union in relation to the activities of its members.[49] Finding in favour of the Railway Company, the House of Lords gave clear endorsement to the realist approach which was then prevalent:[50]

(1859) 7 CBNS 290; *Barwick v English Joint-Stock Bank* (1867)LR 2 Exch 259; *Henderson v M Rly Co* (1871) 24 LTNS 881; *Bank of New South Wales v Owston* (1879) (JC) 4 App Cas 270; *Edwards v Midland Rly* (1880) 6 QBD 287, (1880) 50 LJ (QB) 281; *Abrath v NE Rly Co* (1886) 11 App Cas 250; *Kent v Courage and Co Ltd* (1890) JP 55, 264; *Cornford v Carlton Bank* (1899) 1 QB 392–5.

44 The following civil cases are discussed, *Pharmaceutical Society v The London and Provincial Supply Association* [1874–80] 5 App Cas 857; *Eastern Counties Rly Co v Broom* (1851) 6 Ex 314; *Whitfield v SE Rly Co* (1858) 27 LT QB 229; *Green v London Gen Omnibus Company* (1859)7 CBNS 290; *Barwick v English Joint-Stock Bank*,LR 2 Exch 259; *Henderson v M Rly Co* (1871) 24 LTNS 88; *Bank of New South Wales v Owston* (1879) (JC) 4 App Cas 270; *Edwards v Midland Rly* (1880) 50 LJ (QB) 28; *Abrath v NE Rly Co* (1886) 11 App Cas 250; *Kent v Courage and Co Ltd* (1890) JP 55, 264; *Cornford v Carlton Bank* [1899] 1 QB 392; *Citizens Life Assurance Company v Brown* [1904] AC 423.

45 *Henderson v M Rly Co* (1871) 24 LTNS 881. Baron Bramwell also gave judgment in this case and others in which he strenuously denied that corporations could be malicious.

46 *Abrath v NE Rly Co* (1886) 11 App Cas 250, 254.

47 *Cornford v Carlton Bank* [1899] 1 QB 392.

48 Cecil Thomas Carr, *The General Principles of the Law of Corporations* (Yorke prize essay 1902, Cambridge: Cambridge University Press 1905) 192.

49 *Taff Vale Rly Co v Amalgamated Society of Rly Servants* [1901] AC 426 (HL).

50 Ibid. Of note, Haldane, as King's Counsel, acted for the trade union and his submissions in the Court of Appeal had centred on the proposition that a society could not be sued

The principle on which corporations have been held liable in respect of wrongs committed by servants or agents in the course of their service and for the benefit of the employer – *qui sentit commodum sentire debet et onus* – (see *Mersey Docks and Gibbs* (1866) LR 1 HL 93) is as applicable to the case for trade union as to that of the Corporation. If the contention of the defendant society were well founded, the legislature has authorised the creation of numerous bodies of men capable of owning great wealth and of acting by agents with absolutely no responsibility for the wrongs that they may do to other persons by the use of that wealth and the employment of those agents … [See *Mersey Docks* case LR1 HL 120]. It would require very clear and express words of enactment to induce me to hold that the legislature had in fact legalised the existence of such irresponsible bodies with such wide capacity for evil.[51]

Lord Halsbury, then Lord Chancellor, gave an opinion, with which Lord Macnaghten concurred, stating that, "if the legislature has created a thing which can own property, which can employ servants, and which can inflict injury, it must be taken, I think, to have implicitly given the power to make it suable in a court of law for injuries purposely done by its authority and procurement".[52] Similarly, Maitland had observed that when the House of Lords found that the trade union could be liable for the acts of its members,

---

unless it was incorporated, or the legislature had said it could be sued as if it were incorporated. The ability of a trade union to hold property was facilitated by vesting it in the trustees, Trade Unions Act 1871, s. 8; Trade Unions Act 1876, ss 3, 4 and it could not be inferred that the legislature intended to treat a trade union as if it were a corporate body. Further, he submitted that although the union had no legal entity and it may be practically impossible to sue the members, the plaintiffs could not shortcut suing them by suing the registered name of the trade union instead. For their part, the plaintiffs contended that the status of trade union, created in the Trade Unions Act 1871 contemplated an entity with perpetual succession, a body entitled to hold funds and therefore a legal entity irrespective of incorporation. In the event, Haldane K.C.'s arguments prevailed; A L Smith, M.R., stated that there must be some statute enabling an action to be maintained in the name of the society. However, the House of Lords reversed the decision reasoning by analogy to the tortious liability of corporations. See the comments of David Foxton, 'Corporate Personality in the Great War' (2002) 118 LQR (July) 428–57.

51 *Taff Vale Rly Company v Amalgamated Society of Rly Servants* [1901] AC 426 (HL) 430 (J. Farwell).

52 Ibid 436. In retrospect, however, the House of Lords decision in *Taff Vale*, recognising the collectivity as a social fact, produced ramifications that cannot be understated. If it was, as has been suggested, a politically motivated decision driven by Lord Halsbury, the conservative Lord Chancellor in the unionist government, its ironic consequence was to shift massive public support to the Labour party and had this not been the case, history may have taken an altogether different course, KD Ewing, 'The Politics of the British Constitution' (2000) PL Autumn 405. The Trade Disputes Act 1906 was enacted in an attempt to shore up the political damage effected through the *Taff Vale* decision and the judges, especially the Law Lords, were set to exit from areas of appellate process that appeared to involve policy-making, Robert

it involved a recognition that questions of identity could not be detached from questions of responsibility. If groups are to have a life of their own, they must be willing to be held responsible for what their agents do.[53]

It is pertinent that, contrary to what might be thought today, Carr explicitly recognised that corporate liability had been "readily brought home by the criminal law", in contrast to the civil law.[54] In this respect he pointed to civic communities and cities, endowed with corporate status, which were subject to punishment for failing to repair roads and bridges, almshouses and grammar schools.[55] The punishment of the body was effected by fine and, if further forms of sanction were needed, the crown could take away some of its civic privileges or even curtail its civic existence.[56] Furthermore, referring Pollock's work,[57] Carr observed that the corporate liability could be vicarious[58] and he noted that this principle pervaded the whole of English law where the wrong was committed in the course of service and for the master's benefit.[59]

Stevens, *Law And Politics, The House of Lords As A Judicial Body, 1800–1976* (London: Wydenfelt and Nicholson 1978) 69.

53 Otto Friedrich von Gierke, *Political Theories in the Middle Age*, (trans Frederic William Maitland, Cambridge: Cambridge University Press 1913) translator's Introduction, xxii.

54 Carr explains that the punishment of the individual criminal was, in early times, effected by threatening punishment to a group of individuals. In the days when the modern system of policing was as yet unknown, the group of men was made answerable for the doings of the man. He said that there was the "view of frank pledge", 18 Edw II: Stephen, *General View of Criminal Law*, 10: Stubbs, *Constitutional History* I, 87: Maitland, *Gloucester Pleas* XXXI etc. In the maturity of the system all men were bound to combine themselves into associations of ten, each of whom were security for the good behaviour of the rest. Consequently lawyers were early familiarised with the notions of making a company of men liable to criminal proceedings. These companies were in no sense corporations, the procedure not aimed at an impersonal artificial entity, aimed rather at any members of the group who appeared sufficiently substantial to pay a fine, Cecil Thomas Carr, *The General Principles of the Law of Corporations* (Yorke prize essay 1902, Cambridge: Cambridge University Press 1905) 87.

55 The punishment of the body was effected by amercement, a fine.

56 What the crown had given, it could take away; charters could be forfeited, commercial advantages abolished, elected mayors and magistrates could be deposed and replaced by Royal lieutenants, Cecil Thomas Carr, *The General Principles of the Law of Corporations* (Yorke prize essay 1902, Cambridge: Cambridge University Press 1905) 87–8.

57 F Pollock (1845–1937).

58 It is submitted that where liability is imposed vicariously, it is on a fiction basis rather than in accordance with the realist theory of organisations. However, such an observation may as much reflect the fact that the master and servant relationship was the precursor to the corporate employer and that as the law of master and servant developed there was no reason to allude to theories of realism which only became relevant where there was collective action.

59 *Laugher v Pointer* (1826) 5 B&C 554 cited by Cecil Thomas Carr, *The General Principles of the Law of Corporations* (Yorke prize essay for the year 1902, Cambridge: Cambridge University Press 1905) 97. In support, he quoted Lord Justice Rigby in *Dyer v Munday* (1895) 1 QBD 748 who had said, "I can find no authority for distinguishing in the application of this rule between tortious and criminal acts of the servant".

Although the literature reveals some disagreement about the development of the criminal law in the specific context of the trading corporation,[60] it is generally agreed that proceedings alleging public nuisance were some of the earliest to influence the criminal law's development. Of note, public nuisance

---

60 Notwithstanding Carr's encyclopaedic analysis, academic accounts have focused on the attribution of criminal liability to the corporate form exclusively in the context of the commercial trading entity. On this narrow perspective, Brickey asserts that the general view in the early 16th and 17th centuries was that corporations simply could not be held criminally liable, see Kathleen F Brickey, 'Corporate Criminal Accountability: A Brief History and an Observation' 60 Wash ULQ 393, 396 giving as an example 1 William Blackstone, Commentaries 476. This seems to have the support of the infamous case of 1701 in which Lord Holt is reported to have said that a "corporation is not indictable, but the particular members of it are", *Anonymous Case* (No 935) (1701) 88 Eng Rep 1518, 1518 (KB 1701). It should be noted that the case report comprises just this one sentence and Lord Holt's reasoning cannot be ascertained. While the distinction between civil and criminal law cannot be understood in the same way it is today, it is said that this precedent was still authoritative in the mid-19th century, notwithstanding there were recognised exceptions, see Leigh LH, *The Criminal Liability of Corporations in English Law* 1–12 (LSC Research Monographs, London: Lowe and Brydone Ltd 1969). Kanna and Coffee, for example, submit that there were a number of obstacles to the courts finding corporate liability in the 1700s which included the thinking that corporations could not be morally blameworthy, see Khanna VS, 'Corporate Criminal Liability: What Purpose Does It Serve?' (1996) 109 Harv L Rev 1477 and John Collins Coffee Jr, 'Corporate Criminal Responsibility' in Sanford H Kadish (ed.), *Encyclopaedia of Crime and Justice* (Aspen 1983) 253. An additional obstacle was the ultra vires doctrine which meant that the courts would not hold corporations accountable for acts not provided for in their charters, because the fictional corporate entity had no mind and no body, and later it was said that corporations, other than charter corporations, were creatures endowed with the limited powers that were specified by the incorporating statute or the enabling provisions of the Companies Act and/or by the objects set out in the memorandum of association. Powers were never explicitly conferred enabling corporations to commit crimes, therefore, such acts were ultra vires, see LH Leigh, *The Criminal Liability of Corporations in English Law 1–12* (LSC Research Monographs, Lowe and Brydone Ltd 1969) 8–9; John Collins Coffee Jr, 'Corporate Criminal Responsibility' in Sanford H Kadish (ed.), *Encyclopaedia of Crime and Justice* (Aspen 1983). Similarly, as a matter of procedure, the accused had to be physically brought before the court, LH Leigh, *The Criminal Liability of Corporations in English Law 1–12* (LSC Research Monographs, Lowe and Brydone Ltd 1969) 9–12; Glanville Williams, *Criminal Law: The General Part* (2nd ed, London: Stevens & Sons 1961) 855–7. Thus, prior to the 19th Century, commercial trading corporations lay outside the scope of the criminal law institution, as it then was, because prisoners were required to stand at the bar in person and they could not be represented by lawyers, JWC Turner, *Kenny's Outlines of Criminal Law* (18th ed, Cambridge: Cambridge University Press 1962); *Anonymous Case* (No 935) (1701) 88 ER 1518, note, by Holt C.J. Finally, as corporations could act only through officers and not *in propria persona*, liability had to be vicarious and, according to Leigh, it was a fundamental principle of English common law that a person could not be held vicariously liable for the crimes of another, Leigh LH, *The Criminal Liability of Corporations in English Law* (LSC Research Monographs, Lowe and Brydone Ltd 1969) 3; *R v Huggins* (1730) 2 Ld Raym 1574. That being said, Leigh did recognise exceptions to what he described as the general rule which were developed by analogy with the established master/servant doctrine in the context that a local authority could be held vicariously liable for the strict liability common law offence of public nuisance. Arguably, Leigh is mistaken in this respect given that the corporations themselves were under a statutory

was, in substance, a civil matter albeit technically framed as a criminal offence.[61] The offence would be committed when the local authority failed in its duty to maintain roads, bridges and waterways and examples of cases of this nature date back to the 17th and 18th centuries.[62] Accordingly, culpability was not based on the principle of vicarious liability since the corporation itself was under the duty to perform the act in question[63] and it was in the context of statutory duties that the mid-19th century courts began to convict trading companies.[64] Thus, in *the Birmingham and Gloucester Railway* case of 1842[65] the company was indicted for a "non-feasance" and, in 1846, the *Great North of England Railway Company*[66] was indicted for a positive act, that of misfeasance by public nuisance[67]. It was in this particular case that Denman C.J. famously remarked:

> there can be no effectual means for deterring from an oppressive exercise of power for the purpose of gain, except the remedy by an indictment against those who truly commit it – that is, the Corporation, acting by its majority: and there is no principle which places them beyond the reach of the law for such proceedings.[68]

Although the observation was made in the context of a breach of a statutory duty, Carr affirmed its general landmark importance in that it had "fixed the attitude of the criminal law towards corporations".[69] He also quoted with

duty. Others note the reluctance of the criminal law to adopt the doctrine and it was argued that such a move would be contrary to the criminal law's aim of punishing only the morally culpable, where fault rested on vicarious, not personal, guilt. See Sanford H Kadish, 'Developments in the Law – Corporate Crime: Regulating Corporate Behaviour Through Criminal Sanctions' (1979) 92 Harv L Rev 1227, 1231–42 for a discussion of arguments relating to moral blameworthiness and James R Elkins, 'Corporations and the Criminal Law: An Uneasy Alliance' (1976) 65 Ky L J 73, 97; Laski HJ, 'The Basis of Vicarious Liability' (1916) 26 Yale LJ 105, 130–4.

61 See *R v Stephens* (1866) LR 1 QB 702.
62 E.g. *Case of Langforth Bridge* 79 ER 919, (1634) Cro Car 365; *R v Inhabitants of Great Broughton*, 98 ER 418, (1771) 5 Burr 2700.
63 Elkins JR, 'Corporations and the Criminal Law: An Uneasy Alliance' (1976) 65 Ky LJ 73, 87–8; John Collins Coffee Jr, 'Corporate Criminal Responsibility' in Sanford H Kadish (ed.), *Encyclopaedia of Crime and Justice* 253, 253–4 (Aspen 1983).
64 *R v Birmingham and Gloucester Rly Co* 114 ER 492, (1842) 3 QB 223; *R v Great North of England Rly Co*, 115 ER 1294, (1846) 9 QB 315.
65 *R v Birmingham and Gloucester Rly Co* 114 ER 492, (1842) 3 QB 223.
66 *R v Great North of England Rly Co* 115 ER 1294, (1846) 9 QB 315.
67 See Winn CRN, 'The Criminal Responsibility of Corporations' (1927–29) 3 CLJ 398, 399 who says that the courts were compelled to recognise a like responsibility for acts done in breach of statutory duty as no satisfactory distinction could be drawn between an act and an omission.
68 *R v Great North of England Rly Co* 115 ER 1294, (1846) 9 QB 315, 327.
69 Cecil Thomas Carr, *The General Principles of the Law of Corporations* (Yorke prize essay 1902, Cambridge: Cambridge University Press 1905) 96. In particular, Carr foresaw the possibility of the courts extending a corporation's criminal liability to manslaughter where negligence causes death.

approval Maitland's prediction that, "Someday the historian may have to tell you that the really fictitious fiction of English law was, not that its Corporation was a person, but that its unincorporated body was no person".[70]

Indeed, the potential for corporate prosecution had been expressly provided for much earlier in that statutory reference to a "person" would include a corporate personality, unless a contrary legislative intention appeared.[71] Thereafter, in 1880 the House of Lords had reviewed the scope of the criminal law in relation to corporate entities and, by way of limitation, found that an artificial person still could not commit treason, felony or a misdemeanour involving personal violence.[72] Writing in 1902, two decades later, Carr observed that if corporations "can have a mens rea their criminal liability is almost unbounded".[73]

Although acceptance of the realist nature of organisations was seemingly not in doubt at the outset of the 20th century, it must be acknowledged that the decided cases at that time point to a corporate liability based on vicarious principles established in the context of master and servant law and agency. It is to be conceded that, whilst at first blush these theories, realism and the vicarious attribution of corporate liability, appear to make for incompatible bedfellows, they are certainly not mutually exclusive. Since the acceptance of the realist theory of groups during this époque is not to be doubted, the fact that the cases on corporate liability emerging at this time are based on principles of vicarious liability may simply reflect that they involved wrongdoing that was readily attributable to identifiable individuals whereas instances of crime that were not so reducible had not yet come about. This is plausible given that the early corporate forms were not the Goliaths, with vast, complex and decentralised management structures, that are typical of many corporations in existence today. The analogies drawn with the other areas of law, master and servant and agency, strongly suggest simple pyramidal management systems characteristic of small organisations such that the employer incorporate was considered akin to the individual employer. Indeed, as much is inferred in a 1904 case dealing with the

70 Frederic William Maitland, 'Political Theories of the Middle Age, Introduction' xxxiv in Cecil Thomas Carr, *The General Principles of the Law of Corporations* (Cambridge: Cambridge University Press 1905) 194. Indeed, it should be noted that the landmark judicial decision in *Salomon v Salomon* [1897] AC 22 (HL) was itself the product of the realist influence.

71 Criminal Law Act 1827, s. 14. The Interpretation Act of 1889 also reinforced judicial recognition that corporations could be held criminally culpable. Having already noted the distinct categorisation of statutory and common law offences, whether the same attitude also extended to common law offences is not clear.

72 *Pharmaceutical Society v London & Provincial Supply Association* [1874–80] 5 App Cas 857 (HL).

73 Cecil Thomas Carr, *The General Principles of the Law of Corporations* (Yorke prize essay 1902, Cambridge: Cambridge University Press 1905) 98 and citing *Stephens v Robert Reid and Co Ltd*, 28 Victorian Law Reports 82; *Lawler v P and H Egan Limited* (1901) 2 Ir R 589; *R v Panton* 14 Victorian Law Reports 836. Presumably Carr is here referring to common law offences since the presumption of mens rea applied only to them.

common law offence of malicious publication of defamatory libel[74] in which the Privy Council likened the position of the corporate actor to that of the individual principal. In so doing it strongly reaffirmed that principles of agency law applied as equally to corporations as they did to individuals, such that corporate liability would be vicarious:

> If it is once granted that corporations are for civil purposes to be regarded as persons, i.e., as principals acting by agents and servants, it is difficult to see why the ordinary doctrines of agency and of master and servant are not to be applied to corporations as well as to ordinary individuals. These doctrines have been so applied in a great variety of cases, in questions arising out of contract, and in questions arising out of torts and frauds; and to apply them to one class of libels and to deny their application to another class of libels on the ground that malice cannot be imputed to a body corporate appears to their Lordships to be contrary to sound legal principles. To talk about imputing malice to corporations appears to their Lordships to introduce metaphysical subtleties which are needless and fallacious.[75]

Furthermore, the 1910 edition of *Archbold's* practitioner text set out the general principles of corporate criminality as they were then understood.[76] Affirming the limitations identified earlier,[77] it lists the decided instances in which corporations had been indicted, namely nonfeasance and misfeasance of public duties and the common law libel offences. However, this rehearsal can be read alongside Carr's earlier analysis which indicated that the scope of corporate liability was effectively much broader. Of note, Carr had observed that, "We have therefore arrived at the valuable idea that, if employers were not liable for the wrong done by their servants it would be impossible to bring charges home to a corporation".[78] What is clear is that the imposition of corporate liability was simply not limited by any supervening doctrine, such as the now established "identification" doctrine. That development, and the fictionist approach to the corporate form, was yet to come.

---

74 A common law offence, the punishment was set out in Libel Act 1843, s. 5 see William Feilden Craies and Henry Delacombe Roome, *Archbold's Criminal Pleading, Evidence & Practice* (24th ed, London: Sweet & Maxwell 1910) 1236.

75 *Citizens Life Assurance Company Ltd v Brown* [1904] AC 423 (PC) Aus (Lord Lindley).

76 William Feilden Craies and Henry Delacombe Roome, *Archbold's Criminal Pleading, Evidence & Practice* (24th ed, London: Sweet & Maxwell 1910) 7.

77 An artificial person could not commit treason, felony or a misdemeanour involving personal violence, *Pharmaceutical Society v London & Provincial Supply Association* [1874–80] 5 App Cas 857 (HL).

78 Cecil Thomas Carr, *The General Principles of the Law of Corporations* (Yorke prize essay 1902, Cambridge: Cambridge University Press 1905) 104.

The ascription of vicarious liability,[79] as evidenced in the early cases, may not necessarily appear compatible with realist theory but neither is it fatal or damaging to it. That an organisation has the potential to act autonomously does not mean its individual members never act autonomously. Rather, the issue goes to Harding's tipping point in the spectrum of organisational behaviour and the location of the emergence of the distinct corporate personality.[80] Liability may be more readily recognised at the individual level, at the group level, or even reside in both. Further, the nature of the liability itself may differ according to the particular involvement of the particular actor. Thus, for example, in the context of the modern bribery offence the individual liability is incurred for the bribery conduct while the corporate liability is incurred for failing to prevent that conduct. The early cases, in which corporate liability is attributed vicariously, provide nothing more than examples in which individual members were individually culpable and that, as a matter of law, criminal liability could be attributed to the corporate employer. The capacity for group agency is not diminished by the additional capacity for individual agency within the group context.

---

79 Indeed, the basis of vicarious liability itself remains controversial and there is still disagreement as to whether it means that the master is responsible for the servant or whether the servant's acts are those of the master himself, Celia Wells, *Corporations and Criminal Responsibility* (2nd ed, Oxford: Oxford University Press 2001) referring to Glanville Williams, 'Vicarious Liability: Tort of the Master or of the Servant?' (1956) 72 LQR 522; Brent Fisse, 'The Distinction Between Primary and Vicarious Corporate Criminal Liability' (1967) 41 ALJ 203. Ormerod suggests if the physical act of the employee is construed in law to be the act of the employer, in legal theory it is not really a case of vicarious liability at all, David Ormerod's, *Smith and Hogan's Criminal Law: Cases and Materials* (10th ed, Oxford: Oxford University Press 2009). By way of illustration he says that in an offence of selling such as selling goods with a false trade description, in law the sale is the transfer of ownership of goods from A to B so although the goods are sold by the shop assistant, the seller is the owner of the goods i.e. the employer. In law too, the employer is the possessor of goods and there are numerous offences of possessing various articles and an employer has been held to keep and to use a vehicle when it is in the keeping or use by his employee in circumstances which the law forbids. Whether the particular verb includes the inactive employer is a question of statutory interpretation but it should be noted that the law often has it both ways; so the statute can be construed that the shop assistant has also sold the goods belonging to her employer and be guilty like the principal of the same offence. In the case of selling intoxicating liquor the owner of the liquor, the licensee and the barmaid may all be guilty as principals of the same offence as each has in law sold the liquor, *Allied Domecq Leisure Ltd v Cooper* [1999] Crim L R 230 and *Nottingham City Council v Wolverhampton & Dudley Breweries* [2004] 2 WLR 820. Alternatively, vicarious liability is said to be established by the identification of the conduct of the agent which is then ascribed to the employer, based on the legal relationship existing between them. On this view, vicarious liability is conceived as a structure of legal fiction which states that whatever a person does through an agent, he is deemed to have done himself and the knowledge of the agent is the knowledge of the employer, see Eli Lederman, 'Models for Imposing Corporate Criminal Liability: From Adaptation and Imitation toward Aggregation and the Search for Self-Identity' [2001] Buff Crim LR 642. Blackstone explained the principle in terms of the fiction of an implied command, Blackstone, Commentaries 1, 417.

80 Christopher Harding, *Criminal Enterprise: Individuals, Organisations and Criminal Responsibility* (Cullompton: Willan 2007).

6.3 *Lennard's* [1915] and the turn of the theoretical tide?

The snapshot provided, of the philosophical and legal context in which the landmark judgment was delivered, makes *Lennard's* a surprising decision, seemingly swimming against both the theoretical tide and the judicial willingness to inculpate corporations. Perhaps more curious still is the fact that it was also decided in the absence of any binding precedent. The fictionist approach to organisations that it is said to herald, therefore emerged in contradiction to both the prevailing theoretical landscape and legal principle.

At a personal level, Viscount Haldane L.C., who is reputed to have first articulated the fictionist "directing mind" theory, was also something of a philosopher himself.[81] Profoundly influenced by the German thinkers, with strong realist beliefs, it is a matter of some irony that he has come to be seen as the father of the fiction theory.[82] Although he had been called to the bar in 1879,[83] Haldane nonetheless maintained his interest in philosophy and published his *Essays in Philosophical Criticism* in 1883, in addition to his translation of Schopenhauer's *The World as Will and Idea*. Other philosophical works produced by Haldane include the *Pathway to Reality* (1903), *Reign of Relativity* (1921), *The Philosophy of Humanism* (1922) and *Selected Addresses and Essays* (1928)[84] and evidence of the influence of the German realist theories of organisations is abundant in his work. For example, in his book one, lecture two of the Gifford series, Haldane observed:

> In life we have in the organism this remarkable feature, that the life of the whole is present in each of the parts ... But this whole of life does not in its work resemble a cause operating, *ab extra*, upon the organism, but is more like, more really analogous to, the purpose which the soldiers in an army or the citizens in a State are moved by when they act together. The cells of the body, the cells which make up the totality of the organism, act together

---

81 As a teenager, Haldane had lost the faith shared by his deeply religious parents and had become interested in a mixture of philosophy, theology, natural science and the idealism of TH Green and Georg Hegel, see John T Saywell, *The Lawmakers: Judicial Power and the Shaping of Canadian Federalism* (Osgoode Society for Canadian Legal History, Toronto: University of Toronto Press 2002). However, notwithstanding his publishing success, the New Statesman remarked that Haldane was "a Hegelian who never understood Hegel", "The Haldane Paradox", The New Statesman, 25 August 1928, 30. At 18 years of age he spent six months studying philosophy and geology in Gottingen, Germany and later won prizes and scholarships in philosophy at Edinburgh University.

82 Richard Burdon Haldane, *An Autobiography* (London: Hodder and Stoughton 1929).

83 Law and philosophy merged in his interest in jurisprudential cases and, by 1882, he was appearing before the judicial committee of the Privy Council and before the House of Lords.

84 David Kahan's introduction to Richard Burdon Haldane's 1902–1904 Gifford Lectures: The Pathway to Reality at www.giffordlectures.org/Browse.asp?PubID=TPTPTR&Volume=O&Issue=O&ArticleID=6 accessed 15 May 2014.

purposively, or quasi-purposively, which is a better expression—and I refer to them in order to illustrate to you how really the analogy of the actual purpose of living beings, acting together in a regiment or in a State, is a better analogy to the life of the organism than is the analogy of a machine.[85]

In his second book, he referred once more to the notion of a collective purpose or intention:

> The great result which modern Biology has achieved, lies in the demonstration that the living organism is an aggregate of the living units which are often called cells. But the aggregate is no mechanical aggregate. The cells are less like marbles in a heap than like free citizens living in a state. They act for the fulfilment of a common end, which continues so long as the life of the organism continues, and the fulfilment of which appears to be just that life.[86]

Although realist theory fell from favour as fascism took over in Europe, its association with the totalitarian image of society perhaps leading to its demise,[87] it was extremely fashionable at the time of the *Lennard's* judgment in 1915.[88] Since the articulation of the fictionist "identification principle" of corporate fault attribution marked a considerable departure from the prevailing orthodoxy, and indeed Viscount Haldane L.C.'s own beliefs, the following chapter seeks to explain the development of the law more specifically by reference to the black letter law itself.

Bibliography

Books

Carr CT, *The General Principles of the Law of Corporations* (Yorke prize essay 1902, Cambridge: Cambridge University Press 1905)

Clayton P (ed.), *The Oxford Handbook of Religions and Science* (Oxford: Oxford University Press 2006)

Craies WF and Roome HD, *Archbold's Criminal Pleading, Evidence & Practice* (24th ed, London: Sweet & Maxwell 1910)

Durkheim E, *De La Division Du Travail Social* (1893), *The Division Of Labour in Society* (trans WD Halls, The Free Press 1984)

Durkheim E, *The Elemental Forms of Religious Life* (orig. pub. 1912, Oxford: Oxford University Press 2008)

---

85 Viscount Richard Burdon Haldane, *The Pathway to Reality: Being the Gifford Lectures Delivered in the University of St Andrews in the Session 1902–1904* (Ulan Press 2012) bk 1, lec 2.

86 Viscount Richard Burdon Haldane, *The Pathway to Reality: Being the Gifford Lectures Delivered in the University of St Andrews in the Session 1902 –1904* (Ulan Press 2012) bk 2, lec 3.

87 Christian List and Philip Pettit, *Group Agency* (Oxford: Oxford University Press 2011).

88 *Lennard's Carrying Co Ltd v Asiatic Petroleum Ltd* [1915] AC 705 (HL).

Fisher HAL (ed.), *The Collected Papers of Frederick William Maitland* (Cambridge University Press 1911)

Haldane RB, *An Autobiography* (London: Hodder and Stoughton 1929)

Haldane RB, *The Pathway to Reality: Being the Gifford Lectures Delivered in the University of St Andrews in the Session 1902–1904* (Ulan Press 2012)

Harding C, *Criminal Enterprise: Individuals, Organisations and Criminal Responsibility* (Cullompton: Willan 2007)

Kadish SH (ed.), *Encyclopaedia of Crime and Justice* (Aspen 1983)

Korczynski M et al (eds.), *Social Theory at Work* (Oxford: Oxford University Press 2006)

Leigh LH, *The Criminal Liability of Corporations in English Law* 1–12 (LSC Research Monographs, London: Lowe and Brydone Ltd 1969)

List C and Pettit P, *Group Agency* (Oxford: Oxford University Press 2011)

Ormerod D, *Smith and Hogan's Criminal Law: Cases and Materials* (10th ed, Oxford: Oxford University Press 2009)

Otto T and Bubandt N, *Experiments in Holism, Theory and Practice in Contemporary Anthropology* (Oxford: Wiley-Blackwell 2010)

Saywell JT, *The Lawmakers: Judicial Power and the Shaping of Canadian Federalism* (Osgoode Society for Canadian Legal History, Toronto: University of Toronto Press 2002)

Smuts JC, *Holism and Evolution* (Orig. Pub. 1926, Greenwood Press 1973

Stevens R, *Law And Politics, The House of Lords As A Judicial Body, 1800–1976* (London: Wydenfelt and Nicholson 1978)

Turner JWC, *Kenny's Outlines of Criminal Law* (18th ed, Cambridge: Cambridge University Press 1962)

von Gierke OF, *Political Theories of the Middle Age* (trans Frederic William Maitland, Cambridge: Cambridge University Press 1913)

Wells C, *Corporations and Criminal Responsibility* (2nd ed, Oxford: Oxford University Press 2001)

Williams G, *Criminal Law: The General Part* (2nd ed, London: Stevens & Sons 1961)

Journal articles

Brickey KF, 'Corporate Criminal Accountability: A Brief History and an Observation' 60 Wash ULQ 393

Burns TR and Engdahl E, 'The Social Construction of Consciousness, Part 1: Collective Consciousness and its Socio-Cultural Foundations' (1998) 5(1) Journal of Consciousness Studies 72

Elkins JR, 'Corporations and the Criminal Law: An Uneasy Alliance' (1976) 65 Ky L J 73

Ewing KD, 'The Politics of the British Constitution' (2000) PL Autumn 405

Fisse B, 'The Distinction Between Primary and Vicarious Corporate Criminal Liability' (1967) 41 ALJ 203

Foxton D, 'Corporate Personality in the Great War' (2002) 118 LQR (July) 428

Geldart WM, 'Legal Personality' (1911) 27 LQR 90

Kadish SH, 'Developments in the Law – Corporate Crime: Regulating Corporate Behaviour Through Criminal Sanctions' (1979) 92 Harv L Rev 1227

Khanna VS, 'Corporate Criminal Liability: What Purpose Does It Serve?' (1996) 109 Harv L Rev 1477

Laski HJ, 'The Basis of Vicarious Liability' (1916) 26 Yale LJ 105

Lederman E, '*Models for Imposing Corporate Criminal Liability: From Adaptation and Imitation toward Aggregation and the Search for Self-Identity*' [2001] Buff Crim LR 642
Pollock F, '*Theories of Corporations in Common Law*' (1911) LQR 219
Williams G, '*Vicarious Liability: Tort of the Master or of the Servant?*' (1956) 72 LQR 522
Winn CRN, '*The Criminal Responsibility of Corporations*' (1927–29) 3 CLJ 398

Websites

www.giffordlectures.org/Browse.asp?PubID=TPTPTR&Volume=O&Issue=O&ArticleID=6 accessed 15 May 2014
www.iep.utm.edu/durkheim/internet accessed 15 May 2014

7   The unmasking of the identification principle

7.1 *Lennard's*: viewed in the light of its day

The decision emanating from the House of Lords in *Lennard's*[1] was a surprising one given the prevailing realist ideology, to which Viscount Haldane L. C. was no stranger, and the absence of any binding precedent. The identification doctrine associated with this judgment was described in a recent report by the Law Commission as one that "treats the acts and states of mind of those individuals who are the directing mind and will of the corporation as the acts or state of mind of the corporation itself".[2] Accordingly, the imposition of corporate liability requires a "two step analysis [that] first identifies the perpetrator of the crime, and then asks whether he or she is a person who can be said to embody the company's mind and will".[3] Thus, it has been suggested that the common law developed two main techniques for the attribution of criminal fault, first by vicarious liability arising from the employment or agency relationship and, subsequently, via the identification doctrine.[4] However, considered in the light of the findings in Chapter 6, it is more accurate to say that the common law first developed one mechanism for the attribution of criminal fault and, thereafter, another by which to limit the operation of the first. Put another way, the identification principle constitutes a refinement that serves to limit the broad application of vicarious liability.

In contrast to typical accounts of this area of law,[5] this chapter will demonstrate *Lennard's*[6] was not taken to decide anything remarkable at the time or to develop the law in relation to any general principle of liability, either in the civil

---

1 *Lennard's Carrying Co Ltd v Asiatic Petroleum Ltd* [1915] AC 705 (HL).
2 Law Commission, *Criminal Liability in Regulatory Contexts* (Law Com No 195, 2010) Pt. 5, para 5.9.
3 James Gobert, 'Corporate Criminality: Four Models of Fault' (1994) 14(3) LS 393, 395.
4 Described as the concept of corporate alter ego, see Sullivan GT, 'The Attribution of Culpability to Limited Companies' (1996) 55(3) CLJ 515, 515.
5 David Ormerod, *Smith and Hogan's Criminal Law* (13th ed, Oxford: Oxford University Press 2011) 260.
6 *Lennard's Carrying Co Ltd v Asiatic Petroleum Ltd* [1915] AC 705 (HL).

or criminal law jurisdiction. Indeed, a wider examination reveals that the retrospective interpretation of *Lennard's*[7] places it in stark contrast to the prevailing criminal law which continued to apply the traditional principles of attribution via vicarious liability. That this was the case is demonstrated by reference to the leading substantive and practitioner texts of the period, taken together with a string of well-known authoritative cases that were heard after *Lennard's*.[8] It is clear that the landmark status now afforded to *Lennard's*[9] was due entirely to its subsequent elevation in *Tesco v Nattrass*, decided almost six decades later.[10]

Ironically, if *Lennard's*[11] had established the "identification principle" of corporate fault attribution in 1915, the implications would have been of far less significance than they became over half a century later. In particular, the two evidential presumptions of fault were fully operational in the criminal law during this period.[12] Accordingly, the primary focus of enquiry would have been the manifest appearance of fault, the presumption of intention of natural consequences applying as much to the corporate actor as to the human individual.[13] However, by the time of the *Tesco* prosecution in 1971[14], the enlarged mens rea doctrine had done much to displace both the traditional canons of fault and the evidential presumptions that accompanied them. Specifically, it will be recalled that *Sweet v Parsley*,[15] decided in 1969, two years before *Tesco*,[16] had already effected something of sea change as regards the presumption of voluntariness,[17] while the presumption of intention had been causing considerable concern for the best part of the decade.[18] Thus, with the upgrading of the doctrine of mens rea and the displacement of the evidential fault presumptions, a combination of factors was to influence the development of the principles of corporate fault attribution. One of these may have been the increasing reluctance to convict in the absence of proof of a blameworthy state of mind, as was evidenced by the judicial approach to the so-called "strict liability" offences at the time of the *Tesco* decision.[19] It is plausible that the doctrine of vicarious liability suffered for much the same reason. Similarly, in the absence of the evidential presumption of intention as the mechanism by which corporate blameworthiness might have been proved, the attribution of corporate fault would now have become problematic. In both these respects the recognition of the "identification

---

7 *Ibid*

8 *Ibid.*

9 Ibid.

10 *Tesco Ltd v Nattrass* [1972] AC 153 (HL).

11 *Lennard's Carrying Co Ltd v Asiatic Petroleum Ltd* [1915] AC 705 (HL).

12 See Chapters 3 and 4.

13 *National Coal Board v Gamble* [1958] 1 QB 11.

14 *Tesco Ltd v Nattrass* [1972] AC 153 (HL).

15 *Sweet v Parsley* [1970] AC 132 (HL).

16 *Tesco Ltd v Nattrass* [1972] AC 153 (HL).

17 *Sweet v Parsley* [1970] AC 132 (HL) and see the discussion in Ch. 3.

18 See the discussion above in Ch. 4.

19 *Tesco Ltd v Nattrass* [1972] AC 153 (HL).

principle" provided a ready solution. Not only did the notion of the "directing mind and will" resonate with the modern primacy of the metaphysical enquiry, its attribution to an earlier authority accorded with the orthodoxy of the black letter law methodology.

In *Lennard's* the House of Lords was called to consider whether a corporate shipowner could be liable for loss of the cargo due to the unseaworthy state of one of its ships.[20] Under the relevant merchant shipping provisions, the ship-owner could be liable if it could be shown that he, in this case the owner company, was at "actual fault".[21] The case turned on the meaning of "actual fault" as it applied to a company and their Lordships felt that, properly inter-preted, the term precluded the application of vicarious liability on the part of the employer for the negligent acts of its servant. Echoing the expression of Coke in the *Sutton's Hospital Case*,[22] which was influenced by the ecclesiastical notion that a corporation was incapable of sin,[23] the doctrine was first articulated by Viscount Haldane in broad terms:

> A corporation is an abstraction. It has no mind of its own any more than it has a body of its own; its active and directing will must consequently be sought in the person of somebody who for some purposes may be called an agent, but who is really the directing mind and will of the corporation, the very ego and centre of the personality of the Corporation.[24]

Lord Dunedin gave the only other speech in *Lennard's* and he did not comment on the "directing mind" test at all, although he did refer to the "alter ego" of the company and the fact that the board of directors had entrusted its business to the managing director, who had been at actual fault. Of note, *Ingram & Royle* was cited[25], this case predating *Lennard's*[26] by just two years and in which Scrutton J. had stated that in relation to the same provision:

> The only exceptions to the protection given by the statute are (a) if the fire happened with the actual fault or privity of the owner, which, in the case of a limited company, means the person having management; i.e. Mr Lindley [the director] …".[27]

---

20 *Lennard's Carrying Co Ltd v Asiatic Petroleum Ltd* [1915] AC 705 (HL).
21 Merchant Shipping Act 1894, s. 502.
22 *Sutton's Hospital Case* (1612) [1558–1774] All ER Rep 11, 15 Co Rep 32b.
23 Cecil Thomas Carr, *The General Principles of the Law of Corporations* (Cambridge: Cambridge University Press 1905) referring to Dr Otto von Gierke, *Deutsche Genossenschaftsrecht III*, 279.
24 *Lennard's Carrying Co Ltd v Asiatic Petroleum Ltd* [1915] AC 705, 713.
25 *Ingram & Royle Ltd v Services Martimes du Treport Ltd (No 1)* [1913] 1 KB 538.
26 *Lennard's Carrying Co Ltd v Asiatic Petroleum Ltd* [1915] AC 705 (HL).
27 *Ingram & Royle Ltd v Services Maritimes du Treport Ltd (No 1)* [1913] 1 KB 538, 544.

Unlike Viscount Haldane L.C.'s dicta, there was no elaboration or metaphysical subtlety added. Indeed, Scrutton J.'s comment was obiter and he did not go as far as to provide any reasoning or any authority for the proposition he made, it was simply taken as read.

The facts of *Lennard's* were that faulty ship boilers had caused the fire which destroyed the claimant's cargo. The managing shipowner sought to rely on the said statutory provision since its purpose was to protect shipowners from the acts of their servants and to limit liability for loss and damage. In determining the construction of the particular section, it was held that the owner himself needed to prove that he was not at actual fault. Applied to the corporate owner, it was said that this required the person acting as the alter ego of the company to show that he was not personally at fault. Since the board of directors had placed responsibility for the management of the ship in the managing director, it was the managing director who needed to show that he, acting as the alter ego of the company, was not at fault. In the circumstances, he had failed to do so and accordingly the company was liable for the loss of the cargo.

As regards any theoretical discussion about the liability of organisations, the *Lennard's* judgment was sadly wanting.[28] The authorities referred to were few in number and all concerned civil matters, none of which were exactly on point.[29] Similarly, neither Viscount Haldane L.C. nor Lord Dunedin purported to set out any general principle of corporate criminal liability in what was essentially a consideration of the issue of causation and the interpretation of one particular statutory provision. This is unsurprising in that the criminal liability of corporations was still evolving by analogy with the law of master and servant and that of principal and agent. For example, the 1910 edition of *Archbold's Criminal Pleading* quoted s. 2(1) Interpretation Act 1889, "in the construction of every enactment … the expression 'person' shall, unless a contrary intention appears, include a body corporate"; a contrary intention being inferred in cases of treason, felony, personal violence and where the penalty is imprisonment or corporal punishment.[30] The text then set out various authoritative examples of corporate liability. These included *Whitfield v South East Railway Co* (1858),[31] a case concerning an allegation of malicious libel, in which Lord Campbell C.J. had held that since actions in tort or trespass could lie against a corporation, there must be circumstances in which express malice could also be imputed to a corporation.[32] Similarly, in *Mackay v The*

---

28 *Lennard's Carrying Co Ltd v Asiatic Petroleum Ltd* [1915] AC 705 (HL).
29 Cases referred to are *Wilson v Dickson* (1818) 2 B & Ald 2 which considered the position of individual part owners; *The Warkworth* (1884) LR 9 PD 20; *Norfolk & North America Steam Shipping Co Ltd v Virginia Carolina Chemical Co* [1912] 1 KB 229 (CA); *Ingram & Royle Ltd v Services Martimes du Treport Ltd (No 1)* [1913] 1 KB 538.
30 William Feiden Craies and Henry Delacombe Roome, *Archbold's Criminal Pleading, Evidence and Practice* (24th ed, London: Sweet & Maxwell 1910) 7, 8.
31 *Whitfield v South East Rly Company* (1858) E, B & E 115; 120 ER 451.
32 Express malice was distinguished from malice in law.

Commercial Bank of New Brunswick [1874][33] the Privy Council had decided
that an incorporated bank could be liable in deceit for the false statements of its
cashier, who was acting as a general manager of the bank. It did not doubt that
a corporation could be liable for the fraudulent actions of an agent done in the
course of his service. The Privy Council expressly approved the statement of
Lord Cranworth in *Ranger v Great Western Railway* [1854][34] in which his
Lordship had applied simple agency principles where the employer was a
corporation rather than an individual.

Two years after *Lennard's*,[35] the case of *Mousell Brothers* [1917][36] decided that
a railway company was criminally liable for the acts of its branch manager who
had issued false consignment notes to avoid railway tolls. The decision was said to
be based on the Parliamentary intention to make masters criminally liable for the
acts of their servants, akin to the social welfare legislation relating to the sale of
goods and drugs, where, as a matter of construction, statutes imposed an
absolute liability on the employer.[37] Giving judgment in *Mousell Bros*, Viscount
Reading said:

> I think, looking at the language and the purpose of this Act, that the
> Legislature intended to fix responsibility for this quasi-criminal act upon the
> principal if the forbidden acts were done by his servant within the scope of
> his employment. If that is the true view, there is nothing to distinguish a
> limited company from any other principal, and the Defendants are properly
> made liable for the acts of [the manager].[38]

Considering the corpus of reported judgments of the time, there is nothing to
suggest that the courts were seeking to construct some general principle of
corporate liability.[39] Similarly, while it has been suggested elsewhere that the

---

33 *Mackay v The Commercial Bank of New Brunswick* [1874] LT vol 30, NS 180.
34 *Ranger v Great Western Rly* [1854] 5 HLC 71.
35 *Lennard's Carrying Co Ltd v Asiatic Petroleum Ltd* [1915] AC 705 (HL).
36 *Mousell Bros Ltd v London & North Western Rly Co* [1917] 2 KB 836.
37 See for example the discussion contained in the Law Commission, *Criminal Liability in
   Regulatory Contexts* (Law Com No 195, 2010) Pt. 5, para 5.4 and citing *Mousell Bros Ltd v
   London & North Western Rly Co* [1917] 2 KB 836, 845 (Atkin J).
38 *Mousell Bros Ltd v London & North Western Rly Co* [1917] 2 KB 836, 845.
39 According to Glanville Williams, *Criminal Law: The General Part* (2nd ed, London:
   Stevens & Sons 1961) 274, Mousell was the solitary exception to the principle that the
   vicariously attributed acts do not apply to offences requiring mens rea. Ormerod,
   however, says that the best explanation is that the decision belongs to an intermediate
   stage in the development of corporate criminal responsibility, David Ormerod, *Smith and
   Hogan's Criminal Law, Cases and Materials* (10th ed, Oxford: Oxford University Press
   2009). Later Williams observed that the speech of Lord Evershed in *Vane v Yiannopolous*
   [1965] AC 486 (HL) suggested that *Mousell Bros Ltd v London & North Western Rly Co*
   [1917] 2 KB 836 was to be restrictively interpreted and was no authority for saying that
   every employer is vicariously liable for his employee's offences involving mens rea; rather

"directing mind" theory resurfaced in the civil law in the early 1930s,[40] the 1938 edition of *Archbold's*[41] was drafted in the same terms as the 1910 version. It is of note that it makes no reference whatsoever to *Lennard's*,[42] or indeed to any such theory. In contrast, it set out the provisions of the Criminal Justice Act 1925 which deal with procedural matters in instances where a corporation is charged "alone or with some other person, with an indictable offence".[43] It was not until the Second World War that cases dealing with the question of the basis of criminal responsibility of companies came to the fore again. These included *Triplex Safety Glass*,[44] *ICR Haulage*,[45] *Kent and Sussex Contractors*[46] and *Moore v Bresler*.[47] Again, none of these cases made any reference to *Lennard's* [1915][48] and the decisions reached therein continued to employ traditional agency principles.

In *Triplex Safety Glass* [1939],[49] the Court of Appeal applied agency reasoning in relation to criminal libel and in *Moore v Bresler Ltd*[50] it was held that the corporate employer could be criminally liable if its employees performed an authorised job in an unauthorised, fraudulent way. That same year, in *Kent & Sussex Contractors*,[51] the company was prosecuted for issuing a record, knowing it to be false in a material particular.[52] The facts were that the transport manager had submitted the record in order to obtain petrol coupons with intent to deceive. At first instance it was held that the knowledge of the manager could not be imputed to the company but this was reversed on appeal to the Divisional

---

Mousell was an obscure decision and not clear authority for anything, Glanville Williams, *Text Book of Criminal Law* (2nd ed, London: Stevens & Sons 1961).

40 See RJ Wickins and CA Ong, 'Confusion Worse Confounded: The End of the Directing Mind Theory?' [1997] JBL Nov, 524–56; Ong points to several cases dealing with the liability of companies in negligence where employees had suffered injuries within a factory workplace but regrettably the author does not identify them by name. It should be noted in any event that negligence is not based on subjective mental states but objective assessment.

41 Robert Ernest Ross and Maxwell Turner, *Archbold's Criminal Pleading: Evidence and Practice* (30th ed, London: Sweet & Maxwell 1938) 10.

42 *Lennard's Carrying Co Ltd v Asiatic Petroleum Ltd* [1915] AC 705 (HL).

43 Ross RE and Turner M, *Archbold's Criminal Pleading: Evidence and Practice* (30th ed, London: Sweet & Maxwell 1938) 97.

44 *Triplex Safety Glass Co Ltd v Lancegaye Safety Glass (1934) Ltd* [1939] 2 KB 395 (CA).

45 *R v ICR Haulage Ltd* [1944] KB 551.

46 *DPP v Kent & Sussex Contractors* [1944] KB 146.

47 *Moore v Bresler Ltd* [1944] 2 All ER 515.

48 *Lennard's Carrying Co Ltd v Asiatic Petroleum Ltd* [1915] AC 705 (HL).

49 *Triplex Safety Glass Co Ltd v Lancegaye Safety Glass (1934) Ltd* [1939] 2 KB 395 (CA).

50 *Moore v Bresler Ltd* [1944] 2 All ER 515.

51 *DPP v Kent & Sussex Contractors* [1944] KB 146.

52 Informations were preferred against the respondent company under regulations 82(1)(c) and 82(2) of the Defence (General) Regulations 1939, charging the company with the use of a document which was false in a material particular for the purposes of the Motor Fuel (No 3) Rationing Order, 1941, with intent to deceive, where the document was signed by the transport manager.

Court. Notably, Viscount Caldecote C.J. rehearsed the judgment of Lord Cranworth in *Ranger v Great Western Railway Company* [1854], which stated:

> Strictly speaking a corporation cannot itself be guilty of fraud. But where a corporation is formed for the purpose of carrying on a trade or other speculation not-for-profit, such as forming the railway, these objects can only be accomplished by the agency of individuals; there can be no doubt that if the agents employed conduct themselves fraudulently, so that if they had been acting for private employers the persons for whom they were acting would have been affected by their fraud, the same principles must prevail whether the principal under whom the agent acts is a corporation.[53]

He noted that it was well settled that a corporation could be liable in actions such as fraud, libel or malicious prosecution and he also considered *Pearks, Gunston and Tee Limited v Ward*[54] and Channel J.'s recognition of quasi-criminal offences which imposed absolute liability. With regard to the present case, Viscount Caldecote C.J. stated that where

> the company was charged with doing something with intent to deceive, [and] the second charge was of making a statement which the company knew to be false in a material particular ... (t)he question of mens rea seems to be quite irrelevant. ... There was ample evidence, on the facts as stated in the special case, that the company, by the only people who could act or speak or think for it had done both these things, and I can see nothing in any of the authorities which requires us to say that a company is incapable of being found guilty of the offences with which the company was charged.[55]

Also giving judgment framed in agency terms, Macnaghten J. agreed that a corporation could only have knowledge and form an intention through its human agents but added that circumstances may be such that the knowledge and intention of the agent must be imputed to the body corporate.[56] In the same case, Hallett J. referred to the Interpretation Act 1889 and the Criminal Justice Act 1925 noting that, "There has been a development in the attitude of the Court arising from the large part played in modern times by limited liability companies ... the theoretical difficulty of imputing criminal intention is no longer felt to the same extent".[57] Hallett J. also commented that:

---

53 *Ranger v Great Western Rly* (1854) 10 ER 824 [86].
54 *Pearks, Gunston & Tee Ltd v Ward* [1902] 2 KB 1. The case concerned s. 6 of the Food and Drugs Act 1875, providing that "no person shall sell to the prejudice of the purchaser any article of food or any drug which is not of the nature, substance, and quality of the article demanded by such purchaser".
55 *DPP v Kent & Sussex Contractors* [1944] KB 146, 155–6.
56 Ibid 156.
57 Ibid 157.

if every person desiring to obtain petrol coupons has a duty imposed by statutory authority to furnish honest information, it seems strange and undesirable that a body corporate desiring to obtain petrol coupons and furnishing dishonest information for that purpose should be able to escape the liability which would be incurred in like case by private person.[58]

As regards criminal intent, he quoted from Atkin J.'s judgment in *Mousell*, "I see no difficulty in the fact that an intent to avoid payment is necessary to constitute the offence. That is an intent which the servant might well have, inasmuch as he is the person who has to deal with the particular matter".[59] Hallett J. also referred to *Triplex Safety Glass* in which du Parcq L.J. had taken the view that a body corporate may by its servants or agents be guilty of malice so as to render it liable to conviction for criminal libel.[60]

Subsequently, in the Court of Appeal, the case of *ICR Haulage* [1944][61] involved a charge against the company, its managing director and other employees of common law conspiracy to defraud. Approving the earlier authorities, the company itself was included on the indictment. The Court of Appeal made use of the statement of Macnaghten J. in *DPP v Kent and Sussex Contractors Ltd* [1944] to the effect that the criminal intention of an agent, acting within the scope of his authority, could be imputed to the company.[62] In that same year *Moore v Bresler Ltd*[63] concerned the conviction of the company secretary and sales manager for making use of a document which was false in a material particular with intent to deceive.[64] The Divisional Court found the company itself criminally liable, notwithstanding the company had been the victim of the said fraud and the individuals concerned had not been acting in the company's interests.

While the early cases appear to be context sensitive,[65] they do not purport to establish a general principle of corporate criminal liability, indeed in *ICR Haulage* [1944], Mr Justice Stable was explicit on that point.[66] Furthermore, according with the agency analysis of liability at this time, the 1949 edition of *Archbold's*[67] made no mention of *Lennard's*[68] and it was still absent from the

---

58 *DPP v Kent & Sussex Contractors* [1944] KB 146, 158.
59 *Mousell Brothers Ltd v London & North Western Rly Co* [1917] 2 KB 836, 846.
60 *Triplex Safety Glass Co Ltd v Lancegaye Safety Glass (1934) Ltd* [1939] 2 KB 395 (CA).
61 *R v ICR Haulage Ltd* [1944] KB 551 (CCA).
62 *DPP v Kent & Sussex Contractors* [1944] KB 146.
63 *Moore v Bresler Ltd* [1944] 2 All ER 515.
64 Contrary to Finance (No 2) Act 1940, s. 35(2).
65 See the rehearsal given and comments provided in the Law Commission, *Criminal Liability in Regulatory Contexts* (Law Com No 195, 2010) Pt. 5.
66 *R v ICR Haulage Ltd* [1944] KB 551, 599.
67 TR Fitzwalter Butler and Marston Garsia, *Archbold's Pleading, Evidence and Practice in Criminal Cases* (London: Sweet & Maxwell 1949).
68 *Lennard's Carrying Co Ltd v Asiatic Petroleum Ltd* [1915] AC 705 (HL).

1958 and 1966 editions of *Kenny's Outlines*.[69] However, it was during this period that Lord Goddard C.J., in *Gardner v Akeroyd* [1952], suggested that founding the criminal liability of employers on the basis of vicarious liability might be "odious" and lead to potentially unjust results.[70] Of note, it was in the same year that the next reported reference to the "directing mind and will" was made, in *The Truculent*, and, like its predecessor *Lennard's*,[71] the case was a civil matter.[72] It was not until 1957 that there was a veritable sea change. Brought about in the civil law case of *Bolton (Engineering) Co Ltd*,[73] Denning L.J. claimed that the earlier cases had created a unifying theory which set out an overarching principle for both the civil and the criminal liability of companies. He said:

> So also in the criminal law, in cases where the law requires a guilty mind as a condition of a criminal offence, the guilty mind of the directors or the managers will render the company themselves guilty. This is shown by *R v ICR Haulage Ltd*.[74]

Of course, Denning L.J.'s comment on criminal liability was strictly obiter, *Bolton Engineering* itself concerning a civil matter of landlord and tenant law.[75] *ICR Haulage*[76] had contained no mention of the directing mind theory either explicitly or implicitly and as for *Lennard's*,[77] Denning L.J. observed simply that, "in cases where the law requires personal fault as a condition of liability in tort, the fault of the manager will be the personal fault of the company".[78] However, it was in *Bolton Engineering* that Denning L.J. breathed life into the now infamous anthropomorphic account that has become the touchstone of the doctrine:[79]

---

69 JW Cecil Turner, *Kenny's Outlines of Criminal Law* (17th ed, Cambridge: Cambridge University Press 1958); JW Cecil Turner, *Kenny's Outlines of Criminal Law* (19th ed, Cambridge: Cambridge University Press 1966).
70 *Gardner v Akeroyd* [1952] 2 QB 743, 751 (Lord Goddard C.J.). Considering whether an employer could be vicariously liable for the criminal attempt of an employee it was said, "that it is a necessary doctrine for the proper enforcement of much modern legislation none would deny, but it is not one to be extended. Just as in former days the term "odious" was applied to some forms of estoppel, so might it be to vicarious liability".
71 *Lennard's Carrying Co Ltd v Asiatic Petroleum Ltd* [1915] AC 705 (HL).
72 *Admiralty v Owners of the Divina, The Truculent* [1952] P 1. Like the *Lennard's* case, it concerned a defence afforded to an owner under shipping law.
73 *HL Bolton (Engineering) Co Ltd v T J Graham & Sons Ltd* [1957] 1 QB 159 (CA).
74 Ibid 172.
75 *HL Bolton (Engineering) Co Ltd v T J Graham & Sons Ltd* [1957] 1 QB 159 (CA).
76 *R v ICR Haulage Co Ltd* [1944] 1 KB 551.
77 *Lennard's Carrying Co Ltd v Asiatic Petroleum Ltd* [1915] AC 705 (HL).
78 *HL Bolton (Engineering) Co Ltd v T J Graham & Sons Ltd* [1957] 1 QB 159 (CA) 172.
79 In other contexts, the anthropomorphic analogy was already familiar, e.g. Cecil Thomas Carr, *The General Principles of the Law of Corporations* (Yorke prize essay for the year 1902, Cambridge: Cambridge University Press 1905).

A company in many ways may be likened to a human body. It has a brain and a nerve centre which controls what it does. It also has hands which hold the tools and act in accordance with directions from the centre. Some of the people in the company are mere servants and agents who are nothing more than the hands to do the work and cannot be said to represent the mind or will. Others are directors and managers who represent the directing mind and will of the company, and control what it does. The state of mind of these managers is the state of mind of the company and is treated by the law as such.[80]

Leaving aside the fact that this was a fundamentally problematic analysis for the criminal law, since the actus reus and mens rea seemed to reside in different individuals, the statement must be considered by reference to the principles of criminality as they existed at that time. Thus, as regards the reference to a state of mind, it must be remembered that in the 1950s the presumption of voluntariness and the presumption of intention were still in full sway. Whatever Denning L.J. said, the practice at that time was to assess fault primarily by reference to the overt conduct and its outcome. Accordingly, the full implication of Denning L.J.'s creative analysis of corporate liability would not be felt until much later with the displacement of the evidential presumptions in favour of the expanded notion of mens rea. It must also be noted that Denning L.J.'s innovative interpretation in *Bolton Engineering*[81] did not assert anything like a firm influence on the criminal law until much later, with opinion divided as to any certain development of the legal principle. For example, the 1961 edition of Williams' seminal *Criminal Law* text mentioned a "new concept" in the law of tort, and only tort, where the "acts of the 'organs' of the corporation ... were attributed to the corporation and treated ... as though they were the acts of the corporation itself".[82] In support of this tortious liability Williams quoted at length the dicta of Viscount Haldane L.C. in *Lennard's*,[83] identified that the term "organs" derived from the 1916 *Daimler v Contintental Tyre* case[84] and observed that the alter ego doctrine enabled the state of mind of the organ to be regarded as the company's own. As to the imputation of mens rea under this principle, Williams cited *ICR Haulage Ltd* [1944] in support.[85] That

---

80 *HL Bolton (Engineering) Co Ltd v T J Graham & Sons Ltd* [1957] 1 QB 159 (CA) 172.
81 *HL Bolton (Engineering) Co Ltd v T J Graham & Sons Ltd* [1957] 1 QB 159 (CA).
82 Glanville Williams, *Criminal Law, The General Part* (2nd ed, London: Stevens & Sons 1961) 855.
83 *Lennard's Carrying Co Ltd v Asiatic Petroleum Ltd* [1915] AC 705 (HL).
84 *Daimler Co Ltd v Continental Tyre Co Ltd* [1916] 2 AC 307 (HL), 340.
85 *R v ICR Haulage Co Ltd* [1944] 1 KB 551 (CCA) in Glanville Williams, *Criminal Law, The General Part* (2nd ed, London: Stevens & Sons 1961) 856. Williams also referred to *Law Society v United Service Bureau Ltd* [1934] 1 KB 343, 348 but was critical of the inelegant language, 857.

being said, the 1966 edition of *Kenny's Outlines of Criminal Law* was a little more reticent about recognising a new principle in the criminal law, stating that, "the courts have moved in the direction of making the corporation directly responsible, by the fiction that the elements of criminal liability present in the responsible agent of the corporation can be imputed to the corporation itself".[86] However, the text concluded that the "formulation of clear principles of criminal liability for corporations is urgently needed".[87] Given that Stable J. in *ICR Haulage* had articulated the judgment of the court in the language of the law of agency, there is arguably some weight to be afforded to Kenny's reservations.[88] Furthermore, while Glanville Williams explicitly linked the tortious development in *Lennard's*[89] to the development of the criminal law of corporations[90], not one of the cases he discussed in support had made any reference to *Lennard's*.[91]

The conclusion must be that at the time of the *Tesco v Natrass* prosecution in 1971,[92] *Lennard's*[93] had resurfaced after a period of five decades and was now reinterpreted to provide not only the authority for the identification principle in tort law, but was also read into the criminal case of *ICR Haulage*,[94] a case that had actually been decided on the traditional principles of agency law. Indeed, in its 1985 report, the Law Commission confessed to having been taken aback by the range of situations in which there was (to their knowledge) no direct authority for the criminal law's use of the identification principle prior to *Tesco v Nattrass*.[95]

---

86 JW Cecil Turner, *Kenny's Outlines of Criminal Law* (19th ed, Cambridge: Cambridge University Press 1966) 77–8 and citing R Burrows, 'The Responsibility of Corporations Under Criminal Law' (1948) 1 Journal of Crim Sci 1ff.

87 JW Cecil Turner, *Kenny's Outlines of Criminal Law* (19th ed, Cambridge: Cambridge University Press 1966) 77–8.

88 *R v ICR Haulage Co Ltd* [1944] 1 KB 551 (CCA) 695 (J. Stable) approving the judgment of Macnaghten J in *DPP v Kent & Sussex Contractors Ltd* [1944] 1 KB 146, 156, "It is true that a corporation can only have knowledge and form an intention through its human agents, but circumstances may be such that the knowledge and intention of the agent must be imputed to the body corporate ... If the responsible agent of a company, acting within the scope of his authority, puts forward on its behalf a document which he knows to be false and by which he intends to deceive ... according to the authorities ... his knowledge and intention must be imputed to the company".

89 *Lennard's Carrying Co Ltd v Asiatic Petroleum Ltd* [1915] AC 705 (HL).

90 Glanville Williams, *Criminal Law, The General Part* (2nd ed, London: Stevens & Sons 1961) 857–8.

91 The cases he discusses are *R v ICR Haulage Co Ltd* [1944] 1 KB 551 (CCA); *DPP v Kent and Sussex Contractors Ltd* [1944] KB 146, 155; *Moore v Bresler Ltd* [1944] 2 All ER 515.

92 *Tesco Ltd v Nattrass* [1972] AC 153 (HL).

93 *Lennard's Carrying Co Ltd v Asiatic Petroleum Ltd* [1915] AC 705 (HL).

94 *R v ICR Haulage Ltd* [1944] KB 551 (CCA).

95 Law Commission, *The Codification of the Criminal Law* (Law Com No 143, 1985) Ch. 11, para 11.2 discussing *Tesco Ltd v Nattrass* [1972] AC 153 (HL).

7.2 The elevation of *Lennard's*: viewed retrospectively

As to the landmark case of *Tesco Ltd v Nattrass* [1972],[96] the company was prosecuted under s. 11(2) Trade Descriptions Act 1968 for selling goods at a price higher than that advertised.[97] The supermarket sought to rely on the defence set out at s. 24(1), namely that the offence was committed by another, the store manager, and that the company had taken all reasonable precautions and exercised all due diligence to avoid its commission.[98] In seeking to blame the store manager, Tesco argued that he was another person within the meaning of that provision and could not be viewed as the embodiment of the company itself. With the court finding in favour of the company, it has been suggested that the case emerged in an atmosphere of liberal reform. Lord Reid was certainly highly critical of the creation of absolute offences and the fact that individuals could be convicted of offences for which they were entirely blameless;[99] an injustice, he said, which brought the law into disrepute. It was, of course, Lord Reid who, just two years earlier, had been instrumental in the *Sweet v Parsley* ruling which had expanded the very concept of mens rea.[100]

Of note, in *Tesco* Lord Reid relied particularly upon the dictum of Viscount Haldane L.C. in *Lennard's* [1915][101] and also on that of Denning L.J. in *Bolton Engineering* [1957].[102] In addition, he cited the 1950 case of *Dumfries and Maxwelltown Co-operative Society v Williamson*[103] which had concerned the similar provisions of the Sale of Food (Weights and Measures) Act.[104] Agreeing with Lord Justice-General Cooper's interpretation, he held that vicarious liability should not be imposed for an infringement committed without the consent or

---

96 *Tesco Ltd v Nattrass* [1972] AC 153 (HL).
97 Trade Descriptions Act 1968, s. 11(2) sets out "if any person offering to supply any goods gives, by whatever means, any indication likely to be taken as an indication that the goods are being offered at a price less than at which they are in fact being offered he shall, subject to the provisions of this act, be guilty of an offence".
98 S. 24(1) sets out that, subject to subsection (2), it is a defence for the person charged to prove that (a) the commission of the offence was due to a mistake or to the reliance on information supplied to him or to the act or default of another person, an accident or some other cause beyond his control; and (b) that he took all reasonable precautions and exercised all due diligence to avoid the commission of such an offence by himself or any person under his control.
99 *Sweet v Parsley* [1970] AC 132 (HL), 148 (L. Reid).
100 *Sweet v Parsley* [1970] AC 132 (HL), 148 (L. Reid). See the discussion in Ch. 3.
101 *Lennard's Carrying Co Ltd v Asiatic Petroleum Ltd* [1915] AC 705 (HL).
102 *HL Bolton (Engineering) Co Ltd v TJ Graham & Sons Ltd* [1957] 1 QB 159 (CA), 172.
103 *Dumfries and Maxwelltown Co-operative Society v Williamson* [1950] SC (J) 76, 80.
104 Sale of Food (Weights and Measures) Act 1926, s. 12(5). An employer or principal charged with an offence under the Act may lay information against any other person whom he charges as the actual offender, and may have such person brought before the Court, and, if he proves that he used due diligence to enforce the execution of the Act and that the other person committed the offence without his consent or connivance, the other person shall be summarily convicted and the employer or principal shall be exempt from any penalty.

connivance of the employer. Having relied upon the two civil cases, *Lennards*[105] and *Bolton,*[106] and then *Dumfries,*[107] which had considered the issue of vicarious liability, Lord Reid then reviewed criminal cases which he classified as examples of companies being held liable for the fault of "a superior officer", referring to *DPP v Kent*[108] and *ICR Haulage.*[109] Arguably, the reference to the officers being "superior" was superfluous since both cases had been decided by reference to simple agency theory in which the superiority of the officer involved was of no legal relevance. However, omitting explicit reference to the law of agency, Lord Reid then quoted a passage from the latter case, stating that:

> where in any particular case there is evidence to go to a jury that the criminal act of an agent, including his state of mind, intention, knowledge or belief is the act of the company [it] ... must depend on the nature of the charge, the relative position of the officer or agent, and other relevant facts and circumstances of the case.[110]

As far as this quote is concerned, it is contained in the final paragraph of Stable J.'s judgment in *ICR Haulage* in which he appeared to be talking generally about the need to consider a principal's liability for the acts of his agent on a case-by-case basis.[111] However, Lord Reid relied on the quote to support the recognition of the "directing mind and will theory" for corporate liability which was said to require the culpability of a sufficiently senior officer. Lord Reid went on to cite a further two cases in which companies had not been held responsible for the acts of their servants[112] and, of these, the one reported case had relied solely on the civil case of *Bolton Engineering* [1957].[113] Lord Reid concluded that corporate criminal liability only arose in two circumstances; the first, in the case of a company where the acts are those of responsible

---

105 *Lennard's Carrying Co Ltd v Asiatic Petroleum Ltd* [1915] AC 705 (HL).

106 *HL Bolton (Engineering) Co Ltd v TJ Graham & Sons Ltd* [1957] 1 QB 159 (CA) 172.

107 *Dumfries and Maxwelltown Co-operative Society v Williamson* [1950] SC (J) 76.

108 *DPP v Kent & Sussex Contractors* [1944] KB 146.

109 *R v ICR Haulage Ltd* [1944] KB 551 (CCA).

110 *R v ICR Haulage Ltd* [1944] KB 551 (CCA) 559.

111 *R v ICR Haulage Ltd* [1944] KB 551 (CCA).

112 *John Henshall (Quarries) Ltd v Harvey* [1965] 2 QB 233 in which case a company was not held criminally responsible for the negligence of a servant in charge of the weighbridge and the unreported case of *Magna Plant v Mitchell*, 27th of April 1966 where the fault of the depot engineer, i.e. his knowledge, was not imputed to the company where he was a servant for whose actions the company was not criminally responsible. The facts of Henshall are similar to those of *National Coal Board v Gamble* [1959] 1 QB 11; in the earlier case the issue of the basis of corporate liability was not raised, in the latter case it was held that the employee's knowledge of the overloaded lorry could not be imputed to the company as his were not considered the brains of the company.

113 *HL Bolton (Engineering) Co Ltd v TJ Graham & Sons Ltd* [1957] 1 QB 159 (CA), 172.

officers who form the "brain" of the company and, the second, where the acts are those of a person to whom delegation of management has been passed. Delegation by an individual was, he said quite correctly, another principle which has been recognised in licensing cases but which was anomalous.[114] Bypassing any discussion of the longstanding agency principles or those relating to the law of master and servant, upon which the earlier criminal cases were entirely based,[115] Lord Reid then focused on the anomalous line of authority in relation to delegation liability.

Delegation as a basis of liability had only ever been applied in limited, fact-specific situations such as licensee's breaches where the licensee was absent from the licensed premises.[116] The principle comes into effect when an individual office-holder is under a duty and the performance of the duty is delegated to another.[117] Accordingly, there are obvious overlaps between it and the attribution of liability on the basis of both master and servant and agency law. While this may explain the difficulties encountered by those who have sought to provide a coherent account of the development of a general principle in the attribution of corporate criminal fault, Lord Reid failed to consider the agency and master and servant cases. Appearing to intermingle, and thus confuse, the directing mind theory with that of delegation, Lord Reid asserted that a board of directors could delegate part of their functions of management so as to make their delegate an embodiment of the company. In the instant case, *Tesco v Nattrass*,[118] he held that the Tesco board had never delegated any part of its functions, but had set up a chain of command through regional and district supervisors whilst remaining in control. Accordingly, the acts or omissions of the shop manager were not the acts of the company itself.

7.3 Distinguishing and delimiting the directing mind doctrine

On Lord Reid's analysis in *Tesco v Nattrass*, the identification principle restricted corporate liability to instances of culpability at a very high level within the organisation, namely "the board of directors, the managing director and perhaps other superior officers of a company who carry out functions of management and speak and act as the company".[119] It is this narrowing of corporate liability to a very high level of management that has resulted in the widespread criticism that it is

114 Quoting *Vane v Yiannopolous* [1965] AC 486 (HL) in support.
115 *Triplex Safety Glass Co Ltd v Lancegaye Safety Glass (1934) Ltd* [1939] 2 KB 395 (CA); *Moore v Bresler Ltd* [1944] 2 All ER 515.
116 *Tesco Ltd v Nattrass* [1972] AC 153 (HL) 175.
117 *Allen v Whitehead* [1930] 1 KB 211.
118 *Tesco Ltd v Nattrass* [1972] AC 153 (HL).
119 Ibid 171 (Lord Reid); although it should be noted that all the Law Lords provided a slightly different test for determining who may be identified as the mind of the company.

at odds with the realities of the diffusion of managerial power in large companies and, more troubling still, could provide companies with perverse incentives to decentralise responsibilities so as to make it impossible to identify a senior individual ... in charge of any matter.[120]

This deficiency was addressed to some extent in a line of cases[121] culminating in the Privy Council case of *Meridian Global Funds Management* (1995)[122] in which Lord Hoffman framed the question in a purposive way.[123] Although the flexibility of this approach was applauded by many who recognised that it could resolve the problem of corporate liability in a doctrinally coherent fashion,[124] the approach was short-lived. Argued by the Crown in the corporate manslaughter case *AGs Ref (No 2 of 1999)* [2000],[125] it was ultimately rejected by the Court of Appeal.[126]

---

120 Eilis Ferran, 'Corporate Attribution and the Directing Mind and Will' (2011) 127 LQR (Apr) 239–59; see too Law Commission, *Legislating the Criminal Code: Involuntary Manslaughter* (Law Com No 237, 1996) 1.10–1.21 for issues arising from the narrow basis of attribution of liability to a company for manslaughter.

121 The civil case of *El Ajou v Dollar Land Holdings plc* [1994] 2 All ER 685; *DG of Fair Trading v Pioneer Concrete (UK) Ltd* [1995] 1 AC 456 (HL).

122 *Meridian Global Funds Management Asia Ltd v Securities Commission* [1995] 2 AC 500 (PC) NZ.

123 In determining what acts were to be attributed to the company, the question was a matter of interpretation or construction of that particular substantive rule. Hence, if the court decided that the substantive rule was intended to apply to a company it then had to decide how it would apply and whose act or knowledge or state of mind was for that purpose intended to count as the act, knowledge or state of mind of the company. Lord Hoffman did not reject the directing mind metaphor altogether, he said that it was simply a phrase used by Viscount Haldane in the context of interpreting the particular statute in issue, see Celia Wells, 'Corporate Liability for Crime – Tesco v Nattrass on the Danger List?' (1996) Arch News 1, 5 and Celia Wells, 'The Law Commission Report on Involuntary Manslaughter: The Corporate Manslaughter Proposals: Pragmatism, Paradox and Peninsularity' [1996] Crim LR 545.

124 See for example LS Sealy, 'The Corporate Ego and Agency Untwined' [1995] 54 CLJ 507; Ross Grantham, 'Corporate Knowledge: Identification or Attribution' (1996) 59 MLR 732; Celia Wells, 'Corporate Liability for Crime – Tesco v Nattrass on the Danger List?' (1996) Arch News 1, 5; Celia Wells, 'The Law Commission Report on Involuntary Manslaughter: The Corporate Manslaughter Proposals: Pragmatism, Paradox and Peninsularity' [1996] Crim LR 545. This approach was consistent with the 1994 Court of Appeal decision in the civil case of *El-Ajou v Dollar Land Holdings* [1994] 2 All ER 685 involving the imputation of knowledge to a company in an equitable case alleging "knowing receipt" which also referred to the constitution of the company and to whom powers had been entrusted.

125 *Attorney General's Reference* (No 2 of 1999) [2000] Cr App R 207.

126 Meridian was taken to reaffirm the identification principle, *Meridian Global Funds Management Asia Ltd v Securities Commission* [1995] 2 AC 500 (PC) NZ. The 2009 House of Lords civil case of *Stone & Rolls Ltd v Moore Stephens* [2009] UKHL 39 (HL) (a ruling on auditors' civil liability) continued the use of anthropomorphic metaphors, as did *R v St Regis Paper Co Ltd* [2011] EWCA Crim 2527 (CCA) with emphasis placed on the status of the individual as the "embodiment of" the company.

Arguably, *Tesco*[127] could have been distinguished in future cases on the basis that it provided nothing more than clarity as to the interpretation of the specific piece of legislation with which it was concerned, the Trade Descriptions Act.[128] It has also been suggested that as the sole House of Lords' decision in this area and involving a "public welfare" offence, not requiring proof of mens rea, the "directing mind" argument could have been sidestepped altogether.[129] In this respect, it has been argued that the fact that their Lordships did not do so illustrates as much about the contemporary judicial aversion to strict liability offences as it does about corporate liability for non-regulatory offences.[130] While there certainly appears to be evidence of a judicial agenda of this nature, with the broad expansion of the mens rea doctrine, it is also clear that the full extent of the potential legal implications of *Tesco*[131] would not have been obvious at the time. Much as both of the evidential presumptions were fully operative at the time of the *Lennard's* judgment,[132] the presumption of intention, by reference to the natural and probable consequences of the act, was just beginning to attract attention on a prolific scale in the *Tesco* era. Although *DPP v Smith* [1961] had attracted much criticism,[133] upgrading the rebuttable evidential presumption to the status of an irrebuttable presumption of law, and s. 8 of the Criminal Justice Act 1967 had corrected its misapplication, the terminology of "natural and probable consequences" was to be the subject of heightened judicial attention for some time to come.[134] Although *Tesco v Nattrass*[135] served to link the criminal liability of the company to the blameworthiness of one of its senior officers, the assessment of fault at that time was still focused on the manifest appearance of the conduct. Accordingly, the metaphysical limitations of the identification principle were yet to become evident.

In summary, the 1915 *Lennard's* judgment,[136] addressing as it did the statutory interpretation of a shipping act provision, was in no way remarkable when it was delivered and its subsequent significance as a general principle of corporate liability was a matter of retrospective convenience. Indeed, that the case was to achieve landmark status was not evident at the time of Viscount Haldane's death in 1928 and, of the few memorable cases mentioned by

---

127 *Tesco Ltd v Nattrass* [1972] AC 153 (HL).
128 RJ Wickins and CA Ong, 'Confusion Worse Confounded: The End of the Directing Mind Theory?' [1997] JBL Nov 524–56.
129 Celia Wells, 'Corporations: Culture, Risk and Criminal Liability' (1993) Crim LR Aug 551–66.
130 Ibid.
131 *Tesco Ltd v Nattrass* [1972] AC 153 (HL).
132 *Lennard's Carrying Co Ltd v Asiatic Petroleum Ltd* [1915] AC 705 (HL).
133 *DPP v Smith* [1961] AC 290 (HL).
134 See *Hyam v DPP* [1975] AC 55 (HL), *R v Moloney* [1985] AC 905 (HL), *R v Hancock and Shankland* [1986] AC 455 (HL), *R v Nedrick* [1986] 1 WLR (CA), *R v Woollin* [1999] 1 AC 82 (HL). See the discussion in Ch. 4.
135 *Tesco Ltd v Nattrass* [1972] AC 153 (HL).
136 *Lennard's Carrying Co Ltd v Asiatic Petroleum Ltd* [1915] AC 705 (HL).

Viscount Haldane in his autobiography, *Lennard's* is not one.[137] Indeed, the retrospective interpretation of *Lennard's*[138] places it in stark contrast to the prevailing criminal law which continued to apply the traditional principles of vicarious liability. The landmark status now afforded to *Lennard's*[139] was due entirely to its subsequent elevation in *Tesco*[140] and, it would seem, a court keen to expand the boundaries of the mens rea doctrine yet further. Accordingly, it would appear that the identification doctrine was more the result of a haphazard conjunction of judicial pronouncements, made over a long period of time, than a coherent development of legal principle.

Furthermore, it can be observed that the authorities involving the question of corporate misconduct have tended to involve the misconduct of one or two identifiable individuals, the issue being whether or not these individuals can be taken as the embodiment of the corporation itself for the purpose of liability attribution. As such, and in accordance with black letter law methodology, *Lennard's*[141] and *Tesco*[142] can be distinguished from cases involving widespread misconduct of a systemic nature that is not reducible to the wrongdoing of individuals. Instances of pervasive misconduct within an organisation are rare in the case law, with perhaps the exception of the unsuccessful prosecution of P & O Ferries springing to mind.[143] The court held, and Parliament recognised, that corporate conduct of such a pervasive nature could not be addressed by reference to the identification principle. Accordingly, the bespoke corporate homicide offence was enacted, aligning more to the recognition of a type of aggregate wrongdoing, albeit that fault is confined to management level in this context.[144] While the identification principle might be serviceable in the former cases, it singularly fails in the latter. Recently enacted statutes provide precedent for the departure from the identification principle in specified instances of corporate misconduct and also implicitly accept that a corporation is itself a responsibility-bearing actor for the purpose of the criminal law.[145] While we remain bereft of a fully developed theory of corporations, cases involving criminogenic companies can, and should, be distinguished from those in which individual offenders can be located. In addition to the identification principle, the law can and should develop a new, and additional, approach to corporate criminality. In this respect the use of the orthodox principles of fault, and the evidential presumptions they invoke, provide the foundation upon which the law can progress without disturbing existing principles. The stage is set for a rational reconstruction of the criminal law that can at last provide a unified approach to corporate criminality.

---

137 Richard Burdon Haldane, *An Autobiography* (Hodder and Stoughton 1929).
138 *Lennard's Carrying Co Ltd v Asiatic Petroleum Ltd* [1915] AC 705 (HL).
139 Ibid.
140 *Tesco Ltd v Nattrass* [1972] AC 153 (HL).
141 *Lennard's Carrying Co Ltd v Asiatic Petroleum Ltd* [1915] AC 705 (HL).
142 *Tesco Ltd v Nattrass* [1972] AC 153 (HL).
143 *P & O European Ferries Ltd* (1990) 93 Cr App R 72.
144 Corporate Manslaughter and Corporate Homicide Act 2007.
145 Corporate Manslaughter and Corporate Homicide Act 2007; Bribery Act 2010.

Bibliography

Books

Carr CT, *The General Principles of the Law of Corporations* (Cambridge: Cambridge University Press 1905)

Craies WF and Roome HD, *Archbold's Criminal Pleading, Evidence and Practice* (24th ed, London: Sweet & Maxwell 1910)

Butler TRF and Garsia M, *Archbold's Pleading, Evidence and Practice in Criminal Cases* (London: Sweet & Maxwell 1949)

Haldane RB, *An Autobiography* (Hodder and Stoughton 1929)

Ormerod D, *Smith and Hogan's Criminal Law, Cases and Materials* (10th ed, Oxford: Oxford University Press 2009)

Ormerod D, *Smith and Hogan's Criminal Law* (13th ed, Oxford: Oxford University Press 2011)

Ross RE and Turner M, *Archbold's Criminal Pleading: Evidence and Practice* (30th ed, London: Sweet & Maxwell 1938)

Turner JWC, *Kenny's Outlines of Criminal Law* (17th ed, Cambridge: Cambridge University Press 1958)

Turner JWC, *Kenny's Outlines of Criminal Law* (19th ed, Cambridge: Cambridge University Press 1966)

Williams G, *Criminal Law: The General Part* (2nd ed, London: Stevens & Sons 1961)

Williams G, *Text Book of Criminal Law* (2nd ed, London: Stevens & Sons 1961)

Journal articles

Burrows R, 'The Responsibility of Corporations Under Criminal Law' (1948) 1 Journal of Crim Sci 1ff

Ferran E, 'Corporate Attribution and the Directing Mind and Will' (2011) 127 LQR (Apr) 239

Gobert J, 'Corporate Criminality: Four Models of Fault' (1994) 14(3) LS 393

Grantham R, 'Corporate Knowledge: Identification or Attribution' (1996) 59 MLR 732

Sealy LS, 'The Corporate Ego and Agency Untwined' [1995] 54 CLJ 507

Sullivan GT, 'The Attribution of Culpability to Limited Companies' (1996) 55(3) CLJ 515

Wells C, 'Corporations: Culture, Risk and Criminal Liability' (1993) Crim LR Aug 551

Wells C, 'Corporate Liability for Crime – Tesco v Nattrass on the Danger List?' (1996) Arch News 1

Wells C, 'The Law Commission Report on Involuntary Manslaughter: The Corporate Manslaughter Proposals: Pragmatism, Paradox and Peninsularity' [1996] Crim LR 545

Wickins RJ and Ong CA, 'Confusion Worse Confounded: The End of the Directing Mind Theory?' [1997] JBL Nov, 524

Official materials

Law Commission, *Criminal Liability in Regulatory Contexts* (Law Com No 195, 2010)

Law Commission, *Legislating the Criminal Code: Involuntary Manslaughter* (Law Com No 237, 1996)

Law Commission, *The Codification of the Criminal Law* (Law Com No 143, 1985)

8 Concluding thoughts: corporate fraud and the way forward

The problem of fraud shows no sign of abating, indeed its cost to the UK economy is estimated to have grown from £73 billion in 2011 to a staggering £193 billion in 2016.[1] Furthermore, these figures are likely to be significantly understated if losses from what are currently considered as regulatory breaches, such as the various mis-selling examples that have pervaded the financial services industry, were to be included. Misconduct of this nature requires particular consideration since it is an example of wrongdoing that is better identified as corporate fraud than criminality perpetrated by individuals. Experience demonstrates that the regulatory framework has failed to provide an adequate deterrent and examples of financial misconduct continue to make news, some of the most recent, at the time of writing, being in relation to the provision of finance for vehicle purchases and the so-called "dieselgate" emissions affair. Although regulatory provisions are designed primarily to address conduct that is not harmful in itself, but which may be conducive to harmful outcomes, corporate economic misconduct has nonetheless tended to be treated as a matter for regulatory enforcement. While the criminal law is concerned with serious reprehensible conduct, involving dishonesty and intention, with the fraud-based offences having been specifically identified as meriting the invocation of the criminal jurisdiction, the criminal law has not been employed in cases involving widespread and systemic corporate fraud. In this respect the provisions of the Fraud Act are sufficiently broad that they would catch the economic misconduct however it is performed. Thus, for example, where sales have occurred through false or misleading claims, such as those relating to diesel emissions, the conduct may, if dishonest, amount to fraud by false representation.[2] Where, for example, lenders make loans conditional upon the purchase of inappropriate insurance

---

1 National Fraud Authority, 'Annual Fraud Indicator', March 2012 at www.gov.uk/govern ment/uploads/system/uploads/attachment_data/file/118530/annual-fraud-indicator-2012. pdf accessed Dec 7, 2016 and PKF, Experian and Portsmouth University Centre for Counter Fraud Studies, 'Annual Fraud Indicator' 2016 at www.experian.co.uk/assets/identity-and-fraud/pkfexperian-fraud-indicator-report.pdf accessed Dec 6, 2016.
2 Fraud Act 2006, s. 1(2)(a).

products, there may be a case for considering that a fraud by abuse of position,[3] again if considered dishonest and if the lender's position gives rise to an expectation that the borrower's interests will be safeguarded. However, categorised as regulatory breach, misconduct of this nature has therefore avoided the moral compass and other implications of the mainstream criminal law. That regulation has been preferred to mainstream prosecution is not surprising, not only for reasons of path dependency but also because the criminal law has remained entrenched in the ideology of individualism and has developed no overarching theory of corporate criminality. As the law stands, a corporation can only be convicted of fraud if a person who is recognised as its "directing mind" is himself guilty of the offence. This "identification principle" of fault attribution may be well suited to address wrongdoing perpetrated by small companies, which are typically owner managed, but its application is severely limited in relation to large companies. Similarly, any development that allows for corporate conviction on the basis of a "failure to prevent" fraud, along the lines of the existing corporate bribery offence,[4] will still require that an underlying fraud offence has been committed by an individual member or an associate of the corporation. Again, although this approach is useful to address instances in which the corporation has not prevented the criminality of "rogue" individuals who occupy positions of a lower status, such as may have been the case in the LIBOR and FOREX scandals, whether they are prosecuted or not, this model of corporate liability would have no bite where the wrongdoing in question is not reducible to individuals. Notwithstanding this lacuna, it is clear that both the common law identification principle and the proposed statutory "failure to prevent fraud" have an important part to play in the prosecutorial armoury. Crime committed in the corporate context cannot be accommodated within a one size fits all approach to corporate liability and the offences available must suit the various different agents, the different natures of the offending behaviour and the different types of offence.

In this respect, fraud differs from most other offences. Unlike bribery, for example, fraud is not an activity in itself, but is an otherwise lawful act that is done dishonestly.[5] Under a parasitic model of corporate liability, the corporation will evade liability if the individuals involved in the day to day activity are not themselves dishonest. This is likely to be the situation in relation to examples of misconduct emerging as widespread and pervasive practices, such as in the highly publicised mis-selling scandals which were company and industry wide. While the practices may be considered "dishonest", the honesty of the individual employees involved in the day to day selling, in accordance with their employment duties, is unlikely to be in question. With no underlying criminality at the individual level, the parasitic "failure to prevent" approach to imputing corporate liability, like the identification doctrine, has no application. In any event, misconduct of a systemic

---

3 Fraud Act 2006, s. 1(2)(c).
4 Bribery Act 2010, s. 7.
5 Paul McGrath, *Commercial Fraud and Civil Practice* (Oxford: Oxford University Press 2008).

and widespread nature may be better conceived as a substantive offence of fraud attributable to the corporation itself. To describe the corporate culpability in terms of a "failure to prevent" employees' fraudulent acts in such circumstances would be to attribute the criminal behaviour to innocent, honest, individuals, it would fail the criminal law's expressive function and offend the principle of fair labelling.

In addition to cases where no individual is at fault, there may be other reasons to hold the company liable in preference to its employees. It may be clear that a person or group within the organisation has been at fault but the organisation has obscured internal accountability[6] or it may be that a utilitarian sense of justice militates towards the imposition of corporate liability. This may be, for example, where an organisation tries to inculpate individuals as scapegoats, where employees have in some way been pressured into complying with the deviant behaviour, or where individual fault is a small contributor to a complex and pervasive whole.[7] Other situations may demand that both particular individuals and the corporation are held criminally liable, for the same or different offences. The interrelationship between a particular corporation and its individual members is a unique and highly sophisticated one, involving infinite degrees of interdependence and mutual influence. Naturally, this recognition bears on the issue of determining both agency and responsibility where wrongdoing is identified. However, where organisations exhibit a corporate culture that can be regarded as criminal, the criminal law should be invoked to stigmatise and deter socially harmful behaviour. In this respect, the underlying criminogenic culture can be masked by an apparently diligent approach to compliance, indeed it has been observed that the corporate promotion of good citizenship often goes hand in hand with creative deviance.[8] Similarly, although it is now generally accepted that organisations can and do develop an ethos and personality of their own, and that they have the capacity for agency, the board of directors is ultimately responsible for the corporation's strategic aims, values and standards. It is undesirable that directors can deny knowledge of a widespread dishonest culture, from which they benefit, where such a culture is typical of the various remunerative incentives put in place by the board. The criminalisation of the corporation itself would provide a powerful message to markets whose response would be reflected in both the value of the company and mechanisms employed to effect changes in the board of directors who may, as individuals, be beyond the direct reach of the criminal law.[9] The prospect of reputational damage to both the corporation and its directors, arising as a consequence of criminal enforcement and sanction against

---

6 Brent Fisse, *Howard's Criminal Law* (5th ed, London: Sweet & Maxwell 1990) 591.

7 Ibid 593.

8 William S Laufer, *Corporate Bodies and Guilty Minds* (Chicago: University of Chicago Press 2008) 107, 111.

9 See Stephen Copp and Alison Cronin, Response to the Ministry of Justice Call for Evidence on Corporate Liability for Economic Crime, Jan 2017, yet to be published.

the company, provides a sobering deterrent. In contrast to the identification principle of corporate liability, which encourages managerial distancing and wilful blindness, the availability of the direct imposition of corporate criminal fault provides a strong incentive for directors to effect robust managerial structures that provide the desired internal accountability.[10] Furthermore, by holding the corporation liable it is hoped that internal disciplinary action will be stimulated.[11] From an economic perspective, aside from the market response to corporate investigation and prosecution, the use of a strong anti-fraud law would provide scope for significant cuts in the volume and complexity of company law together with substantial reductions in the increasing financial burden of regulation.[12]

The existing provisions of the Fraud Act 2006 already provide a robust generic offence with the capacity to deal with all types of fraudulent conduct. However, its usefulness in the context of corporate crime is severely diminished in that a corporation can only be convicted of fraud if it is proved that its "directing mind", the corporate alter ego, committed the offence in question. If circumstances are to be recognised in which it is more appropriate to convict the corporation itself of a substantive fraud offence, reflecting both the agency and the liability of the organisational whole, it is necessary to confront the perceived mens rea obstacle such that dishonesty and intention can be directly attributed to a corporation. It is only by doing so that the criminal law will be able to respond to instances of pervasive corporate fraud which are not reducible, or should not be reduced, to individuals acting in the corporate context. In this respect, the historical analysis of the constructs of criminality reveals that the current approach to fault attribution is the product of a gradual distortion of the orthodox doctrine. Linguistic ambiguity in the use of the term "mens rea" has brought about both conceptual confusion and the submergence of the accompanying evidential presumptions. Resulting more from inadvertence than design, the now enlarged version of the mens rea doctrine has displaced not only its former self, as it was originally conceived, but the whole of the voluntariness doctrine that stood as the traditional bedrock of criminal liability. As the notion of mens rea underwent its gradual but dramatic metamorphosis, its metaphysical connotations came to assume greater prominence as the rebuttable evidential presumptions diminished in the overall discourse. Having had particular, although unforeseen, effect in the context of corporate crime, the problem of imputing mens rea to the corporate form became the Gordian knot impeding the development of any overarching theory. That this is so, is largely confirmed by the models of corporate criminality that have been introduced and mooted to date, each of

---

10 E.g. see the prominence now given to the principle of individual and collective accountability in the finance industry, The Fair and Effective Markets Review: Implementation Report at www.bankofengland.co.uk/markets/Documents/femr/implementationreport.pdf accessed May 26, 2017.

11 Brent Fisse, *Howard's Criminal Law* (5th ed, London: Sweet & Maxwell 1990) 591.

12 Stephen Copp and Alison Cronin, 'The Failure of the Criminal Law to Control the Use of Off Balance Sheet Finance During the Banking Crisis' (2015) 36 Co Law 99.

which carefully sidesteps the problem of mens rea and attributes liability on an alternative basis. This is unfortunate in that it is the mens rea element of dishonesty that defines fraud and this must be overcome if a model of corporate fraud, as a substantive offence, is to be achieved.

To this end, and for a general theory of corporate criminality, the rational reconstruction of the traditional doctrines of criminal fault has exciting implications. The voluntariness doctrine, as the primary determinant of criminal fault, with the accompanying evidential presumption of voluntariness, provides the means by which a corporation can be recognised as a responsibility-bearing entity.[13] Similarly, the clear reinstatement of the presumption of intention, itself based on the notion of the rational actor with the capacity to foresee the natural consequences of an act, has obvious application in the context of corporate action. Indeed, the corporation has been identified as the paradigm rational actor and, while corporate policy has been considered the equivalent of intention, the use of the evidential presumptions obviates the need to consider or prove mens rea by reference to individualist metaphysical concepts. In the context of the generic fraud offence,[14] the evidential presumptions therefore facilitate the attribution of both capacity and intent to the corporate actor. The corporation can be presumed to be acting voluntarily and can also be presumed to intend to make a gain[15] since this is the natural consequence of commercial activity. Furthermore, "dishonesty", as the defining characteristic that distinguishes the entrepreneurial from the fraudulent, is also the subject of a longstanding inferential approach.[16] Since the evidential presumptions are rebuttable, they accord with accepted theories of criminality in that they afford a "defence" for those who are not morally blameworthy. The corporate defendant, through its representatives, is as capable as the individual defendant of adducing evidence to refute the presumptions. Although the evidential presumptions involve the "manifest" perception of the harmful behaviour, recent scientific advancements satisfy the subjectivist concerns. Specifically, credence is given to this approach by knowledge that has been gained in the field of modern neuroscience. This challenges both the strict bifurcation of the physical and mental elements of action and also the way in which the subjective mental state of the defendant can be understood. In revealing that the physical and mental realms are not ontologically separate, the actus reus and mens rea construct of criminal liability is shown to be artificial, the mental state is not a distinct metaphysical element. Furthermore, the brain's mirror neuron system operates to provide a person with direct subjective knowledge of another's

13 Discussed above in Ch. 3, literal involuntariness would seem inapplicable to the corporate person.
14 Fraud Act 2006, s. 1.
15 Fraud Act 2006, ss. 2(1)(b)(i) and (ii); 3(b)(i) and (ii) and 4(1)(c)(i) and (ii) set out the intention as either to make a gain for oneself or another or to cause loss to another or expose another to a risk of loss.
16 See Ch. 3.

action simply through observing that action. The startling conclusion is that the manifest assessment of fault, determining whether or not the conduct is blameworthy, through the observance of its outward appearance is entirely compatible with the subjective ideology of the criminal law. Put simply, the mirror neuron system internalises the external. Since the forming of groups and group engagement in collective action is itself an elemental characteristic of human behaviour, it is now also known that the same is true as regards the observance of "group behaviour". The evidential presumptions, based on the "manifest" assessment of behaviour, are consistent with the subjectivist account and are as applicable to group, or corporate, action as they are to individual behaviour.

Since dishonesty is the defining characteristic of fraud, it is likely that the majority of defences raised will turn on this issue and the denial that the conduct in question was dishonest. In that the law determines honesty by reference to prevailing standards of morality, the manifest approach is particularly suited to identifying dishonest practice. In terms of procedural considerations, and the practicality of bringing a prosecution for fraud, the manifest approach to dishonesty has another important advantage. Assessed by inference from the conduct itself, the prosecution is not necessarily dependent upon calling corporate officers and employees to give evidence against their own employer. This avoids the problem of obvious conflicts of interest since the employees who are called to give evidence are likely to be acting for the defence in seeking to rebut the inference of corporate dishonesty. The wheels of justice can turn, unhindered by otherwise difficult dilemmas for employee witnesses that may stem from the incompatibility of their altruistic concerns with their duty of loyalty to the company and the understandable desire to avoid the personal financial sacrifices typically associated with disloyalty. By placing the evidential burden on the defendant corporation to raise a claim that, contrary to its overt appearance, the practice was not dishonest, employees called to give evidence may be confined to the ranks of the defence.

Similarly, experience now growing in the context of corporate bribery demonstrates that the potential use of Deferred Prosecution Agreements encourages frank disclosure and early admissions of corporate guilt. It may be that this success, increased familiarity with the process itself and the implications typical of such agreements,[17] would provide a basis and justification upon which the deferred prosecution mechanism could be extended to instances involving allegations of corporate fraud. Not only incentivising genuine cooperation in any investigation process and the speedy implementation of restorative and compensatory measures, the conditions of these agreements also stimulate prophylactic internal measures addressed at improving the corporate culture and

---

17 The SFO has been involved with DPA applications in relation to corporate bribery matters and the CPS is likely to gain experience in this respect when the corporate tax evasion offence comes into force.

preventing reoffending. While there are fears that the deep governance changes typically required by the terms of the Deferred Prosecution Agreements may lead criminogenic organisations to prefer prosecution over deferment, alternative approaches to corporate "cleansing" are already being mooted in relation to alternative punitive sanctions.[18] Similarly, in the event that criminogenic corporations seek to evade liability[19] by producing individual "scapegoats" to avoid corporate liability for fraud, the corporation may find that, even if successful, it has simply traded a deferred prosecution for the substantive offence, or possible conviction for it, with a conviction for the "failure to prevent fraud" offence that it is proposed should form part of the range of offences available.

As regards the introduction of the new model of liability for corporate fraud, via the "manifest" approach, a survey of the cases involving the common law identification principle reveals that there is no legal precedent in relation to cases involving systemic corporate fraud of the nature under consideration here. Accordingly, using traditional legal methodology, the existing legal authorities can be distinguished on their facts and the door is open to the courts' developing a common law response to this particular genre of corporate fraud. Accordingly, judicial intervention could develop the common law on a case by case basis to provide a unified theory of corporate liability and a response to corporate fraud on the "manifest" basis. In employing traditional legal methodology, this would preserve the overall coherence of the criminal law. However, this may well prove to be a lengthy, uncertain and haphazard process. Furthermore, the opportunity for judicial intervention is itself determined by the prosecuting authorities, and whether the Crown Prosecution Serice (CPS) or the Serious Fraud Office (SFO), who are tasked with bringing prosecutions before the courts, can do so in accordance with the prosecutorial code. The current CPS guidance provides that corporate prosecutions can be brought either on the basis of vicarious liability or direct liability that results from the application of the identification principle.[20] Accordingly, the current form precludes the direct attribution of fault to corporations, absent of a parasitic basis, with no guidance in this respect. However, while the existing approach to prosecution and conviction is still framed in individualist ideology, it is interesting to note that the CPS guide to corporate prosecution contains a principle that implicitly recognises the sophisticated nature of agency in this context:

> Prosecution of a company should not be seen as a substitute for the prosecution of criminally culpable individuals such as directors, officers, employees or shareholders. Prosecuting such individuals provides a strong deterrent against future corporate wrongdoing. Equally when considering

---

18 For example, corporate probation orders.
19 See e.g. William S Laufer, *Corporate Bodies and Guilty Minds* (Chicago: University of Chicago Press, 2006).
20 www.cps.gov.uk/legal/a_to_c/corporate_prosecutions/ accessed Sept 6, 2017.

prosecuting individuals, it is important to consider the possible liability of the company where the criminal conduct is for corporate gain.[21]

From a practical perspective, it would seem that the question of agency will need to precede any question of the choice of offence to be charged and, as a necessary part of that, the mode of fault attribution. The prosecuting authority will want to determine whether it is appropriate to bring proceedings against individuals, the corporation or both. In appropriate circumstances, where there are identifiable culpable individuals, it may be appropriate to bring them to trial, depending on the application of the prosecutorial code and the evidential and public interest tests this involves.[22] It may also be appropriate to bring a prosecution against the corporation and, depending on the circumstances, this may be in addition to those individuals or instead of them. Where there are fraud offences committed by individuals within the corporation, the decision to prosecute the company could therefore take the form of a) a corporate prosecution for a fraud offence under the common law identification principle where there is a guilty "directing mind", b) a "failure to prevent" offence where there are "rogue" lower level employees committing fraud, or c) the substantive fraud offence using the "manifest" model where dishonesty and intent can be directly attributed to the corporation in addition to the liability incurred by individuals. Alternatively, in circumstances where liability is not reducible, and there is no dishonesty on the part of individuals, there may be a corporate prosecution for the substantive fraud offence under the "manifest" model of direct attribution proposed (as above, c).

In principle, it is clear that relatively minor amendments to the existing prosecution guidance would be required. The investigation and prosecution of offences committed by individuals does not present anything new. The application of the identification principle to attribute corporate liability occurs less frequently but it is not new. The "failure to prevent" approach to corporate criminality is also nothing new; introduced first in the Bribery Act 2010 there is now some experience in prosecuting this type of offence, which will increase further with time and with the extension of this model of liability to corporate tax evasion. In this respect, there is also a growing pool of precedent in relation to what might amount to reasonable steps to prevent the commission of the offence, which serves as a corporate defence, and experience is being gained in the application of Deferred Prosecution Agreements. While it would seem that the addition of the proposed "manifest" approach to corporate liability for fraud is novel, even in this respect it must be remembered that the presumptive or inferential approach to evidence of blameworthiness is nothing new. Its application in practice may currently be tacit,[23] but it is of longstanding in

---

21 Ibid General Principles, 8.
22 www.cps.gov.uk/publications/docs/code_2013_accessible_english.pdf accessed Sept 7, 2017.
23 See the discussion in Chs 3 and 4.

both the process of the criminal law generally and in the context of individual prosecution for fraud specifically. The adoption of the manifest approach to corporate prosecution for the substantive fraud offence would not invoke any sea change in procedure and further guidance for prosecutors could be added quite readily in relation to this model of liability. In particular, various principles could be introduced to assist in the determination of agency and whether the conduct is better conceived as corporate or individual fault, or indeed both. Such factors might include the pervasiveness of the conduct within the organisation, the gravity of the individual harm caused in comparison with the gravity or potential gravity of the aggregate harm, whether the harm is confined to specific identifiable victims or whether it is widespread and, if so, whether it has or could have caused indirect harm to the market. Other indicators of corporate blameworthiness may be found in the relationship between the practice and the employees' performance targets and indicators, remuneration and bonus structures, and promotion prospects. The absence of internal accountability measures and the extent to which the employees could be considered truly free agents, with choice afforded by a realistic prospect for gaining reasonably equivalent employment elsewhere, may form part of the consideration. Although economic duress or coercion is not a defence to criminality,[24] and it is not suggested here that it should be, this may also bear on the decision whether to prosecute individuals and/or the corporation, particularly where there appears to be an unexpressed but underlying corporate pressure to comply with a criminogenic culture. While this is not intended as an exhaustive list for prosecution guidance purposes, and other considerations will undoubtedly feature, it is evident that comprehensive guidance can be produced, and updated, on the basis of the existing and growing corpus of knowledge and experience gained in this area. Indeed, the implications of the different responses to individual and corporate crime are already emerging and various consequences will need to be addressed. For example, there are currently concerns that the aims of the Deferred Prosecution Agreements may be frustrated if they are offered in return for corporate cooperation with criminal investigations which may, as a result, lead to the prosecution and conviction of individuals within the organisation. Also, there has yet to be a case where a prosecution is continued after corporate non-compliance with the terms of a deferment agreement. This is an area rich in opportunity for ongoing future development and refinement.

As regards the imperative of legal certainty, corporations themselves will need clear signposting in relation to the introduction of the manifest model of corporate fraud. In this respect, the challenge is much the same as that faced with the introduction of any new corporate offence. Past experience provides a range of broad examples, including market manipulation, corporate manslaughter and the most recent addition of "failure to prevent" bribery and tax evasion

---

24 Depending on the circumstances such a claim may feature in a plea of mitigation at sentencing.

offences. From this an effective publicity and education strategy can be developed in relation to a new corporate fraud offence and it is envisaged that the Ministry of Justice would play a pivotal role, much as it did with the introduction of corporate bribery.[25] Since it is proposed that a corporate "failure to prevent fraud" offence would be introduced alongside the substantive offence based on manifest liability, the dissemination would address both. While the former model is now familiar the latter, in the corporate context, is not. However, in that the essence of any fraud, individual or corporate, is dishonesty the following observations can be made. Notwithstanding initial concerns as regards the principle of certainty, dishonesty itself is not a new concept in the criminal law and, as regards what might amount to corporate dishonesty, illustrative examples could be provided. Further, the law's approach to dishonesty, as a concept, is that it is usually better considered a matter of common sense and, as such, it rarely requires a judicial direction in the courts. There is little reason to suspect that the issue of dishonesty should cause more difficulty in relation to corporate action than it may in the context of individual behaviour. Indeed, the manifest approach to dishonesty makes for a comfortable fit as regards the common law approach to its identification, the first question being whether what was done was dishonest according to the ordinary standards of reasonable and honest people.[26] Although the second question, required only if the first answer is affirmative, asks whether the defendant realised that reasonable and honest people would regard what was done as dishonest, the direction in the *Crown Court Compendium* clearly states that this is answered inferentially.[27] Indeed, if the Supreme Court's judgment in *Ivey v Genting* [2017][28] is followed in the criminal courts, as it is likely to be, this second question will no longer be asked. While there may be initial concern about juries understanding fraud in the corporate context,[29] the test of dishonesty is universal and the corporate arena should not attract a different moral compass. Similarly, it must be remembered that the notion of dishonesty is dynamic, serving as a reflection of the prevailing social morality; as a measure of blameworthiness its value lies much in the fact that it cannot be confined to specificity and delimitation. It has an elegant simplicity that cannot be undermined by otherwise strict compliance with the complex, prescriptive and highly particularised provisions typical of regulation and flies free of the financial burdens that such an approach incurs. Finally, as with any development in the law, the traditional doctrine ensures a steady accretion of precedent which serves as a further touchstone for predicting future liability.

---

25 www.justice.gov.uk/downloads/legislation/bribery-act-2010-guidance.pdf accessed Sept 6, 2017.

26 *R v Ghosh* [1982] QB 1053 (CAA).

27 Indeed, it has been held not to be a misdirection if the jury is not given this second element of the direction, *R v Chitate* [2014] EWCA Crim 1744.

28 *Ivey v Genting Casinos (UK) Ltd t/a Crockfords* [2017] UKSC 67.

29 Whether or not such concerns are corroborated.

Having established that the corporate defendant is an appropriate agent for prosecution, the practical and procedural aspects of a trial for the substantive fraud offence under the "manifest model" differ little from the prosecution of an individual for fraud. Employing the existing generic provision contained in the Fraud Act 2006,[30] the questions for the court are simple. The first is whether the corporate person intended to make a gain for itself or another, or intended to cause a loss to another or expose another to the risk of loss, through either a false representation,[31] a failure to disclose information[32] or an abuse of position.[33] As observed above,[34] the presumption of intention was placed on a statutory footing by s. 8 Criminal Justice Act 1967 and it acknowledges that a person may be presumed to have intended or foreseen the natural and probable consequence of his act, but that the presumption may be rebutted by other evidence raising contrary inferences. As a matter of statutory interpretation this applies equally to organisations since Schedule 1, Interpretation Act 1978 states that where an act refers to a "person" this includes a body of persons incorporate or unincorporated. Corporate intention in relation to fraud could be readily ascertained by the inference that the defendant organisation intended to make a gain as a result of, for example, its sales activity, since this is the natural and probable result of such activity. The second question for the court is whether the conduct was done dishonestly.[35] The presumptive approach to dishonesty is also well established[36] and, like the presumption of intention, can be rebutted by evidence raised by the defendant in person or, where a corporate defendant, through its representatives. Accordingly, in relation to corporate prosecutions for the substantive offence brought under the Fraud Act, Parliament could put the manifest approach beyond doubt with the enactment of an express statutory provision. For example, it may enact a provision such that

> in relation to a charge of fraud contrary to the Fraud Act 2006, a body of persons incorporate or unincorporated may be found to be dishonest and have fraudulent intention, as described in the Act, where this is the obvious inference to be drawn from the corporate conduct and all the evidence.

This would effectively affirm the orthodox presumptive approach, accord with the s. 8 provision as regards its application[37] and draw it together with the relevant part from the Interpretation Act 1978.[38] In this way, the determination of

---

30 Fraud Act 2006, s. 1.
31 Fraud Act 2006, s. 2.
32 Fraud Act 2006, s. 3.
33 Fraud Act 2006, s. 4.
34 See Ch. 4.
35 Fraud Act 2006, ss. 2(1)(a), 3(a) and 4(1)(b).
36 See the discussion in Ch. 4.
37 Criminal Justice Act 1967.
38 Schedule 1.

individual and corporate fault would be expressly placed on the same footing. Such an approach would avoid the various disadvantages associated with the evolution of the common law by judicial intervention but, consistent with the aims of rational reconstruction, would be equally attractive in terms of maintaining overall doctrinal coherence. Advance publication of a predetermined development in the law ensures that the issues of corporate and prosecutorial guidance are properly addressed, in addition to other necessities such as sentencing guidelines.

The statutory approach to substantive corporate fraud under the "manifest" model is plainly preferable to a common law, case by case, development for a number of reasons. Indeed, as regards the introduction of an accompanying corporate "failure to prevent" offence, statutory enactment is absolutely necessary as it constitutes a novel basis for corporate liability for fraud. However, since the "manifest" approach to a substantive corporate fraud offence is, in essence, afforded by a restatement of orthodox principles and presumptions, with no alteration or addition necessary to the substance of the law itself, there may be a more efficient means by which to achieve the legal development required. In principle, the adoption of such an approach to corporate prosecution requires no more than the drafting and introduction of a Criminal Procedure Rule and Practice Direction.[39] This is an attractive option in terms of time, cost and overall efficiency since the Criminal Procedure Rules Committee is made responsible for drafting and maintaining this procedural code.[40] This means that procedural and practice changes can be effected by statutory instrument, without recourse to primary legislation and the lumbering process associated with such enactment. Together with the prosecution and industry guidance suggested to accompany the introduction of the "manifest model", the procedural approach may be the key to providing a simple, effective and doctrinally coherent response to the immediate and burgeoning problem of corporate fraud.

Bibliography

Books

Fisse B, *Howard's Criminal Law* (5th ed, London: Sweet & Maxwell 1990)
Laufer WS, *Corporate Bodies and Guilty Minds* (Chicago: University of Chicago Press 2006)
McGrath P, *Commercial Fraud and Civil Practice* (Oxford: Oxford University Press 2008)

---

39 www.justice.gov.uk/courts/procedure-rules/criminal/notes accessed Sept 9, 2017.
40 The Committee was established under the Courts Act 2003, ss. 69–73 and is chaired by the Lord Chief Justice. It comprises 17 members appointed by the L.C.J. and the Lord Chancellor.

Journal articles

Copp S and Cronin A, '*The Failure of the Criminal Law to Control the Use of Off Balance Sheet Finance During the Banking Crisis*' (2015) 36 Co Law 99

Websites

www.bankofengland.co.uk/markets/Documents/femr/implementationreport.pdf accessed May 26, 2017

www.cps.gov.uk/legal/a_to_c/corporate_prosecutions/ accessed Sept 6, 2017

www.cps.gov.uk/publications/docs/code_2013_accessible_english.pdf accessed Sept 7, 2017

www.experian.co.uk/assets/identity-and-fraud/pkfexperian-fraud-indicator-report.pdf accessed Dec 6, 2016

www.gov.uk/government/uploads/system/uploads/attachment_data/file/118530/annual-fraud-indicator-2012.pdf accessed Dec 7, 2016

www.justice.gov.uk/downloads/legislation/bribery-act-2010-guidance.pdf accessed Sept 6, 2017

www.justice.gov.uk/courts/procedure-rules/criminal/notes accessed Sept 9, 2017

Index

Aberfan disaster 26
absolute liability 150, 152
abuse of position 107, 165, 174
actus non facit reum nisi mens sit rea 30, 60, 82, 112–13
actus reus 16, 34, 36, 48, 52, 56–7, 60–3, 66–70, 82–3, 95, 112–13, 121, 125, 155, 168; and Australian Criminal Code 48; denial 73, 76; term understanding 118–19; validity challenge 57; and voluntariness 60, 62–3, 66–9, 78n127
Agassi, Joseph 18
agency 4n16, 6–7, 22–3, 26, 29, 34, 49, 129, 132, 146, 150–3, 172; corporate 14–15, 25–6, 30, 140, 166–7, 170–2; freedom of 65; human 27; individual 141, 152, 172; law of 129, 132, 139–40, 151–3, 156, 158–60, 166–7, 170–1; moral 21, 27, 29; National Fraud 1; organisational 23, 26, 29, 49, 113, 166–7 *see also* group agency
aggregation 22n107, 46–7, 129, 133, 143, 162; harm 172; liability 47
alter ego 5, 7–8, 31–2, 146n4, 148–9, 155, 167
amino acids 117
Annual Fraud Indicator 1, 3–4, 164n1
appeals 98
appropriation 106n101, 119
Ashworth, Andrew 21, 63n22, 70n70, 120n35
asset seizure 11
atom 117; hydrogen 117; oxygen 117; sub atom 117
attribution of fault 8, 16–17, 24, 29, 35–7, 45, 50–2, 86–7, 103, 112–14, 119–21, 126, 143, 146–8, 159, 160n120, 162, 165, 167, 168, 170–1; of agency 22n107; liability 32, 57, 66, 137n60,

139, 146–7; moral responsibility 120n35; parasitic 17
Austin, John 20, 60n3
Australian Criminal Code 24, 47–8
authorisation theory 129
automatism 63, 69, 81, 83, 119n31
autonomy 15, 28; functional 22–3; individual 21n104, 65; organisational (group) 10, 29, 34

bankruptcy *see* corporate insolvency
belief 23, 64, 70, 75–6, 83, 107, 120, 123, 129–30n11&12, 158; absence 77, 82n165; evaluative 28; mistaken 64n31, 70, 76, 82n166; reasonable 75n103, 77, 80n149, 82n166; shared 129
Bentham, Jeremy 20, 92n28, 104n89
biological naturalism 116
black letter law analysis 34–5, 37, 143, 148, 162
Bonner, James P 28
brain states 115; neural 115
Braithwaite, John 15n70, 22, 49
bribery 10, 32–3, 46, 50–2, 56, 141, 165, 169; Act (2010) 10n44, 50, 171; anti-regime 11, 51; failure to prevent 50, 172–3
building, strict liability offences 71
burden of evidence *see* evidence, burden of
burden of proof 11, 36, 73, 78–81, 87

capacity 37, 63–4, 83, 91, 112–13, 117, 132, 167–8; agency (group/individual) 141, 166; autonomous action 23; blame avoidance 15n70; decision-making 27–8; denial 76; for evil 135; mental 86, 88, 94–5, 124n50; organisational 105; repayment 1n1; survival 23; to choose 65, 120; to commit 65–6, 94